HARRAP'S

SPANISH
pocket
VERBS

D1307475

McGraw Hill

New York Chicago San Francisco Lisbon London Madrid Mexico City
Milan New Delhi San Juan Seoul Singapore Sydney Toronto

ISBN 978-0-07-162780-1
MHID 0-07-162780-4

McGraw-Hill books are available at special quantity discounts to use as
premiums and sales promotions or for use in corporate training programs.
To contact a representative, please visit the Contact Us pages at
www.mhprofessional.com.

Project Editors: Alex Hepworth, Kate Nicholson
With Helen Bleck

Designed by Chambers Harrap Publishers Ltd, Edinburgh
Typeset in Rotis Serif and Meta Plus by Macmillan Publishing Solutions

INTRODUCTION

Chambers concise yet authoritative guide to Spanish verbs is
designed to be a quick, straightforward reference for all learners
of Spanish. It opens with some essential grammatical information,
explaining in accessible terms how different verb types are
conjugated and how the various tenses are used. The main body
of the book is then comprised of verb tables, showing the full
conjugation of over 200 Spanish verbs which can be used as models
for all the others. In the extensive bilingual index, verbs are cross-
referred to the table whose model they follow, while those used as
models themselves are clearly marked.

This new edition has been updated with a smart two-colour design
to make consultation even easier and more enjoyable. Suitable for
everyone from beginners to experienced language learners, this
pocket reference is an essential companion for anyone wishing to
communicate effectively in Spanish.

 CONTENTS

A GLOSSARY OF GRAMMATICAL TERMS		5
GRAMMATICAL INFORMATION		8
A.	TYPES OF VERB	8
B.	USE OF TENSES	8
C.	SER AND ESTAR	18
VERB TABLES		20
INDEX OF SPANISH VERBS		232
ENGLISH-SPANISH INDEX		258

IMPERATIVE   A **MOOD** used for giving orders (eg **stop!**, **don't go!**) or for making suggestions (eg **let's go**).

INDICATIVE   The 'normal' form of a verb as in **I like**, **he came**, **we are trying**. It is opposed to the **SUBJUNCTIVE**, **CONDITIONAL** and **IMPERATIVE**.

INDIRECT OBJECT   An indirect object follows a verb indirectly, with a linking preposition (usually **to**), eg **I spoke to my friend/to him**. In English this is not always expressed. *See also* **DIRECT OBJECT**.

INFINITIVE   The infinitive is the 'basic' form of the verb as found in dictionaries. In English it is often preceded by **to**, eg **to eat**, **to finish**, **to take**. In Spanish, all infinitives end in -ar, -er or -ir: **hablar**, **comer**, **vivir**.

MOOD   The name given to the four main areas within which a verb is conjugated. *See* **INDICATIVE**, **SUBJUNCTIVE**, **CONDITIONAL**, **IMPERATIVE**.

PASSIVE   A verb is used in the passive when the subject of the verb does not perform the action but is subjected to it. In English, the passive is formed with a part of the verb **to be** and the **PAST PARTICIPLE** of the verb, eg **he was rewarded**.

PAST PARTICIPLE   The past participle of a verb is the form which is used after **to have** in English, eg **I have** *eaten*, **I have** *said*, **you have** *tried*.

PERSON   In any **TENSE**, there are three persons in the singular (1st: **I** ..., 2nd: **you** ..., 3rd: **he/she/it** ...), and three in the plural (1st: **we** ..., 2nd: **you** ..., 3rd: **they** ...). Note that in Spanish the 3rd person is also used with the pronouns **usted** and **ustedes** (both 'you').

PRESENT PARTICIPLE   The present participle is the verb form which ends in **-ing** in English, and **-ando** or **-iendo** in Spanish.

REFLEXIVE   Reflexive verbs 'reflect' the action back onto the subject (eg **I dressed myself**). They are always found with a reflexive pronoun and are more common in Spanish than in English. In the **INFINITIVE**, Spanish reflexive verbs have the preposition **se** attached to the end.

SUBJECT   The subject is the person or thing carrying out the action of a verb. In the sentences **the train left early** and **she bought a CD**, *the train* and *she* are the subjects.

SUBJUNCTIVE   The subjunctive is a verb form which is rarely used in English (eg **if I** *were* **you, God** *save* **the Queen**). It is more common in Spanish.

SUBORDINATE CLAUSE   A group of words with a subject and a verb which is dependent on another clause, ie it cannot stand alone. For example, in **he said he would leave**, *he would leave* is the subordinate clause dependent on *he said*.

STEM   *See* VERB STEM.

TENSE   Verbs are used in tenses, which indicate when an action takes place, eg in the present, the past, the future.

VERB STEM   The stem of a verb is its 'basic unit' to which the various endings are added. To find the stem of a Spanish verb remove the -ar, -er or -ir from the infinitive, thus the stem of **hablar** is habl-, comer > com-, vivir > viv-.

VOICE   The two voices of a verb are its **ACTIVE** and **PASSIVE** forms.

GRAMMATICAL INFORMATION

A TYPES OF VERB

There are three conjugations for Spanish verbs. The ending of the infinitive indicates which conjugation the verb belongs to.

all verbs ending in -ar belong to the first conjugation, eg hablar
all verbs ending in -er belong to the second conjugation, eg comer
all verbs ending in -ir belong to the third conjugation, eg vivir

All regular verbs follow the pattern of one of these conjugations.

Models for these and for a considerable number of irregular verbs are given in the verb tables of this book.

B USE OF TENSES

Tenses are formed by adding various endings to the stem of the verb (ie the verb minus -ar, -er, -ir).

The following section gives explanations and examples of usage of the various verb tenses and moods that are listed in the verb tables in this book.

1 The PRESENT TENSE is used (as in English):

i) to express present states:

estoy enfermo
I am ill

ii) to express general or universal truths:

la vida es dura   **el tiempo es oro**
life is difficult   time is money

iii) to express the future:

vuelvo ahora mismo	**mañana mismo lo termino**
I'll be right back	I will finish it tomorrow

iv) to translate the English present progressive:

vivo en Glasgow	**estudio español**
I am living in Glasgow	I am studying Spanish

The **PRESENT PROGRESSIVE** is formed with the present tense of **ESTAR** plus the present participle of the verb (for example: **¿qué estas haciendo?** what are you doing?; **están escuchando la radio** they're listening to the radio). It is used:

i) when an activity is actually taking place:

estoy escribiendo una carta
I am writing a letter

ii) for an activity begun in the past and continuing into the present even if it is not happening at the moment:

estoy escribiendo un libro
I am writing a book

2 The **IMPERFECT TENSE** is used:

i) to express something that was going on in the past:

hacía mucho ruido
it was making a lot of noise

ii) to refer specially to something that continued over a period of time as opposed to something that happened at a specific point in time:

mientras veíamos la televisión, un ladrón entró por la ventana
while we were watching television, a thief came in through the window

iii) to describe a habitual action that used to take place in the past:

cuando era pequeño iba de vacaciones a Mallorca
when I was young I used to go on holiday to Majorca

iv) to describe or set the background of a story:

el sol brillaba
the sun was shining

The **IMPERFECT PROGRESSIVE**. Like the present tense, the imperfect has a progressive form, formed with the imperfect of **ESTAR** plus the present participle of the verb:

estábamos tomando el sol
we were sunbathing

3 The **PERFECT TENSE** is generally used (as in English) to express an action in the past without referring to a particular time. It usually describes an action that continues into the present or relates to the present:

he conocido a tu hermano
I have met your brother

hemos estado en una discoteca
we have been to a club

4 The **PRETERITE** is used to express an action that has been completed in the past:

ayer fui a la discoteca	**Pedro me llamó por teléfono**
yesterday I went to the club	Peter phoned me

5 The **PLUPERFECT TENSE** is used:

i) (as in English) to express what someone had done or had been doing or something that had happened or had been happening in the past:

mi amiga había llamado por teléfono
my friend had phoned

ii) to express a past action completed before another past action:

cuando llegué Elena ya se había marchado
when I arrived Elena had already gone

6 The FUTURE TENSE is used as in English to express future matters:

este verano iré a España
this summer I'll go to Spain

The future can also be expressed by using the verb ir in the present plus the preposition a followed by an infinitive:

voy a estudiar
I am going to study

van a comer con unos amigos
they are going to eat with some friends

Note that the future is often expressed by the present tense in Spanish (*see* **1. iii** above).

7 The FUTURE PERFECT TENSE:

i) is used to indicate that an action in the future will be completed by the time a second action applies:

lo habré terminado antes de que lleguen
I will have finished it before they arrive

ii) can be used in Spanish to express a supposition about the present:

lo habrá olvidado
he'll have forgotten it

8 The PRESENT CONDITIONAL is used:

i) in certain phrases to express a wish:

me gustaría conocer a tu hermano
I would like to meet your brother

ii) to refer to what would happen or what someone would do under certain circumstances:

si pasara eso, me pondría muy contento
if that happened, I would be very pleased

9 The PAST CONDITIONAL is used to express what would have happened if something else had not interfered:

si hubieras llegado antes, lo habrías visto
if you had arrived earlier, you would have seen it

10 The PAST ANTERIOR is used in literary Spanish, and is preceded by an adverb expressing time:

cuando hubo terminado, se levantó
when he had finished, he got up

11 The SUBJUNCTIVE is mainly used:

i) in conditional statements where the condition is unlikely to be fulfilled:

si tuviera más tiempo, iría de paseo
if I had more time, I would go for a walk

si me lo hubiera pedido, le habría prestado el dinero
if he had asked me, I would have lent him the money

si fuera mi cumpleaños
if it were my birthday

ii) in subordinate clauses following verbs that express a subjective idea or opinion:

siento que no puedas venir
I am sorry you can't come

mi madre quiere que vaya a la Universidad
my mother wants me to go to university

iii) with impersonal expressions:

es fácil que suspenda el examen
it's likely that she'll fail the exam

iv) with expressions of doubt:

no creo que quiera ir al cine
I don't think he will want to go to the cinema

dudo que lo sepa
I doubt whether he knows it

v) after relative clauses with indefinite, negative or interrogative antecedents:

¿conoces a alguien que no quiera ganar mucho dinero?
do you know anybody who doesn't want to earn a lot of money?

aquí no hay nadie que hable alemán
there is nobody here who can speak German

vi) in indefinite expressions when they imply an action in the future:

quienquiera que venga, le diré que no puede entrar
whoever comes, I'll tell him he can't come in

dondequiera que esté, le encontraré
wherever he is, I'll find him

vii) with verbs that imply a command or advice:

mi amiga me dijo que fuera a verla
my friend told me to go and see her

Carmen me aconsejó que dejara de fumar
Carmen advised me to stop smoking

viii) after certain conjunctions when they imply a future or uncertain action:

aunque llueva iré a los toros
even if it rains I'll go to the bullfight

The subjunctive is used with adverbs of time when the verb in the main clause is in the future, as we don't know if the action will take place:

en cuanto venga, se lo diré
as soon as he comes, I'll tell him

antes de que se vaya, hablaré con ella
before she goes, I'll talk to her

The choice of tense for the subjunctive depends on the tense of the main clause:

indicative tense of main clause	subjunctive tense of subordinate clause
present future imperative	present
imperfect preterite conditional	imperfect
present future	perfect

quiero que me escribas
I want you to write to me
me gustaría que me escribieras
I would like you to write to me
nos pedirá que lo terminemos
he will ask us to finish it

me dijo que viniera
he told me to come

dudo que haya llegado
I doubt whether he's arrived

12 The **PRESENT PARTICIPLE** is not very commonly used by itself.

i) It is used with the verb **estar** to form the progressive tenses:

estoy estudiando español
I am studying Spanish

estábamos comiendo una paella
we were eating a paella

ii) On its own it can be used to express the idea of 'by doing':

leyendo se aprende mucho
you learn a lot by reading

13 The **PAST PARTICIPLE**, apart from its use to form the compound tenses, is also used on its own as an adjective:

ese condenado coche
that damned car

14 The IMPERATIVE is used to give orders or to make suggestions:

ven aquí
come here!

deja de hacer el tonto
stop being silly

ten cuidado
be careful

vámonos
let's go

The second persons of the imperative, when used in the NEGATIVE, are formed by using the second persons of the present subjunctive:

no corras tanto
don't run so much

15 The INFINITIVE is used:

i) after a preposition:

se fue sin hablar conmigo
he left without speaking to me

al abrir la puerta
on opening the door

ii) as the direct object of another verb:

pueden Vds pasar
you can go in

me gusta bailar
I like dancing

iii) as a noun (sometimes with an article):

el comer tanto no es bueno
eating so much is not good

16 The PASSIVE VOICE is formed by using the verb **ser** plus the past participle. The agent or person that executes the action is introduced by **por**. In the passive voice the past participle agrees with the subject:

el perro fue atropellado por un coche
the dog was run over by a car

las cartas han sido destruidas por el fuego
the letters have been destroyed by the fire

The passive voice is less commonly used in Spanish than in English and passive ideas can be expressed by:

i) using the reflexive pronoun **se** with the third person of the verb:

esa casa ya se ha vendido
that house has already been sold

ii) using the third person plural of the verb:

nos invitaron a una fiesta
we were invited to a party

iii) changing the roles of subject and agent:

la policía arrestó a los ladrones
the thieves were caught by the police

mi profesora escribió ese libro
that book was written by my teacher

An example of the full conjugation of a passive verb is given on the following page.

PRESENT
1. soy amado
2. eres amado
3. es amado
1. somos amados
2. sois amados
3. son amados

IMPERFECT
era amado
eras amado
era amado
éramos amados
erais amados
eran amados

FUTURE
seré amado
serás amado
será amado
seremos amados
seréis amados
serán amados

PRETERITE
1. fui amado
2. fuiste amado
3. fue amado
1. fuimos amados
2. fuisteis amados
3. fueron amados

PERFECT
he sido amado
has sido amado
ha sido amado
hemos sido amados
habéis sido amados
han sido amados

PLUPERFECT
había sido amado
habías sido amado
había sido amado
habíamos sido amados
habíais sido amados
habían sido amados

PAST ANTERIOR
hube sido amado *etc*

FUTURE PERFECT
habré sido amado *etc*

CONDITIONAL

IMPERATIVE

PRESENT
1. sería amado
2. serías amado
3. sería amado
1. seríamos amados
2. seríais amados
3. serían amados

PAST
habría sido amado
habrías sido amado
habría sido amado
habríamos sido amados
habríais sido amados
habrían sido amados

SUBJUNCTIVE

PRESENT
1. sea amado
2. seas amado
3. sea amado
1. seamos amados
2. seáis amados
3. sean amados

IMPERFECT
fu-era/ese amado
fu-eras/eses amado
fu-era/ese amado
fu-éramos/ésemos amados
fu-erais/eseis amados
fu-eran/esen amados

PLUPERFECT
hubiera sido amado
hubieras sido amado
hubiera sido amado
hubiéramos sido amados
hubierais sido amados
hubieran sido amados

PERFECT   haya sido amado *etc*

INFINITIVE

PARTICIPLE

PRESENT
ser amado

PRESENT
siendo amado

PAST
haber sido amado

PAST
sido amado

C SER AND ESTAR

Both verbs translate the verb 'to be'.

SER is used to express:

i) identity:

soy Elena
I am Elena

es mi prima
she is my cousin

ii) origin or nationality:

él es de Madrid
he is from Madrid

mis amigos son escoceses
my friends are Scottish

iii) inherent quality or characteristics:

la playa es grande
the beach is big

mi profesor es muy amable
my teacher is very kind

iv) occupation:

mi novio es arquitecto
my boyfriend is an architect

v) possession:

ese libro es de Teresa
that book is Teresa's

vi) the material from which something is made:

la mesa es de madera
the table is made of wood

vii) expressions of time:

es la una y media
it's half past one

mañana es domingo
tomorrow is Sunday

viii) most impersonal expressions:

es mejor levantarse temprano
it's better to get up early

ix) to form the passive voice (*see* **B. 16** above)

ESTAR is used:

i) to indicate where someone or something is:

el hotel está en la calle principal
the hotel is in the main street

España está en Europa
Spain is in Europe

ii) to express a temporary state or condition:

ese hombre está borracho	**el agua está fría**
that man is drunk	the water is cold

iii) to form the progressive tenses:

estamos viendo la televisión
we are watching television

Some words change their meaning when used with ser or estar:

estoy listo	**es listo**
I am ready	he is clever

Note: In the verb tables the numbers 1, 2, 3 indicate the first, second and third person of the verb. In each block the second 1, 2, 3 are the plural forms. Note that the formal second person pronouns usted and ustedes – 'you' in the singular and plural – are used with the third person of the verb.

For an important note on the use of the imperative see **B.14** above.

The pluperfect subjunctive is shown with the hubiera form of the auxiliary. The alternative hubiese form can also be used - see haber (**verb table 111**) for the full conjugation.

ABANDONAR

1 *to abandon*

PRESENT	IMPERFECT	FUTURE
1. abandono	abandonaba	abandonaré
2. abandonas	abandonabas	abandonarás
3. abandona	abandonaba	abandonará
1. abandonamos	abandonábamos	abandonaremos
2. abandonáis	abandonabais	abandonaréis
3. abandonan	abandonaban	abandonarán

PRETERITE	PERFECT	PLUPERFECT
1. abandoné	he abandonado	había abandonado
2. abandonaste	has abandonado	habías abandonado
3. abandonó	ha abandonado	había abandonado
1. abandonamos	hemos abandonado	habíamos abandonado
2. abandonasteis	habéis abandonado	habíais abandonado
3. abandonaron	han abandonado	habían abandonado

PAST ANTERIOR	FUTURE PERFECT
hube abandonado *etc*	habré abandonado *etc*

CONDITIONAL

IMPERATIVE

PRESENT	PAST	
1. abandonaría	habría abandonado	
2. abandonarías	habrías abandonado	(tú) abandona
3. abandonaría	habría abandonado	(Vd) abandone
1. abandonaríamos	habríamos abandonado	(nosotros) abandonemos
2. abandonaríais	habríais abandonado	(vosotros) abandonad
3. abandonarían	habrían abandonado	(Vds) abandonen

SUBJUNCTIVE

PRESENT	IMPERFECT	PLUPERFECT
1. abandone	abandon-ara/ase	hubiera abandonado
2. abandones	abandon-aras/ases	hubieras abandonado
3. abandone	abandon-ara/ase	hubiera abandonado
1. abandonemos	abandon-áramos/ásemos	hubiéramos abandonado
2. abandonéis	abandon-arais/aseis	hubierais abandonado
3. abandonen	abandon-aran/asen	hubieran abandonado

PERFECT   haya abandonado *etc*

INFINITIVE

PARTICIPLE

PRESENT	PRESENT
abandonar	abandonando

PAST	PAST
haber abandonado	abandonado

PRESENT	IMPERFECT	FUTURE
1.	abolía	aboliré
2.	abolías	abolirás
3.	abolía	abolirá
1. abolimos	abolíamos	aboliremos
2. abolís	abolíais	aboliréis
3.	abolían	abolirán

PRETERITE	PERFECT	PLUPERFECT
1. abolí	he abolido	había abolido
2. aboliste	has abolido	habías abolido
3. abolió	ha abolido	había abolido
1. abolimos	hemos abolido	habíamos abolido
2. abolisteis	habéis abolido	habíais abolido
3. abolieron	han abolido	habían abolido

PAST ANTERIOR	FUTURE PERFECT
hube abolido *etc*	habré abolido *etc*

CONDITIONAL

IMPERATIVE

PRESENT	PAST	
1. aboliría	habría abolido	
2. abolirías	habrías abolido	
3. aboliría	habría abolido	
1. aboliríamos	habríamos abolido	(nosotros) abolamos
2. aboliríais	habríais abolido	(vosotros) abolid
3. abolirían	habrían abolido	

SUBJUNCTIVE

PRESENT	IMPERFECT	PLUPERFECT
1.	abol-iera/iese	hubiera abolido
2.	abol-ieras/ieses	hubieras abolido
3.	abol-iera/iese	hubiera abolido
1.	abol-iéramos/iésemos	hubiéramos abolido
2.	abol-ierais/ieseis	hubierais abolido
3.	abol-ieran/iesen	hubieran abolido

PERFECT   haya abolido *etc*

INFINITIVE

PARTICIPLE

PRESENT	PRESENT
abolir	aboliendo
PAST	PAST
haber abolido	abolido

ABORRECER
3 *to loathe*

PRESENT	IMPERFECT	FUTURE
1. aborrezco	aborrecía	aborreceré
2. aborreces	aborrecías	aborrecerás
3. aborrece	aborrecía	aborrecerá
1. aborrecemos	aborrecíamos	aborreceremos
2. aborrecéis	aborrecíais	aborreceréis
3. aborrecen	aborrecían	aborrecerán

PRETERITE	PERFECT	PLUPERFECT
1. aborrecí	he aborrecido	había aborrecido
2. aborreciste	has aborrecido	habías aborrecido
3. aborreció	ha aborrecido	había aborrecido
1. aborrecimos	hemos aborrecido	habíamos aborrecido
2. aborrecisteis	habéis aborrecido	habíais aborrecido
3. aborrecieron	han aborrecido	habían aborrecido

PAST ANTERIOR	FUTURE PERFECT
hube aborrecido *etc*	habré aborrecido *etc*

CONDITIONAL

PRESENT	PAST
1. aborrecería	habría aborrecido
2. aborrecerías	habrías aborrecido
3. aborrecería	habría aborrecido
1. aborreceríamos	habríamos aborrecido
2. aborreceríais	habríais aborrecido
3. aborrecerían	habrían aborrecido

IMPERATIVE

(tú) aborrece
(Vd) aborrezca
(nosotros) aborrezcamos
(vosotros) aborreced
(Vds) aborrezcan

SUBJUNCTIVE

PRESENT	IMPERFECT	PLUPERFECT
1. aborrezca	aborrec-iera/iese	hubiera aborrecido
2. aborrezcas	aborrec-ieras/ieses	hubieras aborrecido
3. aborrezca	aborrec-iera/iese	hubiera aborrecido
1. aborrezcamos	aborrec-iéramos/iésemos	hubiéramos aborrecido
2. aborrezcáis	aborrec-ierais/ieseis	hubierais aborrecido
3. aborrezcan	aborrec-ieran/iesen	hubieran aborrecido

PERFECT   haya aborrecido *etc*

INFINITIVE

PRESENT
aborrecer

PAST
haber aborrecido

PARTICIPLE

PRESENT
aborreciendo

PAST
aborrecido

PRESENT	IMPERFECT	FUTURE
1. abro	abría	abriré
2. abres	abrías	abrirás
3. abre	abría	abrirá
1. abrimos	abríamos	abriremos
2. abrís	abríais	abriréis
3. abren	abrían	abrirán

PRETERITE	PERFECT	PLUPERFECT
1. abrí	he abierto	había abierto
2. abriste	has abierto	habías abierto
3. abrió	ha abierto	había abierto
1. abrimos	hemos abierto	habíamos abierto
2. abristeis	habéis abierto	habíais abierto
3. abrieron	han abierto	habían abierto

PAST ANTERIOR		FUTURE PERFECT
hube abierto *etc*		habré abierto *etc*

CONDITIONAL

IMPERATIVE

PRESENT	PAST	
1. abriría	habría abierto	
2. abrirías	habrías abierto	(tú) abre
3. abriría	habría abierto	(Vd) abra
1. abriríamos	habríamos abierto	(nosotros) abramos
2. abriríais	habríais abierto	(vosotros) abrid
3. abrirían	habrían abierto	(Vds) abran

SUBJUNCTIVE

PRESENT	IMPERFECT	PLUPERFECT
1. abra	abr-iera/iese	hubiera abierto
2. abras	abr-ieras/ieses	hubieras abierto
3. abra	abr-iera/iese	hubiera abierto
1. abramos	abr-iéramos/iésemos	hubiéramos abierto
2. abráis	abr-ierais/ieseis	hubierais abierto
3. abran	abr-ieran/iesen	hubieran abierto

PERFECT	haya abierto *etc*

INFINITIVE

PARTICIPLE

PRESENT	PRESENT
abrir	abriendo

PAST	PAST
haber abierto	abierto

ACABAR
5   *to finish*

PRESENT	IMPERFECT	FUTURE
1. acabo	acababa	acabaré
2. acabas	acababas	acabarás
3. acaba	acababa	acabará
1. acabamos	acabábamos	acabaremos
2. acabáis	acababais	acabaréis
3. acaban	acababan	acabarán

PRETERITE	PERFECT	PLUPERFECT
1. acabé	he acabado	había acabado
2. acabaste	has acabado	habías acabado
3. acabó	ha acabado	había acabado
1. acabamos	hemos acabado	habíamos acabado
2. acabasteis	habéis acabado	habíais acabado
3. acabaron	han acabado	habían acabado

PAST ANTERIOR	FUTURE PERFECT
hube acabado *etc*	habré acabado *etc*

CONDITIONAL   IMPERATIVE

PRESENT	PAST	IMPERATIVE
1. acabaría	habría acabado	
2. acabarías	habrías acabado	(tú) acaba
3. acabaría	habría acabado	(Vd) acabe
1. acabaríamos	habríamos acabado	(nosotros) acabemos
2. acabaríais	habríais acabado	(vosotros) acabad
3. acabarían	habrían acabado	(Vds) acaben

SUBJUNCTIVE

PRESENT	IMPERFECT	PLUPERFECT
1. acabe	acab-ara/ase	hubiera acabado
2. acabes	acab-aras/ases	hubieras acabado
3. acabe	acab-ara/ase	hubiera acabado
1. acabemos	acab-áramos/ásemos	hubiéramos acabado
2. acabéis	acab-arais/aseis	hubierais acabado
3. acaben	acab-aran/asen	hubieran acabado

PERFECT	haya acabado *etc*

INFINITIVE   PARTICIPLE

PRESENT	PRESENT
acabar	acabando

PAST	PAST
haber acabado	acabado

PRESENT	IMPERFECT	FUTURE
1. acentúo	acentuaba	acentuaré
2. acentúas	acentuabas	acentuarás
3. acentúa	acentuaba	acentuará
1. acentuamos	acentuábamos	acentuaremos
2. acentuáis	acentuabais	acentuaréis
3. acentúan	acentuaban	acentuarán

PRETERITE	PERFECT	PLUPERFECT
1. acentué	he acentuado	había acentuado
2. acentuaste	has acentuado	habías acentuado
3. acentuó	ha acentuado	había acentuado
1. acentuamos	hemos acentuado	habíamos acentuado
2. acentuasteis	habéis acentuado	habíais acentuado
3. acentuaron	han acentuado	habían acentuado

PAST ANTERIOR	FUTURE PERFECT
hube acentuado *etc*	habré acentuado *etc*

CONDITIONAL

IMPERATIVE

PRESENT	PAST	
1. acentuaría	habría acentuado	
2. acentuarías	habrías acentuado	(tú) acentúa
3. acentuaría	habría acentuado	(Vd) acentúe
1. acentuaríamos	habríamos acentuado	(nosotros) acentuemos
2. acentuaríais	habríais acentuado	(vosotros) acentuad
3. acentuarían	habrían acentuado	(Vds) acentúen

SUBJUNCTIVE

PRESENT	IMPERFECT	PLUPERFECT
1. acentúe	acentu-ara/ase	hubiera acentuado
2. acentúes	acentu-aras/ases	hubieras acentuado
3. acentúe	acentu-ara/ase	hubiera acentuado
1. acentuemos	acentu-áramos/ásemos	hubiéramos acentuado
2. acentuéis	acentu-arais/aseis	hubierais acentuado
3. acentúen	acentu-aran/asen	hubieran acentuado

PERFECT	haya acentuado *etc*

INFINITIVE

PARTICIPLE

PRESENT	PRESENT
acentuar	acentuando

PAST	PAST
haber acentuado	acentuado

ACERCARSE

7 *to approach*

PRESENT	IMPERFECT	FUTURE
1. me acerco	me acercaba	me acercaré
2. te acercas	te acercabas	te acercarás
3. se acerca	se acercaba	se acercará
1. nos acercamos	nos acercábamos	nos acercaremos
2. os acercáis	os acercabais	os acercaréis
3. se acercan	se acercaban	se acercarán

PRETERITE	PERFECT	PLUPERFECT
1. me acerqué	me he acercado	me había acercado
2. te acercaste	te has acercado	te habías acercado
3. se acercó	se ha acercado	se había acercado
1. nos acercamos	nos hemos acercado	nos habíamos acercado
2. os acercasteis	os habéis acercado	os habíais acercado
3. se acercaron	se han acercado	se habían acercado

PAST ANTERIOR	FUTURE PERFECT
me hube acercado *etc*	me habré acercado *etc*

CONDITIONAL

IMPERATIVE

PRESENT	PAST	
1. me acercaría	me habría acercado	
2. te acercarías	te habrías acercado	(tú) acércate
3. se acercaría	se habría acercado	(Vd) acérquese
1. nos acercaríamos	nos habríamos acercado	(nosotros) acerquémonos
2. os acercaríais	os habríais acercado	(vosotros) acercaos
3. se acercarían	se habrían acercado	(Vds) acérquense

SUBJUNCTIVE

PRESENT	IMPERFECT	PLUPERFECT
1. me acerque	me acerc-ara/ase	me hubiera acercado
2. te acerques	te acerc-aras/ases	te hubieras acercado
3. se acerque	se acerc-ara/ase	se hubiera acercado
1. nos acerquemos	nos acerc-áramos/ásemos	nos hubiéramos acercado
2. os acerquéis	os acerc-arais/aseis	os hubierais acercado
3. se acerquen	se acerc-aran/asen	se hubieran acercado

PERFECT me haya acercado *etc*

INFINITIVE

PARTICIPLE

PRESENT	PRESENT
acercarse	acercándose

PAST	PAST
haberse acercado	acercado

PRESENT	**IMPERFECT**	**FUTURE**
1. me acuerdo	me acordaba	me acordaré
2. te acuerdas	te acordabas	te acordarás
3. se acuerda	se acordaba	se acordará
1. nos acordamos	nos acordábamos	nos acordaremos
2. os acordáis	os acordabais	os acordaréis
3. se acuerdan	se acordaban	se acordarán

PRETERITE	**PERFECT**	**PLUPERFECT**
1. me acordé	me he acordado	me había acordado
2. te acordaste	te has acordado	te habías acordado
3. se acordó	se ha acordado	se había acordado
1. nos acordamos	nos hemos acordado	nos habíamos acordado
2. os acordasteis	os habéis acordado	os habíais acordado
3. se acordaron	se han acordado	se habían acordado

PAST ANTERIOR	**FUTURE PERFECT**
me hube acordado *etc*	me habré acordado *etc*

CONDITIONAL

IMPERATIVE

PRESENT	**PAST**	
1. me acordaría	me habría acordado	
2. te acordarías	te habrías acordado	(tú) acuérdate
3. se acordaría	se habría acordado	(Vd) acuérdese
1. nos acordaríamos	nos habríamos acordado	(nosotros) acordémonos
2. os acordaríais	os habríais acordado	(vosotros) acordaos
3. se acordarían	se habrían acordado	(Vds) acuérdense

SUBJUNCTIVE

PRESENT	**IMPERFECT**	**PLUPERFECT**
1. me acuerde	me acord-ara/ase	me hubiera acordado
2. te acuerdes	te acord-aras/ases	te hubieras acordado
3. se acuerde	se acord-ara/ase	se hubiera acordado
1. nos acordemos	nos acord-áramos/ásemos	nos hubiéramos acordado
2. os acordéis	os acord-arais/aseis	os hubierais acordado
3. se acuerden	se acord-aran/asen	se hubieran acordado

PERFECT me haya acordado *etc*

INFINITIVE

PARTICIPLE

PRESENT	**PRESENT**
acordarse	acordándose

PAST	**PAST**
haberse acordado	acordado

PRESENT	IMPERFECT	FUTURE
1. adquiero	adquiría	adquiriré
2. adquieres	adquirías	adquirirás
3. adquiere	adquiría	adquirirá
1. adquirimos	adquiríamos	adquiriremos
2. adquirís	adquiríais	adquiriréis
3. adquieren	adquirían	adquirirán

PRETERITE	PERFECT	PLUPERFECT
1. adquirí	he adquirido	había adquirido
2. adquiriste	has adquirido	habías adquirido
3. adquirió	ha adquirido	había adquirido
1. adquirimos	hemos adquirido	habíamos adquirido
2. adquiristeis	habéis adquirido	habíais adquirido
3. adquirieron	han adquirido	habían adquirido

PAST ANTERIOR	FUTURE PERFECT
hube adquirido *etc*	habré adquirido *etc*

CONDITIONAL

IMPERATIVE

PRESENT	PAST	
1. adquiriría	habría adquirido	
2. adquirirías	habrías adquirido	(tú) adquiere
3. adquiriría	habría adquirido	(Vd) adquiera
1. adquiriríamos	habríamos adquirido	(nosotros) adquiramos
2. adquiriríais	habríais adquirido	(vosotros) adquirid
3. adquirirían	habrían adquirido	(Vds) adquieran

SUBJUNCTIVE

PRESENT	IMPERFECT	PLUPERFECT
1. adquiera	adquir-iera/iese	hubiera adquirido
2. adquieras	adquir-ieras/ieses	hubieras adquirido
3. adquiera	adquir-iera/iese	hubiera adquirido
1. adquiramos	adquir-iéramos/iésemos	hubiéramos adquirido
2. adquiráis	adquir-ierais/ieseis	hubierais adquirido
3. adquieran	adquir-ieran/iesen	hubieran adquirido

PERFECT haya adquirido *etc*

INFINITIVE

PARTICIPLE

PRESENT	PRESENT
adquirir	adquiriendo

PAST	PAST
haber adquirido	adquirido

PRESENT	IMPERFECT	FUTURE
1. agüero	agoraba	agoraré
2. agüeras	agorabas	agorarás
3. agüera	agoraba	agorará
1. agoramos	agorábamos	agoraremos
2. agoráis	agorabais	agoraréis
3. agüeran	agoraban	agorarán

PRETERITE	PERFECT	PLUPERFECT
1. agoré	he agorado	había agorado
2. agoraste	has agorado	habías agorado
3. agoró	ha agorado	había agorado
1. agoramos	hemos agorado	habíamos agorado
2. agorasteis	habéis agorado	habíais agorado
3. agoraron	han agorado	habían agorado

PAST ANTERIOR	FUTURE PERFECT
hube agorado *etc*	habré agorado *etc*

CONDITIONAL

IMPERATIVE

PRESENT	PAST	
1. agoraría	habría agorado	
2. agorarías	habrías agorado	(tú) agüera
3. agoraría	habría agorado	(Vd) agüere
1. agoraríamos	habríamos agorado	(nosotros) agoremos
2. agoraríais	habríais agorado	(vosotros) agorad
3. agorarían	habrían agorado	(Vds) agüeren

SUBJUNCTIVE

PRESENT	IMPERFECT	PLUPERFECT
1. agüere	agor-ara/ase	hubiera agorado
2. agüeres	agor-aras/ases	hubieras agorado
3. agüere	agor-ara/ase	hubiera agorado
1. agoremos	agor-áramos/ásemos	hubiéramos agorado
2. agoréis	agor-arais/aseis	hubierais agorado
3. agüeren	agor-aran/asen	hubieran agorado

PERFECT   haya agorado *etc*

INFINITIVE

PARTICIPLE

PRESENT	PRESENT
agorar	agorando

PAST	PAST
haber agorado	agorado

AGRADECER

11 *to be grateful for; to thank*

PRESENT	IMPERFECT	FUTURE
1. agradezco	agradecía	agradeceré
2. agradeces	agradecías	agradecerás
3. agradece	agradecía	agradecerá
1. agradecemos	agradecíamos	agradeceremos
2. agradecéis	agradecíais	agradeceréis
3. agradecen	agradecían	agradecerán

PRETERITE	PERFECT	PLUPERFECT
1. agradecí	he agradecido	había agradecido
2. agradeciste	has agradecido	habías agradecido
3. agradeció	ha agradecido	había agradecido
1. agradecimos	hemos agradecido	habíamos agradecido
2. agradecisteis	habéis agradecido	habíais agradecido
3. agradecieron	han agradecido	habían agradecido

PAST ANTERIOR	FUTURE PERFECT
hube agradecido *etc*	habré agradecido *etc*

CONDITIONAL

IMPERATIVE

PRESENT	PAST	
1. agradecería	habría agradecido	
2. agradecerías	habrías agradecido	(tú) agradece
3. agradecería	habría agradecido	(Vd) agradezca
1. agradeceríamos	habríamos agradecido	(nosotros) agradezcamos
2. agradeceríais	habríais agradecido	(vosotros) agradeced
3. agradecerían	habrían agradecido	(Vds) agradezcan

SUBJUNCTIVE

PRESENT	IMPERFECT	PLUPERFECT
1. agradezca	agradec-iera/iese	hubiera agradecido
2. agradezcas	agradec-ieras/ieses	hubieras agradecido
3. agradezca	agradec-iera/iese	hubiera agradecido
1. agradezcamos	agradec-iéramos/iésemos	hubiéramos agradecido
2. agradezcáis	agradec-ierais/ieseis	hubierais agradecido
3. agradezcan	agradec-ieran/iesen	hubieran agradecido

PERFECT	haya agradecido *etc*

INFINITIVE	PARTICIPLE
PRESENT	PRESENT
agradecer	agradeciendo
PAST	PAST
haber agradecido	agradecido

PRESENT	IMPERFECT	FUTURE
1. alcanzo	alcanzaba	alcanzaré
2. alcanzas	alcanzabas	alcanzarás
3. alcanza	alcanzaba	alcanzará
1. alcanzamos	alcanzábamos	alcanzaremos
2. alcanzáis	alcanzabais	alcanzaréis
3. alcanzan	alcanzaban	alcanzarán

PRETERITE	PERFECT	PLUPERFECT
1. alcancé	he alcanzado	había alcanzado
2. alcanzaste	has alcanzado	habías alcanzado
3. alcanzó	ha alcanzado	había alcanzado
1. alcanzamos	hemos alcanzado	habíamos alcanzado
2. alcanzasteis	habéis alcanzado	habíais alcanzado
3. alcanzaron	han alcanzado	habían alcanzado

PAST ANTERIOR	FUTURE PERFECT
hube alcanzado *etc*	habré alcanzado *etc*

CONDITIONAL

IMPERATIVE

PRESENT	PAST	
1. alcanzaría	habría alcanzado	
2. alcanzarías	habrías alcanzado	(tú) alcanza
3. alcanzaría	habría alcanzado	(Vd) alcance
1. alcanzaríamos	habríamos alcanzado	(nosotros) alcancemos
2. alcanzaríais	habríais alcanzado	(vosotros) alcanzad
3. alcanzarían	habrían alcanzado	(Vds) alcancen

SUBJUNCTIVE

PRESENT	IMPERFECT	PLUPERFECT
1. alcance	alcanz-ara/ase	hubiera alcanzado
2. alcances	alcanz-aras/ases	hubieras alcanzado
3. alcance	alcanz-ara/ase	hubiera alcanzado
1. alcancemos	alcanz-áramos/ásemos	hubiéramos alcanzado
2. alcancéis	alcanz-arais/aseis	hubierais alcanzado
3. alcancen	alcanz-aran/asen	hubieran alcanzado

PERFECT	haya alcanzado *etc*

INFINITIVE

PARTICIPLE

PRESENT	PRESENT
alcanzar	alcanzando

PAST	PAST
haber alcanzado	alcanzado

ALMORZAR
13 *to have lunch*

PRESENT	IMPERFECT	FUTURE
1. almuerzo	almorzaba	almorzaré
2. almuerzas	almorzabas	almorzarás
3. almuerza	almorzaba	almorzará
1. almorzamos	almorzábamos	almorzaremos
2. almorzáis	almorzabais	almorzaréis
3. almuerzan	almorzaban	almorzarán

PRETERITE	PERFECT	PLUPERFECT
1. almorcé	he almorzado	había almorzado
2. almorzaste	has almorzado	habías almorzado
3. almorzó	ha almorzado	había almorzado
1. almorzamos	hemos almorzado	habíamos almorzado
2. almorzasteis	habéis almorzado	habíais almorzado
3. almorzaron	han almorzado	habían almorzado

PAST ANTERIOR	FUTURE PERFECT
hube almorzado *etc*	habré almorzado *etc*

CONDITIONAL

IMPERATIVE

PRESENT	PAST	
1. almorzaría	habría almorzado	
2. almorzarías	habrías almorzado	(tú) almuerza
3. almorzaría	habría almorzado	(Vd) almuerce
1. almorzaríamos	habríamos almorzado	(nosotros) almorcemos
2. almorzaríais	habríais almorzado	(vosotros) almorzad
3. almorzarían	habrían almorzado	(Vds) almuercen

SUBJUNCTIVE

PRESENT	IMPERFECT	PLUPERFECT
1. almuerce	almorz-ara/ase	hubiera almorzado
2. almuerces	almorz-aras/ases	hubieras almorzado
3. almuerce	almorz-ara/ase	hubiera almorzado
1. almorcemos	almorz-áramos/ásemos	hubiéramos almorzado
2. almorcéis	almorz-arais/aseis	hubierais almorzado
3. almuercen	almorz-aran/asen	hubieran almorzado

PERFECT haya almorzado *etc*

INFINITIVE

PARTICIPLE

PRESENT	PRESENT
almorzar	almorzando

PAST	PAST
haber almorzado	almorzado

PRESENT	IMPERFECT	FUTURE
1. amanezco	amanecía	amaneceré
2. amaneces	amanecías	amanecerás
3. amanece	amanecía	amanecerá
1. amanecemos	amanecíamos	amaneceremos
2. amanecéis	amanecíais	amaneceréis
3. amanecen	amanecían	amanecerán

PRETERITE	PERFECT	PLUPERFECT
1. amanecí	he amanecido	había amanecido
2. amaneciste	has amanecido	habías amanecido
3. amaneció	ha amanecido	había amanecido
1. amanecimos	hemos amanecido	habíamos amanecido
2. amanecisteis	habéis amanecido	habíais amanecido
3. amanecieron	han amanecido	habían amanecido

PAST ANTERIOR		FUTURE PERFECT
hube amanecido *etc*		habré amanecido *etc*

CONDITIONAL

IMPERATIVE

PRESENT	PAST	
1. amanecería	habría amanecido	
2. amanecerías	habrías amanecido	(tú) amanece
3. amanecería	habría amanecido	(Vd) amanezca
1. amaneceríamos	habríamos amanecido	(nosotros) amanezcamos
2. amaneceríais	habríais amanecido	(vosotros) amaneced
3. amanecerían	habrían amanecido	(Vds) amanezcan

SUBJUNCTIVE

PRESENT	IMPERFECT	PLUPERFECT
1. amanezca	amanec-iera/iese	hubiera amanecido
2. amanezcas	amanec-ieras/ieses	hubieras amanecido
3. amanezca	amanec-iera/iese	hubiera amanecido
1. amanezcamos	amanec-iéramos/iésemos	hubiéramos amanecido
2. amanezcáis	amanec-ierais/ieseis	hubierais amanecido
3. amanezcan	amanec-ieran/iesen	hubieran amanecido

PERFECT   haya amanecido *etc*

INFINITIVE	PARTICIPLE	NOTE
PRESENT	**PRESENT**	Normally used in third person singular.
amanecer	amaneciendo	
PAST	**PAST**	
haber amanecido	amanecido	

PRESENT	IMPERFECT	FUTURE
1. ando	andaba	andaré
2. andas	andabas	andarás
3. anda	andaba	andará
1. andamos	andábamos	andaremos
2. andáis	andabais	andaréis
3. andan	andaban	andarán

PRETERITE	PERFECT	PLUPERFECT
1. anduve	he andado	había andado
2. anduviste	has andado	habías andado
3. anduvo	ha andado	había andado
1. anduvimos	hemos andado	habíamos andado
2. anduvisteis	habéis andado	habíais andado
3. anduvieron	han andado	habían andado

PAST ANTERIOR	FUTURE PERFECT
hube andado *etc*	habré andado *etc*

CONDITIONAL		IMPERATIVE

PRESENT	PAST	
1. andaría	habría andado	
2. andarías	habrías andado	(tú) anda
3. andaría	habría andado	(Vd) ande
1. andaríamos	habríamos andado	(nosotros) andemos
2. andaríais	habríais andado	(vosotros) andad
3. andarían	habrían andado	(Vds) anden

SUBJUNCTIVE

PRESENT	IMPERFECT	PLUPERFECT
1. ande	anduv-iera/iese	hubiera andado
2. andes	anduv-ieras/ieses	hubieras andado
3. ande	anduv-iera/iese	hubiera andado
1. andemos	anduv-iéramos/iésemos	hubiéramos andado
2. andéis	anduv-ierais/ieseis	hubierais andado
3. anden	anduv-ieran/iesen	hubieran andado

PERFECT	haya andado *etc*

INFINITIVE	PARTICIPLE

PRESENT	PRESENT
andar	andando

PAST	PAST
haber andado	andado

PRESENT	IMPERFECT	FUTURE
3. anochece	anochecía	anochecerá

PRETERITE	PERFECT	PLUPERFECT
3. anocheció	ha anochecido	había anochecido

PAST ANTERIOR		FUTURE PERFECT
hubo anochecido		habrá anochecido

CONDITIONAL		IMPERATIVE

PRESENT	PAST	
3. anochecería	habría anochecido	

SUBJUNCTIVE		

PRESENT	IMPERFECT	PLUPERFECT
3. anochezca	anochec-iera/iese	hubiera anochecido
PERFECT	haya anochecido	

INFINITIVE	PARTICIPLE

PRESENT	PRESENT
anochecer	anocheciendo
PAST	PAST
haber anochecido	anochecido

ANUNCIAR
17 *to announce*

PRESENT	IMPERFECT	FUTURE
1. anuncio	anunciaba	anunciaré
2. anuncias	anunciabas	anunciarás
3. anuncia	anunciaba	anunciará
1. anunciamos	anunciábamos	anunciaremos
2. anunciáis	anunciabais	anunciaréis
3. anuncian	anunciaban	anunciarán

PRETERITE	PERFECT	PLUPERFECT
1. anuncié	he anunciado	había anunciado
2. anunciaste	has anunciado	habías anunciado
3. anunció	ha anunciado	había anunciado
1. anunciamos	hemos anunciado	habíamos anunciado
2. anunciasteis	habéis anunciado	habíais anunciado
3. anunciaron	han anunciado	habían anunciado

PAST ANTERIOR	FUTURE PERFECT
hube anunciado *etc*	habré anunciado *etc*

CONDITIONAL

IMPERATIVE

PRESENT	PAST	
1. anunciaría	habría anunciado	
2. anunciarías	habrías anunciado	(tú) anuncia
3. anunciaría	habría anunciado	(Vd) anuncie
1. anunciaríamos	habríamos anunciado	(nosotros) anunciemos
2. anunciaríais	habríais anunciado	(vosotros) anunciad
3. anunciarían	habrían anunciado	(Vds) anuncien

SUBJUNCTIVE

PRESENT	IMPERFECT	PLUPERFECT
1. anuncie	anunci-ara/ase	hubiera anunciado
2. anuncies	anunci-aras/ases	hubieras anunciado
3. anuncie	anunci-ara/ase	hubiera anunciado
1. anunciemos	anunci-áramos/ásemos	hubiéramos anunciado
2. anunciéis	anunci-arais/aseis	hubierais anunciado
3. anuncien	anunci-aran/asen	hubieran anunciado

PERFECT   haya anunciado *etc*

INFINITIVE

PARTICIPLE

PRESENT	PRESENT
anunciar	anunciando

PAST	PAST
haber anunciado	anunciado

PRESENT
1. aparezco
2. apareces
3. aparece
1. aparecemos
2. aparecéis
3. aparecen

IMPERFECT
aparecía
aparecías
aparecía
aparecíamos
aparecíais
aparecían

FUTURE
apareceré
aparecerás
aparecerá
apareceremos
apareceréis
aparecerán

PRETERITE
1. aparecí
2. apareciste
3. apareció
1. aparecimos
2. aparecisteis
3. aparecieron

PERFECT
he aparecido
has aparecido
ha aparecido
hemos aparecido
habéis aparecido
han aparecido

PLUPERFECT
había aparecido
habías aparecido
había aparecido
habíamos aparecido
habíais aparecido
habían aparecido

PAST ANTERIOR
hube aparecido *etc*

FUTURE PERFECT
habré aparecido *etc*

CONDITIONAL

PRESENT
1. aparecería
2. aparecerías
3. aparecería
1. apareceríamos
2. apareceríais
3. aparecerían

PAST
habría aparecido
habrías aparecido
habría aparecido
habríamos aparecido
habríais aparecido
habrían aparecido

IMPERATIVE

(tú) aparece
(Vd) aparezca
(nosotros) aparezcamos
(vosotros) apareced
(Vds) aparezcan

SUBJUNCTIVE

PRESENT
1. aparezca
2. aparezcas
3. aparezca
1. aparezcamos
2. aparezcáis
3. aparezcan

IMPERFECT
aparec-iera/iese
aparec-ieras/ieses
aparec-iera/iese
aparec-iéramos/iésemos
aparec-ierais/ieseis
aparec-ieran/iesen

PLUPERFECT
hubiera aparecido
hubieras aparecido
hubiera aparecido
hubiéramos aparecido
hubierais aparecido
hubieran aparecido

PERFECT   haya aparecido *etc*

INFINITIVE

PRESENT
aparecer

PAST
haber aparecido

PARTICIPLE

PRESENT
apareciendo

PAST
aparecido

APETECER

19 *to feel like*

PRESENT	IMPERFECT	FUTURE
1. apetezco	apetecía	apeteceré
2. apeteces	apetecías	apetecerás
3. apetece	apetecía	apetecerá
1. apetecemos	apetecíamos	apeteceremos
2. apetecéis	apetecíais	apeteceréis
3. apetecen	apetecían	apetecerán

PRETERITE	PERFECT	PLUPERFECT
1. apetecí	he apetecido	había apetecido
2. apeteciste	has apetecido	habías apetecido
3. apeteció	ha apetecido	había apetecido
1. apetecimos	hemos apetecido	habíamos apetecido
2. apetecisteis	habéis apetecido	habíais apetecido
3. apetecieron	han apetecido	habían apetecido

PAST ANTERIOR
hube apetecido *etc*

FUTURE PERFECT
habré apetecido *etc*

CONDITIONAL

IMPERATIVE

PRESENT	PAST	
1. apetecería	habría apetecido	
2. apetecerías	habrías apetecido	(tú) apetece
3. apetecería	habría apetecido	(Vd) apetezca
1. apeteceríamos	habríamos apetecido	(nosotros) apetezcamos
2. apeteceríais	habríais apetecido	(vosotros) apeteced
3. apetecerían	habrían apetecido	(Vds) apetezcan

SUBJUNCTIVE

PRESENT	IMPERFECT	PLUPERFECT
1. apetezca	apetec-iera/iese	hubiera apetecido
2. apetezcas	apetec-ieras/ieses	hubieras apetecido
3. apetezca	apetec-iera/iese	hubiera apetecido
1. apetezcamos	apetec-iéramos/iésemos	hubiéramos apetecido
2. apetezcáis	apetec-ierais/ieseis	hubierais apetecido
3. apetezcan	apetec-ieran/iesen	hubieran apetecido

PERFECT   haya apetecido *etc*

INFINITIVE

PARTICIPLE

NOTE

PRESENT	PRESENT	
apetecer	apeteciendo	

PAST — haber apetecido

PAST — apetecido

Normally used in third person only;
I feel like = me apetece

PRESENT	IMPERFECT	FUTURE
1. aprieto	apretaba	apretaré
2. aprietas	apretabas	apretarás
3. aprieta	apretaba	apretará
1. apretamos	apretábamos	apretaremos
2. apretáis	apretabais	apretaréis
3. aprietan	apretaban	apretarán

PRETERITE	PERFECT	PLUPERFECT
1. apreté	he apretado	había apretado
2. apretaste	has apretado	habías apretado
3. apretó	ha apretado	había apretado
1. apretamos	hemos apretado	habíamos apretado
2. apretasteis	habéis apretado	habíais apretado
3. apretaron	han apretado	habían apretado

PAST ANTERIOR		FUTURE PERFECT
hube apretado *etc*		habré apretado *etc*

CONDITIONAL

IMPERATIVE

PRESENT	PAST	
1. apretaría	habría apretado	
2. apretarías	habrías apretado	(tú) aprieta
3. apretaría	habría apretado	(Vd) apriete
1. apretaríamos	habríamos apretado	(nosotros) apretemos
2. apretaríais	habríais apretado	(vosotros) apretad
3. apretarían	habrían apretado	(Vds) aprieten

SUBJUNCTIVE

PRESENT	IMPERFECT	PLUPERFECT
1. apriete	apret-ara/ase	hubiera apretado
2. aprietes	apret-aras/ases	hubieras apretado
3. apriete	apret-ara/ase	hubiera apretado
1. apretemos	apret-áramos/ásemos	hubiéramos apretado
2. apretéis	apret-arais/aseis	hubierais apretado
3. aprieten	apret-aran/asen	hubieran apretado
PERFECT	haya apretado *etc*	

INFINITIVE

PARTICIPLE

PRESENT	PRESENT
apretar	apretando

PAST	PAST
haber apretado	apretado

APROBAR

21 *to approve; to pass*

PRESENT	IMPERFECT	FUTURE
1. apruebo	aprobaba	aprobaré
2. apruebas	aprobabas	aprobarás
3. aprueba	aprobaba	aprobará
1. aprobamos	aprobábamos	aprobaremos
2. aprobáis	aprobabais	aprobaréis
3. aprueban	aprobaban	aprobarán

PRETERITE	PERFECT	PLUPERFECT
1. aprobé	he aprobado	había aprobado
2. aprobaste	has aprobado	habías aprobado
3. aprobó	ha aprobado	había aprobado
1. aprobamos	hemos aprobado	habíamos aprobado
2. aprobasteis	habéis aprobado	habíais aprobado
3. aprobaron	han aprobado	habían aprobado

PAST ANTERIOR		FUTURE PERFECT
hube aprobado *etc*		habré aprobado *etc*

CONDITIONAL

IMPERATIVE

PRESENT	PAST	
1. aprobaría	habría aprobado	
2. aprobarías	habrías aprobado	
3. aprobaría	habría aprobado	(tú) aprueba
1. aprobaríamos	habríamos aprobado	(Vd) apruebe
2. aprobaríais	habríais aprobado	(nosotros) aprobemos
3. aprobarían	habrían aprobado	(vosotros) aprobad
		(Vds) aprueben

SUBJUNCTIVE

PRESENT	IMPERFECT	PLUPERFECT
1. apruebe	aprob-ara/ase	hubiera aprobado
2. apruebes	aprob-aras/ases	hubieras aprobado
3. apruebe	aprob-ara/ase	hubiera aprobado
1. aprobemos	aprob-áramos/ásemos	hubiéramos aprobado
2. aprobéis	aprob-arais/aseis	hubierais aprobado
3. aprueben	aprob-aran/asen	hubieran aprobado
PERFECT	haya aprobado *etc*	

INFINITIVE

PARTICIPLE

PRESENT	PRESENT
aprobar	aprobando

PAST	PAST
haber aprobado	aprobado

PRESENT	IMPERFECT	FUTURE
1. arguyo	argüía	argüiré
2. arguyes	argüías	argüirás
3. arguye	argüía	argüirá
1. argüimos	argüíamos	argüiremos
2. argüís	argüíais	argüiréis
3. arguyen	argüían	argüirán

PRETERITE	PERFECT	PLUPERFECT
1. argüí	he argüido	había argüido
2. argüiste	has argüido	habías argüido
3. arguyó	ha argüido	había argüido
1. argüimos	hemos argüido	habíamos argüido
2. argüisteis	habéis argüido	habíais argüido
3. arguyeron	han argüido	habían argüido

PAST ANTERIOR		FUTURE PERFECT
hube argüido *etc*		habré argüido *etc*

CONDITIONAL

IMPERATIVE

PRESENT	PAST	
1. argüiría	habría argüido	
2. argüirías	habrías argüido	(tú) arguye
3. argüiría	habría argüido	(Vd) arguya
1. argüiríamos	habríamos argüido	(nosotros) arguyamos
2. argüiríais	habríais argüido	(vosotros) argüid
3. argüirían	habrían argüido	(Vds) arguyan

SUBJUNCTIVE

PRESENT	IMPERFECT	PLUPERFECT
1. arguya	argu-yera/yese	hubiera argüido
2. arguyas	argu-yeras/yeses	hubieras argüido
3. arguya	argu-yera/yese	hubiera argüido
1. arguyamos	argu-yéramos/yésemos	hubiéramos argüido
2. arguyáis	argu-yerais/yeseis	hubierais argüido
3. arguyan	argu-yeran/yesen	hubieran argüido

PERFECT	haya argüido *etc*

INFINITIVE

PARTICIPLE

PRESENT	PRESENT
argüir	arguyendo

PAST	PAST
haber argüido	argüido

ARRANCAR
23 *to pull up*

PRESENT	IMPERFECT	FUTURE
1. arranco	arrancaba	arrancaré
2. arrancas	arrancabas	arrancarás
3. arranca	arrancaba	arrancará
1. arrancamos	arrancábamos	arrancaremos
2. arrancáis	arrancabais	arrancaréis
3. arrancan	arrancaban	arrancarán

PRETERITE	PERFECT	PLUPERFECT
1. arranqué	he arrancado	había arrancado
2. arrancaste	has arrancado	habías arrancado
3. arrancó	ha arrancado	había arrancado
1. arrancamos	hemos arrancado	habíamos arrancado
2. arrancasteis	habéis arrancado	habíais arrancado
3. arrancaron	han arrancado	habían arrancado

PAST ANTERIOR		FUTURE PERFECT
hube arrancado *etc*		habré arrancado *etc*

CONDITIONAL

IMPERATIVE

PRESENT	PAST	
1. arrancaría	habría arrancado	
2. arrancarías	habrías arrancado	(tú) arranca
3. arrancaría	habría arrancado	(Vd) arranque
1. arrancaríamos	habríamos arrancado	(nosotros) arranquemos
2. arrancaríais	habríais arrancado	(vosotros) arrancad
3. arrancarían	habrían arrancado	(Vds) arranquen

SUBJUNCTIVE

PRESENT	IMPERFECT	PLUPERFECT
1. arranque	arranc-ara/ase	hubiera arrancado
2. arranques	arranc-aras/ases	hubieras arrancado
3. arranque	arranc-ara/ase	hubiera arrancado
1. arranquemos	arranc-áramos/ásemos	hubiéramos arrancado
2. arranquéis	arranc-arais/aseis	hubierais arrancado
3. arranquen	arranc-aran/asen	hubieran arrancado

PERFECT	haya arrancado *etc*

INFINITIVE

PARTICIPLE

PRESENT	PRESENT
arrancar	arrancando

PAST	PAST
haber arrancado	arrancado

PRESENT	IMPERFECT	FUTURE
1. arreglo	arreglaba	arreglaré
2. arreglas	arreglabas	arreglarás
3. arregla	arreglaba	arreglará
1. arreglamos	arreglábamos	arreglaremos
2. arregláis	arreglabais	arreglaréis
3. arreglan	arreglaban	arreglarán

PRETERITE	PERFECT	PLUPERFECT
1. arreglé	he arreglado	había arreglado
2. arreglaste	has arreglado	habías arreglado
3. arregló	ha arreglado	había arreglado
1. arreglamos	hemos arreglado	habíamos arreglado
2. arreglasteis	habéis arreglado	habíais arreglado
3. arreglaron	han arreglado	habían arreglado

PAST ANTERIOR		FUTURE PERFECT
hube arreglado *etc*		habré arreglado *etc*

CONDITIONAL

IMPERATIVE

PRESENT	PAST	
1. arreglaría	habría arreglado	
2. arreglarías	habrías arreglado	(tú) arregla
3. arreglaría	habría arreglado	(Vd) arregle
1. arreglaríamos	habríamos arreglado	(nosotros) arreglemos
2. arreglaríais	habríais arreglado	(vosotros) arreglad
3. arreglarían	habrían arreglado	(Vds) arreglen

SUBJUNCTIVE

PRESENT	IMPERFECT	PLUPERFECT
1. arregle	arregl-ara/ase	hubiera arreglado
2. arregles	arregl-aras/ases	hubieras arreglado
3. arregle	arregl-ara/ase	hubiera arreglado
1. arreglemos	arregl-áramos/ásemos	hubiéramos arreglado
2. arregléis	arregl-arais/aseis	hubierais arreglado
3. arreglen	arregl-aran/asen	hubieran arreglado
PERFECT	haya arreglado *etc*	

INFINITIVE

PARTICIPLE

PRESENT	PRESENT
arreglar	arreglando
PAST	PAST
haber arreglado	arreglado

ASCENDER

25 *to ascend*

PRESENT	IMPERFECT	FUTURE
1. asciendo	ascendía	ascenderé
2. asciendes	ascendías	ascenderás
3. asciende	ascendía	ascenderá
1. ascendemos	ascendíamos	ascenderemos
2. ascendéis	ascendíais	ascenderéis
3. ascienden	ascendían	ascenderán

PRETERITE	PERFECT	PLUPERFECT
1. ascendí	he ascendido	había ascendido
2. ascendiste	has ascendido	habías ascendido
3. ascendió	ha ascendido	había ascendido
1. ascendimos	hemos ascendido	habíamos ascendido
2. ascendisteis	habéis ascendido	habíais ascendido
3. ascendieron	han ascendido	habían ascendido

PAST ANTERIOR	FUTURE PERFECT
hube ascendido *etc*	habré ascendido *etc*

CONDITIONAL

IMPERATIVE

PRESENT	PAST	
1. ascendería	habría ascendido	
2. ascenderías	habrías ascendido	(tú) asciende
3. ascendería	habría ascendido	(Vd) ascienda
1. ascenderíamos	habríamos ascendido	(nosotros) ascendamos
2. ascenderíais	habríais ascendido	(vosotros) ascended
3. ascenderían	habrían ascendido	(Vds) asciendan

SUBJUNCTIVE

PRESENT	IMPERFECT	PLUPERFECT
1. ascienda	ascend-iera/iese	hubiera ascendido
2. asciendas	ascend-ieras/ieses	hubieras ascendido
3. ascienda	ascend-iera/iese	hubiera ascendido
1. ascendamos	ascend-iéramos/iésemos	hubiéramos ascendido
2. ascendáis	ascend-ierais/ieseis	hubierais ascendido
3. asciendan	ascend-ieran/iesen	hubieran ascendido

PERFECT	haya ascendido *etc*

INFINITIVE

PARTICIPLE

PRESENT	PRESENT
ascender	ascendiendo

PAST	PAST
haber ascendido	ascendido

PRESENT	**IMPERFECT**	**FUTURE**
1. asgo	asía	asiré
2. ases	asías	asirás
3. ase	asía	asirá
1. asimos	asíamos	asiremos
2. asís	asíais	asiréis
3. asen	asían	asirán

PRETERITE	**PERFECT**	**PLUPERFECT**
1. así	he asido	había asido
2. asiste	has asido	habías asido
3. asió	ha asido	había asido
1. asimos	hemos asido	habíamos asido
2. asisteis	habéis asido	habíais asido
3. asieron	han asido	habían asido

PAST ANTERIOR	**FUTURE PERFECT**
hube asido *etc*	habré asido *etc*

CONDITIONAL

IMPERATIVE

PRESENT	**PAST**	
1. asiría	habría asido	
2. asirías	habrías asido	(tú) ase
3. asiría	habría asido	(Vd) asga
1. asiríamos	habríamos asido	(nosotros) asgamos
2. asiríais	habríais asido	(vosotros) asid
3. asirían	habrían asido	(Vds) asgan

SUBJUNCTIVE

PRESENT	**IMPERFECT**	**PLUPERFECT**
1. asga	as-iera/iese	hubiera asido
2. asgas	as-ieras/ieses	hubieras asido
3. asga	as-iera/iese	hubiera asido
1. asgamos	as-iéramos/iésemos	hubiéramos asido
2. asgáis	as-ierais/ieseis	hubierais asido
3. asgan	as-ieran/iesen	hubieran asido

PERFECT   haya asido *etc*

INFINITIVE

PARTICIPLE

PRESENT	**PRESENT**
asir	asiendo

PAST	**PAST**
haber asido	asido

ATERRIZAR
27 *to land*

PRESENT	IMPERFECT	FUTURE
1. aterrizo	aterrizaba	aterrizaré
2. aterrizas	aterrizabas	aterrizarás
3. aterriza	aterrizaba	aterrizará
1. aterrizamos	aterrizábamos	aterrizaremos
2. aterrizáis	aterrizabais	aterrizaréis
3. aterrizan	aterrizaban	aterrizarán

PRETERITE	PERFECT	PLUPERFECT
1. aterricé	he aterrizado	había aterrizado
2. aterrizaste	has aterrizado	habías aterrizado
3. aterrizó	ha aterrizado	había aterrizado
1. aterrizamos	hemos aterrizado	habíamos aterrizado
2. aterrizasteis	habéis aterrizado	habíais aterrizado
3. aterrizaron	han aterrizado	habían aterrizado

PAST ANTERIOR	FUTURE PERFECT
hube aterrizado *etc*	habré aterrizado *etc*

CONDITIONAL

IMPERATIVE

PRESENT	PAST	
1. aterrizaría	habría aterrizado	
2. aterrizarías	habrías aterrizado	
3. aterrizaría	habría aterrizado	(tú) aterriza
1. aterrizaríamos	habríamos aterrizado	(Vd) aterrice
2. aterrizaríais	habríais aterrizado	(nosotros) aterricemos
3. aterrizarían	habrían aterrizado	(vosotros) aterrizad
		(Vds) aterricen

SUBJUNCTIVE

PRESENT	IMPERFECT	PLUPERFECT
1. aterrice	aterriz-ara/ase	hubiera aterrizado
2. aterrices	aterriz-aras/ases	hubieras aterrizado
3. aterrice	aterriz-ara/ase	hubiera aterrizado
1. aterricemos	aterriz-áramos/ásemos	hubiéramos aterrizado
2. aterricéis	aterriz-arais/aseis	hubierais aterrizado
3. aterricen	aterriz-aran/asen	hubieran aterrizado

PERFECT   haya aterrizado *etc*

INFINITIVE

PARTICIPLE

PRESENT	PRESENT
aterrizar	aterrizando

PAST	PAST
haber aterrizado	aterrizado

PRESENT	IMPERFECT	FUTURE
1. atravieso	atravesaba	atravesaré
2. atraviesas	atravesabas	atravesarás
3. atraviesa	atravesaba	atravesará
1. atravesamos	atravesábamos	atravesaremos
2. atravesáis	atravesabais	atravesaréis
3. atraviesan	atravesaban	atravesarán

PRETERITE	PERFECT	PLUPERFECT
1. atravesé	he atravesado	había atravesado
2. atravesaste	has atravesado	habías atravesado
3. atravesó	ha atravesado	había atravesado
1. atravesamos	hemos atravesado	habíamos atravesado
2. atravesasteis	habéis atravesado	habíais atravesado
3. atravesaron	han atravesado	habían atravesado

PAST ANTERIOR
hube atravesado *etc*

FUTURE PERFECT
habré atravesado *etc*

CONDITIONAL

IMPERATIVE

PRESENT	PAST	
1. atravesaría	habría atravesado	
2. atravesarías	habrías atravesado	(tú) atraviesa
3. atravesaría	habría atravesado	(Vd) atraviese
1. atravesaríamos	habríamos atravesado	(nosotros) atravesemos
2. atravesaríais	habríais atravesado	(vosotros) atravesad
3. atravesarían	habrían atravesado	(Vds) atraviesen

SUBJUNCTIVE

PRESENT	IMPERFECT	PLUPERFECT
1. atraviese	atraves-ara/ase	hubiera atravesado
2. atravieses	atraves-aras/ases	hubieras atravesado
3. atraviese	atraves-ara/ase	hubiera atravesado
1. atravesemos	atraves-áramos/ásemos	hubiéramos atravesado
2. atraveséis	atraves-arais/aseis	hubierais atravesado
3. atraviesen	atraves-aran/asen	hubieran atravesado

PERFECT   haya atravesado *etc*

INFINITIVE

PARTICIPLE

PRESENT	PRESENT
atravesar	atravesando

PAST	PAST
haber atravesado	atravesado

PRESENT
1. me avergüenzo
2. te avergüenzas
3. se avergüenza
1. nos avergonzamos
2. os avergonzáis
3. se avergüenzan

IMPERFECT
me avergonzaba
te avergonzabas
se avergonzaba
nos avergonzábamos
os avergonzabais
se avergonzaban

FUTURE
me avergonzaré
te avergonzarás
se avergonzará
nos avergonzaremos
os avergonzaréis
se avergonzarán

PRETERITE
1. me avergoncé
2. te avergonzaste
3. se avergonzó
1. nos avergonzamos
2. os avergonzasteis
3. se avergonzaron

PERFECT
me he avergonzado
te has avergonzado
se ha avergonzado
nos hemos avergonzado
os habéis avergonzado
se han avergonzado

PLUPERFECT
me había avergonzado
te habías avergonzado
se había avergonzado
nos habíamos avergonzado
os habíais avergonzado
se habían avergonzado

PAST ANTERIOR
me hube avergonzado *etc*

FUTURE PERFECT
me habré avergonzado *etc*

CONDITIONAL

PRESENT
1. me avergonzaría
2. te avergonzarías
3. se avergonzaría
1. nos avergonzaríamos
   (nosotros) avergoncémonos
2. os avergonzaríais
3. se avergonzarían

PAST
me habría avergonzado
te habrías avergonzado
se habría avergonzado
nos habríamos
  avergonzado
os habríais avergonzado
se habrían avergonzado

IMPERATIVE

(tú) avergüénzate
(Vd) avergüéncese

(vosotros) avergonzaos

(Vds) avergüéncense

SUBJUNCTIVE

PRESENT
1. me avergüence
2. te avergüences
3. se avergüence
1. nos avergoncemos

2. os avergoncéis
3. se avergüencen

IMPERFECT
me avergonz-ara/ase
te avergonz-aras/ases
se avergonz-ara/ase
nos avergonz-áramos/
  ásemos
os avergonz-arais/aseis
se avergonz-aran/asen

PLUPERFECT
me hubiera avergonzado
te hubieras avergonzado
se hubiera avergonzado
nos hubiéramos
  avergonzado
os hubierais avergonzado
se hubieran avergonzado

PERFECT me haya avergonzado *etc*

INFINITIVE

PRESENT
avergonzarse

PAST
haberse avergonzado

PARTICIPLE

PRESENT
avergonzándose

PAST
avergonzado

PRESENT
1. averiguo
2. averiguas
3. averigua
1. averiguamos
2. averiguáis
3. averiguan

IMPERFECT
averiguaba
averiguabas
averiguaba
averiguábamos
averiguabais
averiguaban

FUTURE
averiguaré
averiguarás
averiguará
averiguaremos
averiguaréis
averiguarán

PRETERITE
1. averigüé
2. averiguaste
3. averiguó
1. averiguamos
2. averiguasteis
3. averiguaron

PERFECT
he averiguado
has averiguado
ha averiguado
hemos averiguado
habéis averiguado
han averiguado

PLUPERFECT
había averiguado
habías averiguado
había averiguado
habíamos averiguado
habíais averiguado
habían averiguado

PAST ANTERIOR
hube averiguado *etc*

FUTURE PERFECT
habré averiguado *etc*

CONDITIONAL

PRESENT
1. averiguaría
2. averiguarías
3. averiguaría
1. averiguaríamos
2. averiguaríais
3. averiguarían

PAST
habría averiguado
habrías averiguado
habría averiguado
habríamos averiguado
habríais averiguado
habrían averiguado

IMPERATIVE

(tú) averigua
(Vd) averigüe
(nosotros) averigüemos
(vosotros) averiguad
(Vds) averigüen

SUBJUNCTIVE

PRESENT
1. averigüe
2. averigües
3. averigüe
1. averigüemos
2. averigüéis
3. averigüen

IMPERFECT
averigu-ara/ase
averigu-aras/ases
averigu-ara/ase
averigu-áramos/ásemos
averigu-arais/aseis
averigu-aran/asen

PLUPERFECT
hubiera averiguado
hubieras averiguado
hubiera averiguado
hubiéramos averiguado
hubierais averiguado
hubieran averiguado

PERFECT   haya averiguado *etc*

INFINITIVE

PRESENT
averiguar

PAST
haber averiguado

PARTICIPLE

PRESENT
averiguando

PAST
averiguado

BAJAR
31
to get down; to get off

PRESENT	IMPERFECT	FUTURE
1. bajo	bajaba	bajaré
2. bajas	bajabas	bajarás
3. baja	bajaba	bajará
1. bajamos	bajábamos	bajaremos
2. bajáis	bajabais	bajaréis
3. bajan	bajaban	bajarán

PRETERITE	PERFECT	PLUPERFECT
1. bajé	he bajado	había bajado
2. bajaste	has bajado	habías bajado
3. bajó	ha bajado	había bajado
1. bajamos	hemos bajado	habíamos bajado
2. bajasteis	habéis bajado	habíais bajado
3. bajaron	han bajado	habían bajado

PAST ANTERIOR	FUTURE PERFECT
hube bajado *etc*	habré bajado *etc*

CONDITIONAL

IMPERATIVE

PRESENT	PAST	
1. bajaría	habría bajado	
2. bajarías	habrías bajado	(tú) baja
3. bajaría	habría bajado	(Vd) baje
1. bajaríamos	habríamos bajado	(nosotros) bajemos
2. bajaríais	habríais bajado	(vosotros) bajad
3. bajarían	habrían bajado	(Vds) bajen

SUBJUNCTIVE

PRESENT	IMPERFECT	PLUPERFECT
1. baje	baj-ara/ase	hubiera bajado
2. bajes	baj-aras/ases	hubieras bajado
3. baje	baj-ara/ase	hubiera bajado
1. bajemos	baj-áramos/ásemos	hubiéramos bajado
2. bajéis	baj-arais/aseis	hubierais bajado
3. bajen	baj-aran/asen	hubieran bajado

PERFECT	haya bajado *etc*

INFINITIVE

PARTICIPLE

PRESENT	PRESENT
bajar	bajando

PAST	PAST
haber bajado	bajado

PRESENT	**IMPERFECT**	**FUTURE**
1. me baño	me bañaba	me bañaré
2. te bañas	te bañabas	te bañarás
3. se baña	se bañaba	se bañará
1. nos bañamos	nos bañábamos	nos bañaremos
2. os bañáis	os bañabais	os bañaréis
3. se bañan	se bañaban	se bañarán

PRETERITE	**PERFECT**	**PLUPERFECT**
1. me bañé	me he bañado	me había bañado
2. te bañaste	te has bañado	te habías bañado
3. se bañó	se ha bañado	se había bañado
1. nos bañamos	nos hemos bañado	nos habíamos bañado
2. os bañasteis	os habéis bañado	os habíais bañado
3. se bañaron	se han bañado	se habían bañado

PAST ANTERIOR		**FUTURE PERFECT**
me hube bañado *etc*		me habré bañado *etc*

CONDITIONAL		*IMPERATIVE*
PRESENT	**PAST**	
1. me bañaría	me habría bañado	
2. te bañarías	te habrías bañado	(tú) báñate
3. se bañaría	se habría bañado	(Vd) báñase
1. nos bañaríamos	nos habríamos bañado	(nosotros) bañémonos
2. os bañaríais	os habríais bañado	(vosotros) bañaos
3. se bañarían	se habrían bañado	(Vds) báñense

SUBJUNCTIVE		
PRESENT	**IMPERFECT**	**PLUPERFECT**
1. me bañe	me bañ-ara/ase	me hubiera bañado
2. te bañes	te bañ-aras/ases	te hubieras bañado
3. se bañe	se bañ-ara/ase	se hubiera bañado
1. nos bañemos	nos bañ-áramos/ásemos	nos hubiéramos bañado
2. os bañéis	os bañ-arais/aseis	os hubierais bañado
3. se bañen	se bañ-aran/asen	se hubieran bañado
PERFECT	me haya bañado *etc*	

INFINITIVE	*PARTICIPLE*
PRESENT	**PRESENT**
bañarse	bañándose
PAST	**PAST**
haberse bañado	bañado

BEBER
33 to drink

PRESENT	IMPERFECT	FUTURE
1. bebo	bebía	beberé
2. bebes	bebías	beberás
3. bebe	bebía	beberá
1. bebemos	bebíamos	beberemos
2. bebéis	bebíais	beberéis
3. beben	bebían	beberán

PRETERITE	PERFECT	PLUPERFECT
1. bebí	he bebido	había bebido
2. bebiste	has bebido	habías bebido
3. bebió	ha bebido	había bebido
1. bebimos	hemos bebido	habíamos bebido
2. bebisteis	habéis bebido	habíais bebido
3. bebieron	han bebido	habían bebido

PAST ANTERIOR		FUTURE PERFECT
hube bebido *etc*		habré bebido *etc*

CONDITIONAL		IMPERATIVE

PRESENT	PAST	
1. bebería	habría bebido	
2. beberías	habrías bebido	(tú) bebe
3. bebería	habría bebido	(Vd) beba
1. beberíamos	habríamos bebido	(nosotros) bebamos
2. beberíais	habríais bebido	(vosotros) bebed
3. beberían	habrían bebido	(Vds) beban

SUBJUNCTIVE

PRESENT	IMPERFECT	PLUPERFECT
1. beba	beb-iera/iese	hubiera bebido
2. bebas	beb-ieras/ieses	hubieras bebido
3. beba	beb-iera/iese	hubiera bebido
1. bebamos	beb-iéramos/iésemos	hubiéramos bebido
2. bebáis	beb-ierais/ieseis	hubierais bebido
3. beban	beb-ieran/iesen	hubieran bebido
PERFECT	haya bebido *etc*	

INFINITIVE	PARTICIPLE	

PRESENT	PRESENT
beber	bebiendo

PAST	PAST
haber bebido	bebido

PRESENT	**IMPERFECT**	**FUTURE**
1. bendigo	bendecía	bendeciré
2. bendices	bendecías	bendecirás
3. bendice	bendecía	bendecirá
1. bendecimos	bendecíamos	bendeciremos
2. bendecís	bendecíais	bendeciréis
3. bendicen	bendecían	bendecirán

PRETERITE	**PERFECT**	**PLUPERFECT**
1. bendije	he bendecido	había bendecido
2. bendijiste	has bendecido	habías bendecido
3. bendijo	ha bendecido	había bendecido
1. bendijimos	hemos bendecido	habíamos bendecido
2. bendijisteis	habéis bendecido	habíais bendecido
3. bendijeron	han bendecido	habían bendecido

PAST ANTERIOR	**FUTURE PERFECT**
hube bendecido *etc*	habré bendecido *etc*

CONDITIONAL

IMPERATIVE

PRESENT	**PAST**	
1. bendeciría	habría bendecido	
2. bendecirías	habrías bendecido	(tú) bendice
3. bendeciría	habría bendecido	(Vd) bendiga
1. bendeciríamos	habríamos bendecido	(nosotros) bendigamos
2. bendeciríais	habríais bendecido	(vosotros) bendecid
3. bendecirían	habrían bendecido	(Vds) bendigan

SUBJUNCTIVE

PRESENT	**IMPERFECT**	**PLUPERFECT**
1. bendiga	bendij-era/ese	hubiera bendecido
2. bendigas	bendij-eras/eses	hubieras bendecido
3. bendiga	bendij-era/ese	hubiera bendecido
1. bendigamos	bendij-éramos/ésemos	hubiéramos bendecido
2. bendigáis	bendij-erais/eseis	hubierais bendecido
3. bendigan	bendij-eran/esen	hubieran bendecido

PERFECT   haya bendecido *etc*

INFINITIVE

PARTICIPLE

PRESENT	**PRESENT**
bendecir	bendiciendo
PAST	**PAST**
haber bendecido	bendecido

BUSCAR
35   *to look for*

PRESENT	IMPERFECT	FUTURE
1. busco	buscaba	buscaré
2. buscas	buscabas	buscarás
3. busca	buscaba	buscará
1. buscamos	buscábamos	buscaremos
2. buscáis	buscabais	buscaréis
3. buscan	buscaban	buscarán

PRETERITE	PERFECT	PLUPERFECT
1. busqué	he buscado	había buscado
2. buscaste	has buscado	habías buscado
3. buscó	ha buscado	había buscado
1. buscamos	hemos buscado	habíamos buscado
2. buscasteis	habéis buscado	habíais buscado
3. buscaron	han buscado	habían buscado

PAST ANTERIOR	FUTURE PERFECT
hube buscado *etc*	habré buscado *etc*

CONDITIONAL   IMPERATIVE

PRESENT	PAST	
1. buscaría	habría buscado	
2. buscarías	habrías buscado	(tú) busca
3. buscaría	habría buscado	(Vd) busque
1. buscaríamos	habríamos buscado	(nosotros) busquemos
2. buscaríais	habríais buscado	(vosotros) buscad
3. buscarían	habrían buscado	(Vds) busquen

SUBJUNCTIVE

PRESENT	IMPERFECT	PLUPERFECT
1. busque	busc-ara/ase	hubiera buscado
2. busques	busc-aras/ases	hubieras buscado
3. busque	busc-ara/ase	hubiera buscado
1. busquemos	busc-áramos/ásemos	hubiéramos buscado
2. busquéis	busc-arais/aseis	hubierais buscado
3. busquen	busc-aran/asen	hubieran buscado

PERFECT   haya buscado *etc*

INFINITIVE   PARTICIPLE

PRESENT	PRESENT
buscar	buscando

PAST	PAST
haber buscado	buscado

PRESENT	IMPERFECT	FUTURE
1. quepo	cabía	cabré
2. cabes	cabías	cabrás
3. cabe	cabía	cabrá
1. cabemos	cabíamos	cabremos
2. cabéis	cabíais	cabréis
3. caben	cabían	cabrán

PRETERITE	PERFECT	PLUPERFECT
1. cupe	he cabido	había cabido
2. cupiste	has cabido	habías cabido
3. cupe	ha cabido	había cabido
1. cupimos	hemos cabido	habíamos cabido
2. cupisteis	habéis cabido	habíais cabido
3. cupieron	han cabido	habían cabido

PAST ANTERIOR	FUTURE PERFECT
hube cabido *etc*	habré cabido *etc*

CONDITIONAL

IMPERATIVE

PRESENT	PAST	
1. cabría	habría cabido	
2. cabrías	habrías cabido	(tú) cabe
3. cabría	habría cabido	(Vd) quepa
1. cabríamos	habríamos cabido	(nosotros) quepamos
2. cabríais	habríais cabido	(vosotros) cabed
3. cabrían	habrían cabido	(Vds) quepan

SUBJUNCTIVE

PRESENT	IMPERFECT	PLUPERFECT
1. quepa	cup-iera/iese	hubiera cabido
2. quepas	cup-ieras/ieses	hubieras cabido
3. quepa	cup-iera/iese	hubiera cabido
1. quepamos	cup-iéramos/iésemos	hubiéramos cabido
2. quepáis	cup-ierais/ieseis	hubierais cabido
3. quepan	cup-ieran/iesen	hubieran cabido

PERFECT	haya cabido *etc*

INFINITIVE

PARTICIPLE

PRESENT	PRESENT
caber	cabiendo

PAST	PAST
haber cabido	cabido

PRESENT	IMPERFECT	FUTURE
1. caigo	caía	caeré
2. caes	caías	caerás
3. cae	caía	caerá
1. caemos	caíamos	caeremos
2. caéis	caíais	caeréis
3. caen	caían	caerán

PRETERITE	PERFECT	PLUPERFECT
1. caí	he caído	había caído
2. caíste	has caído	habías caído
3. cayó	ha caído	había caído
1. caímos	hemos caído	habíamos caído
2. caísteis	habéis caído	habíais caído
3. cayeron	han caído	habían caído

PAST ANTERIOR	FUTURE PERFECT
hube caído *etc*	habré caído *etc*

CONDITIONAL

IMPERATIVE

PRESENT	PAST	
1. caería	habría caído	
2. caerías	habrías caído	(tú) cae
3. caería	habría caído	(Vd) caiga
1. caeríamos	habríamos caído	(nosotros) caigamos
2. caeríais	habríais caído	(vosotros) caed
3. caerían	habrían caído	(Vds) caigan

SUBJUNCTIVE

PRESENT	IMPERFECT	PLUPERFECT
1. caiga	ca-yera/yese	hubiera caído
2. caigas	ca-yeras/yeses	hubieras caído
3. caiga	ca-yera/yese	hubiera caído
1. caigamos	ca-yéramos/yésemos	hubiéramos caído
2. caigáis	ca-yerais/yeseis	hubierais caído
3. caigan	ca-yeran/yesen	hubieran caído

PERFECT	haya caído *etc*

INFINITIVE

PARTICIPLE

PRESENT	PRESENT
caer	cayendo

PAST	PAST
haber caído	caído

PRESENT	IMPERFECT	FUTURE
1. cargo	cargaba	cargaré
2. cargas	cargabas	cargarás
3. carga	cargaba	cargará
1. cargamos	cargábamos	cargaremos
2. cargáis	cargabais	cargaréis
3. cargan	cargaban	cargarán

PRETERITE	PERFECT	PLUPERFECT
1. cargué	he cargado	había cargado
2. cargaste	has cargado	habías cargado
3. cargó	ha cargado	había cargado
1. cargamos	hemos cargado	habíamos cargado
2. cargasteis	habéis cargado	habíais cargado
3. cargaron	han cargado	habían cargado

PAST ANTERIOR		FUTURE PERFECT
hube cargado *etc*		habré cargado *etc*

CONDITIONAL

IMPERATIVE

PRESENT	PAST	
1. cargaría	habría cargado	
2. cargarías	habrías cargado	(tú) carga
3. cargaría	habría cargado	(Vd) cargue
1. cargaríamos	habríamos cargado	(nosotros) carguemos
2. cargaríais	habríais cargado	(vosotros) cargad
3. cargarían	habrían cargado	(Vds) carguen

SUBJUNCTIVE

PRESENT	IMPERFECT	PLUPERFECT
1. cargue	carg-ara/ase	hubiera cargado
2. cargues	carg-aras/ases	hubieras cargado
3. cargue	carg-ara/ase	hubiera cargado
1. carguemos	carg-áramos/ásemos	hubiéramos cargado
2. carguéis	carg-arais/aseis	hubierais cargado
3. carguen	carg-aran/asen	hubieran cargado
PERFECT	haya cargado *etc*	

INFINITIVE	PARTICIPLE
PRESENT	**PRESENT**
cargar	cargando
PAST	**PAST**
haber cargado	cargado

CAZAR
39 to hunt

PRESENT	IMPERFECT	FUTURE
1. cazo	cazaba	cazaré
2. cazas	cazabas	cazarás
3. caza	cazaba	cazará
1. cazamos	cazábamos	cazaremos
2. cazáis	cazabais	cazaréis
3. cazan	cazaban	cazarán

PRETERITE	PERFECT	PLUPERFECT
1. cacé	he cazado	había cazado
2. cazaste	has cazado	habías cazado
3. cazó	ha cazado	había cazado
1. cazamos	hemos cazado	habíamos cazado
2. cazasteis	habéis cazado	habíais cazado
3. cazaron	han cazado	habían cazado

PAST ANTERIOR	FUTURE PERFECT
hube cazado *etc*	habré cazado *etc*

CONDITIONAL

PRESENT	PAST
1. cazaría	habría cazado
2. cazarías	habrías cazado
3. cazaría	habría cazado
1. cazaríamos	habríamos cazado
2. cazaríais	habríais cazado
3. cazarían	habrían cazado

IMPERATIVE

(tú) caza
(Vd) cace
(nosotros) cacemos
(vosotros) cazad
(Vds) cacen

SUBJUNCTIVE

PRESENT	IMPERFECT	PLUPERFECT
1. cace	caz-ara/ase	hubiera cazado
2. caces	caz-aras/ases	hubieras cazado
3. cace	caz-ara/ase	hubiera cazado
1. cacemos	caz-áramos/ásemos	hubiéramos cazado
2. cacéis	caz-arais/aseis	hubierais cazado
3. cacen	caz-aran/asen	hubieran cazado

PERFECT haya cazado *etc*

INFINITIVE

PRESENT	PARTICIPLE PRESENT
cazar	cazando

PAST	PAST
haber cazado	cazado

PRESENT	IMPERFECT	FUTURE
1. cierro	cerraba	cerraré
2. cierras	cerrabas	cerrarás
3. cierra	cerraba	cerrará
1. cerramos	cerrábamos	cerraremos
2. cerráis	cerrabais	cerraréis
3. cierran	cerraban	cerrarán

PRETERITE	PERFECT	PLUPERFECT
1. cerré	he cerrado	había cerrado
2. cerraste	has cerrado	habías cerrado
3. cerró	ha cerrado	había cerrado
1. cerramos	hemos cerrado	habíamos cerrado
2. cerrasteis	habéis cerrado	habíais cerrado
3. cerraron	han cerrado	habían cerrado

PAST ANTERIOR		FUTURE PERFECT
hube cerrado *etc*		habré cerrado *etc*

CONDITIONAL

IMPERATIVE

PRESENT	PAST	
1. cerraría	habría cerrado	
2. cerrarías	habrías cerrado	
3. cerraría	habría cerrado	(tú) cierra
1. cerraríamos	habríamos cerrado	(Vd) cierre
2. cerraríais	habríais cerrado	(nosotros) cerremos
3. cerrarían	habrían cerrado	(vosotros) cerrad
		(Vds) cierren

SUBJUNCTIVE

PRESENT	IMPERFECT	PLUPERFECT
1. cierre	cerr-ara/ase	hubiera cerrado
2. cierres	cerr-aras/ases	hubieras cerrado
3. cierre	cerr-ara/ase	hubiera cerrado
1. cerremos	cerr-áramos/ásemos	hubiéramos cerrado
2. cerréis	cerr-arais/aseis	hubierais cerrado
3. cierren	cerr-aran/asen	hubieran cerrado
PERFECT	haya cerrado *etc*	

INFINITIVE

PARTICIPLE

PRESENT	PRESENT
cerrar	cerrando

PAST	PAST
haber cerrado	cerrado

COCER
41 _to boil_

PRESENT	IMPERFECT	FUTURE
1. cuezo	cocía	coceré
2. cueces	cocías	cocerás
3. cuece	cocía	cocerá
1. cocemos	cocíamos	coceremos
2. cocéis	cocíais	coceréis
3. cuecen	cocían	cocerán

PRETERITE	PERFECT	PLUPERFECT
1. cocí	he cocido	había cocido
2. cociste	has cocido	habías cocido
3. coció	ha cocido	había cocido
1. cocimos	hemos cocido	habíamos cocido
2. cocisteis	habéis cocido	habíais cocido
3. cocieron	han cocido	habían cocido

PAST ANTERIOR		FUTURE PERFECT
hube cocido _etc_		habré cocido _etc_

CONDITIONAL

IMPERATIVE

PRESENT	PAST	
1. cocería	habría cocido	
2. cocerías	habrías cocido	(tú) cuece
3. cocería	habría cocido	(Vd) cueza
1. coceríamos	habríamos cocido	(nosotros) cozamos
2. coceríais	habríais cocido	(vosotros) coced
3. cocerían	habrían cocido	(Vds) cuezan

SUBJUNCTIVE

PRESENT	IMPERFECT	PLUPERFECT
1. cueza	coc-iera/iese	hubiera cocido
2. cuezas	coc-ieras/ieses	hubieras cocido
3. cueza	coc-iera/iese	hubiera cocido
1. cozamos	coc-iéramos/iésemos	hubiéramos cocido
2. cozáis	coc-ierais/ieseis	hubierais cocido
3. cuezan	coc-ieran/iesen	hubieran cocido

PERFECT   haya cocido _etc_

INFINITIVE

PARTICIPLE

PRESENT	PRESENT
cocer	cociendo

PAST	PAST
haber cocido	cocido

PRESENT	IMPERFECT	FUTURE
1. cojo	cogía	cogeré
2. coges	cogías	cogerás
3. coge	cogía	cogerá
1. cogemos	cogíamos	cogeremos
2. cogéis	cogíais	cogeréis
3. cogen	cogían	cogerán

PRETERITE	PERFECT	PLUPERFECT
1. cogí	he cogido	había cogido
2. cogiste	has cogido	habías cogido
3. cogió	ha cogido	había cogido
1. cogimos	hemos cogido	habíamos cogido
2. cogisteis	habéis cogido	habíais cogido
3. cogieron	han cogido	habían cogido

PAST ANTERIOR	FUTURE PERFECT
hube cogido *etc*	habré cogido *etc*

CONDITIONAL

IMPERATIVE

PRESENT	PAST	
1. cogería	habría cogido	
2. cogerías	habrías cogido	(tú) coge
3. cogería	habría cogido	(Vd) coja
1. cogeríamos	habríamos cogido	(nosotros) cojamos
2. cogeríais	habríais cogido	(vosotros) coged
3. cogerían	habrían cogido	(Vds) cojan

SUBJUNCTIVE

PRESENT	IMPERFECT	PLUPERFECT
1. coja	cog-iera/iese	hubiera cogido
2. cojas	cog-ieras/ieses	hubieras cogido
3. coja	cog-iera/iese	hubiera cogido
1. cojamos	cog-iéramos/iésemos	hubiéramos cogido
2. cojáis	cog-ierais/ieseis	hubierais cogido
3. cojan	cog-ieran/iesen	hubieran cogido

PERFECT	haya cogido *etc*

INFINITIVE

PARTICIPLE

PRESENT	PRESENT
coger	cogiendo

PAST	PAST
haber cogido	cogido

COLGAR
43 to hang

PRESENT	IMPERFECT	FUTURE
1. cuelgo	colgaba	colgaré
2. cuelgas	colgabas	colgarás
3. cuelga	colgaba	colgará
1. colgamos	colgábamos	colgaremos
2. colgáis	colgabais	colgaréis
3. cuelgan	colgaban	colgarán

PRETERITE	PERFECT	PLUPERFECT
1. colgué	he colgado	había colgado
2. colgaste	has colgado	habías colgado
3. colgó	ha colgado	había colgado
1. colgamos	hemos colgado	habíamos colgado
2. colgasteis	habéis colgado	habíais colgado
3. colgaron	han colgado	habían colgado

PAST ANTERIOR	FUTURE PERFECT
hube colgado *etc*	habré colgado *etc*

CONDITIONAL

IMPERATIVE

PRESENT	PAST	
1. colgaría	habría colgado	
2. colgarías	habrías colgado	(tú) cuelga
3. colgaría	habría colgado	(Vd) cuelgue
1. colgaríamos	habríamos colgado	(nosotros) colguemos
2. colgaríais	habríais colgado	(vosotros) colgad
3. colgarían	habrían colgado	(Vds) cuelguen

SUBJUNCTIVE

PRESENT	IMPERFECT	PLUPERFECT
1. cuelgue	colg-ara/ase	hubiera colgado
2. cuelgues	colg-aras/ases	hubieras colgado
3. cuelgue	colg-ara/ase	hubiera colgado
1. colguemos	colg-áramos/ásemos	hubiéramos colgado
2. colguéis	colg-arais/aseis	hubierais colgado
3. cuelguen	colg-aran/asen	hubieran colgado

PERFECT   haya colgado *etc*

INFINITIVE

PARTICIPLE

PRESENT	PRESENT
colgar	colgando

PAST	PAST
haber colgado	colgado

PRESENT
1. comienzo
2. comienzas
3. comienza
1. comenzamos
2. comenzáis
3. comienzan

IMPERFECT
comenzaba
comenzabas
comenzaba
comenzábamos
comenzabais
comenzaban

FUTURE
comenzaré
comenzarás
comenzará
comenzaremos
comenzaréis
comenzarán

PRETERITE
1. comencé
2. comenzaste
3. comenzó
1. comenzamos
2. comenzasteis
3. comenzaron

PERFECT
he comenzado
has comenzado
ha comenzado
hemos comenzado
habéis comenzado
han comenzado

PLUPERFECT
había comenzado
habías comenzado
había comenzado
habíamos comenzado
habíais comenzado
habían comenzado

PAST ANTERIOR
hube comenzado *etc*

FUTURE PERFECT
habré comenzado *etc*

CONDITIONAL

PRESENT
1. comenzaría
2. comenzarías
3. comenzaría
1. comenzaríamos
2. comenzaríais
3. comenzarían

PAST
habría comenzado
habrías comenzado
habría comenzado
habríamos comenzado
habríais comenzado
habrían comenzado

IMPERATIVE

(tú) comienza
(Vd) comience
(nosotros) comencemos
(vosotros) comenzad
(Vds) comiencen

SUBJUNCTIVE

PRESENT
1. comience
2. comiences
3. comience
1. comencemos
2. comencéis
3. comiencen

IMPERFECT
comenz-ara/ase
comenz-aras/ases
comenz-ara/ase
comenz-áramos/ásemos
comenz-arais/aseis
comenz-aran/asen

PLUPERFECT
hubiera comenzado
hubieras comenzado
hubiera comenzado
hubiéramos comenzado
hubierais comenzado
hubieran comenzado

PERFECT haya comenzado *etc*

INFINITIVE

PRESENT
comenzar

PAST
haber comenzado

PARTICIPLE

PRESENT
comenzando

PAST
comenzado

PRESENT	IMPERFECT	FUTURE
1. como	comía	comeré
2. comes	comías	comerás
3. come	comía	comerá
1. comemos	comíamos	comeremos
2. coméis	comíais	comeréis
3. comen	comían	comerán

PRETERITE	PERFECT	PLUPERFECT
1. comí	he comido	había comido
2. comiste	has comido	habías comido
3. comió	ha comido	había comido
1. comimos	hemos comido	habíamos comido
2. comisteis	habéis comido	habíais comido
3. comieron	han comido	habían comido

PAST ANTERIOR		FUTURE PERFECT
hube comido *etc*		habré comido *etc*

CONDITIONAL		IMPERATIVE

PRESENT	PAST	
1. comería	habría comido	
2. comerías	habrías comido	(tú) come
3. comería	habría comido	(Vd) coma
1. comeríamos	habríamos comido	(nosotros) comamos
2. comeríais	habríais comido	(vosotros) comed
3. comerían	habrían comido	(Vds) coman

SUBJUNCTIVE

PRESENT	IMPERFECT	PLUPERFECT
1. coma	com-iera/iese	hubiera comido
2. comas	com-ieras/ieses	hubieras comido
3. coma	com-iera/iese	hubiera comido
1. comamos	com-iéramos/iésemos	hubiéramos comido
2. comáis	com-ierais/ieseis	hubierais comido
3. coman	com-ieran/iesen	hubieran comido

PERFECT	haya comido *etc*

INFINITIVE	PARTICIPLE

PRESENT	PRESENT
comer	comiendo

PAST	PAST
haber comido	comido

PRESENT	**IMPERFECT**	**FUTURE**
3. compete	competía	competerá
3. competen	competían	competerán

PRETERITE	**PERFECT**	**PLUPERFECT**
3. competió	ha competido	había competido
3. competieron	han competido	habían competido

PAST ANTERIOR	**FUTURE PERFECT**
hubo competido	habrá competido
hubieron competido	habrán competido

CONDITIONAL		*IMPERATIVE*

PRESENT	**PAST**
3. competería	habría competido
3. competerían	habrían competido

SUBJUNCTIVE

PRESENT	**IMPERFECT**	**PLUPERFECT**
3. competa	compet-iera/iese	hubiera competido
3. competan	compet-ieran/iesen	hubieran competido
PERFECT	haya competido *etc*	

INFINITIVE	*PARTICIPLE*

PRESENT	**PRESENT**
competer	competiendo

PAST	**PAST**
haber competido	competido

PRESENT	IMPERFECT	FUTURE
1. compro	compraba	compraré
2. compras	comprabas	comprarás
3. compra	compraba	comprará
1. compramos	comprábamos	compraremos
2. compráis	comprabais	compraréis
3. compran	compraban	comprarán

PRETERITE	PERFECT	PLUPERFECT
1. compré	he comprado	había comprado
2. compraste	has comprado	habías comprado
3. compró	ha comprado	había comprado
1. compramos	hemos comprado	habíamos comprado
2. comprasteis	habéis comprado	habíais comprado
3. compraron	han comprado	habían comprado

PAST ANTERIOR		FUTURE PERFECT
hube comprado *etc*		habré comprado *etc*

CONDITIONAL

IMPERATIVE

PRESENT	PAST	
1. compraría	habría comprado	
2. comprarías	habrías comprado	(tú) compra
3. compraría	habría comprado	(Vd) compre
1. compraríamos	habríamos comprado	(nosotros) compremos
2. compraríais	habríais comprado	(vosotros) comprad
3. comprarían	habrían comprado	(Vds) compren

SUBJUNCTIVE

PRESENT	IMPERFECT	PLUPERFECT
1. compre	compr-ara/ase	hubiera comprado
2. compres	compr-aras/ases	hubieras comprado
3. compre	compr-ara/ase	hubiera comprado
1. compremos	compr-áramos/ásemos	hubiéramos comprado
2. compréis	compr-arais/aseis	hubierais comprado
3. compren	compr-aran/asen	hubieran comprado

PERFECT   haya comprado *etc*

INFINITIVE

PARTICIPLE

PRESENT	PRESENT
comprar	comprando

PAST	PAST
haber comprado	comprado

PRESENT	**IMPERFECT**	**FUTURE**
1. concibo	concebía	concebiré
2. concibes	concebías	concebirás
3. concibe	concebía	concebirá
1. concebimos	concebíamos	concebiremos
2. concebís	concebíais	concebiréis
3. conciben	concebían	concebirán

PRETERITE	**PERFECT**	**PLUPERFECT**
1. concebí	he concebido	había concebido
2. concebiste	has concebido	habías concebido
3. concibió	ha concebido	había concebido
1. concebimos	hemos concebido	habíamos concebido
2. concebisteis	habéis concebido	habíais concebido
3. concibieron	han concebido	habían concebido

PAST ANTERIOR	**FUTURE PERFECT**
hube concebido *etc*	habré concebido *etc*

CONDITIONAL

IMPERATIVE

PRESENT	**PAST**	
1. concebiría	habría concebido	
2. concebirías	habrías concebido	(tú) concibe
3. concebiría	habría concebido	(Vd) conciba
1. concebiríamos	habríamos concebido	(nosotros) concibamos
2. concebiríais	habríais concebido	(vosotros) concebid
3. concebirían	habrían concebido	(Vds) conciban

SUBJUNCTIVE

PRESENT	**IMPERFECT**	**PLUPERFECT**
1. conciba	concib-iera/iese	hubiera concebido
2. concibas	concib-ieras/ieses	hubieras concebido
3. conciba	concib-iera/iese	hubiera concebido
1. concibamos	concib-iéramos/iésemos	hubiéramos concebido
2. concibáis	concib-ierais/ieseis	hubierais concebido
3. conciban	concib-ieran/iesen	hubieran concebido

PERFECT	haya concebido *etc*

INFINITIVE

PARTICIPLE

PRESENT	**PRESENT**
concebir	concibiendo

PAST	**PAST**
haber concebido	concebido

CONCERNIR
49 *to concern*

PRESENT	IMPERFECT	FUTURE
3. concierne	concernía	concernirá
3. conciernen	concernían	concernirán

PRETERITE	PERFECT	PLUPERFECT
3. concernió	ha concernido	había concernido
3. concernieron	han concernido	habían concernido

PAST ANTERIOR		FUTURE PERFECT
hubo concernido		habrá concernido
hubieron concernido		habrán concernido

CONDITIONAL

IMPERATIVE

PRESENT	PAST
3. conceriría	habría concernido
3. concernirían	habrían concernido

SUBJUNCTIVE

PRESENT	IMPERFECT	PLUPERFECT
3. concierna	concern-iera/iese	hubiera concernido
3. conciernan	concern-ieran/iesen	hubieran concernido
PERFECT	haya concernido *etc*	

INFINITIVE

PARTICIPLE

PRESENT	PRESENT
concernir	concerniendo
PAST	PAST
haber concernido	concernido

PRESENT	IMPERFECT	FUTURE
1. conduzco	conducía	conduciré
2. conduces	conducías	conducirás
3. conduce	conducía	conducirá
1. conducimos	conducíamos	conduciremos
2. conducís	conducíais	conduciréis
3. conducen	conducían	conducirán

PRETERITE	PERFECT	PLUPERFECT
1. conduje	he conducido	había conducido
2. condujiste	has conducido	habías conducido
3. condujo	ha conducido	había conducido
1. condujimos	hemos conducido	habíamos conducido
2. condujisteis	habéis conducido	habíais conducido
3. condujeron	han conducido	habían conducido

PAST ANTERIOR	FUTURE PERFECT
hube conducido *etc*	habré conducido *etc*

CONDITIONAL

IMPERATIVE

PRESENT	PAST	
1. conduciría	habría conducido	
2. conducirías	habrías conducido	(tú) conduce
3. conduciría	habría conducido	(Vd) conduzca
1. conduciríamos	habríamos conducido	(nosotros) conduzcamos
2. conduciríais	habríais conducido	(vosotros) conducid
3. conducirían	habrían conducido	(Vds) conduzcan

SUBJUNCTIVE

PRESENT	IMPERFECT	PLUPERFECT
1. conduzca	conduj-era/ese	hubiera conducido
2. conduzcas	conduj-eras/eses	hubieras conducido
3. conduzca	conduj-era/ese	hubiera conducido
1. conduzcamos	conduj-éramos/ésemos	hubiéramos conducido
2. conduzcáis	conduj-erais/eseis	hubierais conducido
3. conduzcan	conduj-eran/esen	hubieran conducido

PERFECT	haya conducido *etc*

INFINITIVE

PARTICIPLE

PRESENT	PRESENT
conducir	conduciendo

PAST	PAST
haber conducido	conducido

CONOCER
51 *to know*

PRESENT	IMPERFECT	FUTURE
1. conozco	conocía	conoceré
2. conoces	conocías	conocerás
3. conoce	conocía	conocerá
1. conocemos	conocíamos	conoceremos
2. conocéis	conocíais	conoceréis
3. conocen	conocían	conocerán

PRETERITE	PERFECT	PLUPERFECT
1. conocí	he conocido	había conocido
2. conociste	has conocido	habías conocido
3. conoció	ha conocido	había conocido
1. conocimos	hemos conocido	habíamos conocido
2. conocisteis	habéis conocido	habíais conocido
3. conocieron	han conocido	habían conocido

PAST ANTERIOR		FUTURE PERFECT
hube conocido *etc*		habré conocido *etc*

CONDITIONAL

IMPERATIVE

PRESENT	PAST	
1. conocería	habría conocido	
2. conocerías	habrías conocido	(tú) conoce
3. conocería	habría conocido	(Vd) conozca
1. conoceríamos	habríamos conocido	(nosotros) conozcamos
2. conoceríais	habríais conocido	(vosotros) conoced
3. conocerían	habrían conocido	(Vds) conozcan

SUBJUNCTIVE

PRESENT	IMPERFECT	PLUPERFECT
1. conozca	conoc-iera/iese	hubiera conocido
2. conozcas	conoc-ieras/ieses	hubieras conocido
3. conozca	conoc-iera/iese	hubiera conocido
1. conozcamos	conoc-iéramos/iésemos	hubiéramos conocido
2. conozcáis	conoc-ierais/ieseis	hubierais conocido
3. conozcan	conoc-ieran/iesen	hubieran conocido

PERFECT   haya conocido *etc*

INFINITIVE

PARTICIPLE

PRESENT	PRESENT
conocer	conociendo

PAST	PAST
haber conocido	conocido

PRESENT	IMPERFECT	FUTURE
1. consuelo	consolaba	consolaré
2. consuelas	consolabas	consolarás
3. consuela	consolaba	consolará
1. consolamos	consolábamos	consolaremos
2. consoláis	consolabais	consolaréis
3. consuelan	consolaban	consolarán

PRETERITE	PERFECT	PLUPERFECT
1. consolé	he consolado	había consolado
2. consolaste	has consolado	habías consolado
3. consoló	ha consolado	había consolado
1. consolamos	hemos consolado	habíamos consolado
2. consolasteis	habéis consolado	habíais consolado
3. consolaron	han consolado	habían consolado

PAST ANTERIOR		FUTURE PERFECT
hube consolado *etc*		habré consolado *etc*

CONDITIONAL

IMPERATIVE

PRESENT	PAST	
1. consolaría	habría consolado	
2. consolarías	habrías consolado	(tú) consuela
3. consolaría	habría consolado	(Vd) consuele
1. consolaríamos	habríamos consolado	(nosotros) consolemos
2. consolaríais	habríais consolado	(vosotros) consolad
3. consolarían	habrían consolado	(Vds) consuelen

SUBJUNCTIVE

PRESENT	IMPERFECT	PLUPERFECT
1. consuele	consol-ara/ase	hubiera consolado
2. consueles	consol-aras/ases	hubieras consolado
3. consuele	consol-ara/ase	hubiera consolado
1. consolemos	consol-áramos/ásemos	hubiéramos consolado
2. consoléis	consol-arais/aseis	hubierais consolado
3. consuelen	consol-aran/asen	hubieran consolado

PERFECT   haya consolado *etc*

INFINITIVE	PARTICIPLE
PRESENT	**PRESENT**
consolar	consolando
PAST	**PAST**
haber consolado	consolado

CONSTRUIR
53 *to build*

PRESENT	IMPERFECT	FUTURE
1. construyo	construía	construiré
2. construyes	construías	construirás
3. construye	construía	construirá
1. construimos	construíamos	construiremos
2. construís	construíais	construiréis
3. construyen	construían	construirán

PRETERITE	PERFECT	PLUPERFECT
1. construí	he construido	había construido
2. construiste	has construido	habías construido
3. construyó	ha construido	había construido
1. construimos	hemos construido	habíamos construido
2. construisteis	habéis construido	habíais construido
3. construyeron	han construido	habían construido

PAST ANTERIOR		FUTURE PERFECT
hube construido *etc*		habré construido *etc*

CONDITIONAL

PRESENT	PAST
1. construiría	habría construido
2. construirías	habrías construido
3. construiría	habría construido
1. construiríamos	habríamos construido
2. construiríais	habíais construido
3. construirían	habrían construido

IMPERATIVE

(tú) construye
(Vd) construya
(nosotros) construyamos
(vosotros) construid
(Vds) construyan

SUBJUNCTIVE

PRESENT	IMPERFECT	PLUPERFECT
1. construya	constru-yera/yese	hubiera construido
2. construyas	constru-yeras/yeses	hubieras construido
3. construya	constru-yera/yese	hubiera construido
1. construyamos	constru-yéramos/yésemos	hubiéramos construido
2. construyáis	constru-yerais/yeseis	hubierais construido
3. construyan	constru-yeran/yesen	hubieran construido

PERFECT   haya construido *etc*

INFINITIVE

PRESENT
construir

PAST
haber construido

PARTICIPLE

PRESENT
construyendo

PAST
construido

PRESENT	IMPERFECT	FUTURE
1. cuento	contaba	contaré
2. cuentas	contabas	contarás
3. cuenta	contaba	contará
1. contamos	contábamos	contaremos
2. contáis	contabais	contaréis
3. cuentan	contaban	contarán

PRETERITE	PERFECT	PLUPERFECT
1. conté	he contado	había contado
2. contaste	has contado	habías contado
3. contó	ha contado	había contado
1. contamos	hemos contado	habíamos contado
2. contasteis	habéis contado	habíais contado
3. contaron	han contado	habían contado

PAST ANTERIOR		FUTURE PERFECT
hube contado *etc*		habré contado *etc*

CONDITIONAL

IMPERATIVE

PRESENT	PAST	
1. contaría	habría contado	
2. contarías	habrías contado	
3. contaría	habría contado	(tú) cuenta
1. contaríamos	habríamos contado	(Vd) cuente
2. contaríais	habríais contado	(nosotros) contemos
3. contarían	habrían contado	(vosotros) contad
		(Vds) cuenten

SUBJUNCTIVE

PRESENT	IMPERFECT	PLUPERFECT
1. cuente	cont-ara/ase	hubiera contado
2. cuentes	cont-aras/ases	hubieras contado
3. cuente	cont-ara/ase	hubiera contado
1. contemos	cont-áramos/ásemos	hubiéramos contado
2. contéis	cont-arais/aseis	hubierais contado
3. cuenten	cont-aran/asen	hubieran contado
PERFECT	haya contado *etc*	

INFINITIVE

PARTICIPLE

PRESENT	PRESENT
contar	contando

PAST	PAST
haber contado	contado

CONTESTAR
55 to answer

PRESENT	IMPERFECT	FUTURE
1. contesto	contestaba	contestaré
2. contestas	contestabas	contestarás
3. contesta	contestaba	contestará
1. contestamos	contestábamos	contestaremos
2. contestáis	contestabais	contestaréis
3. contestan	contestaban	contestarán

PRETERITE	PERFECT	PLUPERFECT
1. contesté	he contestado	había contestado
2. contestaste	has contestado	habías contestado
3. contestó	ha contestado	había contestado
1. contestamos	hemos contestado	habíamos contestado
2. contestasteis	habéis contestado	habíais contestado
3. contestaron	han contestado	habían contestado

PAST ANTERIOR
hube contestado *etc*

FUTURE PERFECT
habré contestado *etc*

CONDITIONAL

IMPERATIVE

PRESENT	PAST	
1. contestaría	habría contestado	
2. contestarías	habrías contestado	(tú) contesta
3. contestaría	habría contestado	(Vd) conteste
1. contestaríamos	habríamos contestado	(nosotros) contestemos
2. contestaríais	habríais contestado	(vosotros) contestad
3. contestarían	habrían contestado	(Vds) contesten

SUBJUNCTIVE

PRESENT	IMPERFECT	PLUPERFECT
1. conteste	contest-ara/ase	hubiera contestado
2. contestes	contest-aras/ases	hubieras contestado
3. conteste	contest-ara/ase	hubiera contestado
1. contestemos	contest-áramos/ásemos	hubiéramos contestado
2. contestéis	contest-arais/aseis	hubierais contestado
3. contesten	contest-aran/asen	hubieran contestado

PERFECT   haya contestado *etc*

INFINITIVE

PARTICIPLE

PRESENT	PRESENT
contestar	contestando

PAST	PAST
haber contestado	contestado

PRESENT
1. continúo
2. continúas
3. continúa
1. continuamos
2. continuáis
3. continúan

IMPERFECT
continuaba
continuabas
continuaba
continuábamos
continuabais
continuaban

FUTURE
continuaré
continuarás
continuará
continuaremos
continuaréis
continuarán

PRETERITE
1. continué
2. continuaste
3. continuó
1. continuamos
2. continuasteis
3. continuaron

PERFECT
he continuado
has continuado
ha continuado
hemos continuado
habéis continuado
han continuado

PLUPERFECT
había continuado
habías continuado
había continuado
habíamos continuado
habíais continuado
habían continuado

PAST ANTERIOR
hube continuado *etc*

FUTURE PERFECT
habré continuado *etc*

CONDITIONAL

PRESENT
1. continuaría
2. continuarías
3. continuaría
1. continuaríamos
2. continuaríais
3. continuarían

PAST
habría continuado
habrías continuado
habría continuado
habríamos continuado
habríais continuado
habrían continuado

IMPERATIVE

(tú) continúa
(Vd) continúe
(nosotros) continuemos
(vosotros) continuad
(Vds) continúen

SUBJUNCTIVE

PRESENT
1. continúe
2. continúes
3. continúe
1. continuemos
2. continuéis
3. continúen

IMPERFECT
continu-ara/ase
continu-aras/ases
continu-ara/ase
continu-áramos/ásemos
continu-arais/aseis
continu-aran/asen

PLUPERFECT
hubiera continuado
hubieras continuado
hubiera continuado
hubiéramos continuado
hubierais continuado
hubieran continuado

PERFECT   haya continuado *etc*

INFINITIVE

PRESENT
continuar

PAST
haber continuado

PARTICIPLE

PRESENT
continuando

PAST
continuado

PRESENT	IMPERFECT	FUTURE
1. corrijo	corregía	corregiré
2. corriges	corregías	corregirás
3. corrige	corregía	corregirá
1. corregimos	corregíamos	corregiremos
2. corrregís	corregíais	corregiréis
3. corrigen	corregían	corregirán

PRETERITE	PERFECT	PLUPERFECT
1. corregí	he corregido	había corregido
2. corregiste	has corregido	habías corregido
3. corrigió	ha corregido	había corregido
1. corregimos	hemos corregido	habíamos corregido
2. corregisteis	habéis corregido	habíais corregido
3. corrigieron	han corregido	habían corregido

PAST ANTERIOR		FUTURE PERFECT
hube corregido *etc*		habré corregido *etc*

CONDITIONAL

IMPERATIVE

PRESENT	PAST	
1. corregiría	habría corregido	
2. corregirías	habrías corregido	
3. corregiría	habría corregido	(tú) corrige
1. corregiríamos	habríamos corregido	(Vd) corrija
2. corregiríais	habríais corregido	(nosotros) corrijamos
3. corregirían	habrían corregido	(vosotros) corregid
		(Vds) corrijan

SUBJUNCTIVE

PRESENT	IMPERFECT	PLUPERFECT
1. corrija	corrig-iera/iese	hubiera corregido
2. corrijas	corrig-ieras/ieses	hubieras corregido
3. corrija	corrig-iera/iese	hubiera corregido
1. corrijamos	corrig-iéramos/iésemos	hubiéramos corregido
2. corrijáis	corrig-ierais/ieseis	hubierais corregido
3. corrijan	corrig-ieran/iesen	hubieran corregido
PERFECT	haya corregido *etc*	

INFINITIVE

PARTICIPLE

PRESENT	PRESENT
corregir	corrigiendo
PAST	PAST
haber corregido	corregido

PRESENT	IMPERFECT	FUTURE
1. corro	corría	correré
2. corres	corrías	correrás
3. corre	corría	correrá
1. corremos	corríamos	correremos
2. corréis	corríais	correréis
3. corren	corrían	correrán

PRETERITE	PERFECT	PLUPERFECT
1. corrí	he corrido	había corrido
2. corriste	has corrido	habías corrido
3. corrió	ha corrido	había corrido
1. corrimos	hemos corrido	habíamos corrido
2. corristeis	habéis corrido	habíais corrido
3. corrieron	han corrido	habían corrido

PAST ANTERIOR	FUTURE PERFECT
hube corrido *etc*	habré corrido *etc*

CONDITIONAL

IMPERATIVE

PRESENT	PAST	
1. correría	habría corrido	
2. correrías	habrías corrido	(tú) corre
3. correría	habría corrido	(Vd) corra
1. correríamos	habríamos corrido	(nosotros) corramos
2. correríais	habríais corrido	(vosotros) corred
3. correrían	habrían corrido	(Vds) corran

SUBJUNCTIVE

PRESENT	IMPERFECT	PLUPERFECT
1. corra	corr-iera/iese	hubiera corrido
2. corras	corr-ieras/ieses	hubieras corrido
3. corra	corr-iera/iese	hubiera corrido
1. corramos	corr-iéramos/iésemos	hubiéramos corrido
2. corráis	corr-ierais/ieseis	hubierais corrido
3. corran	corr-ieran/iesen	hubieran corrido

PERFECT	haya corrido *etc*

INFINITIVE	PARTICIPLE
PRESENT	PRESENT
correr	corriendo
PAST	PAST
haber corrido	corrido

COSTAR
59 *to cost*

PRESENT	IMPERFECT	FUTURE
1. cuesto	costaba	costaré
2. cuestas	costabas	costarás
3. cuesta	costaba	costará
1. costamos	costábamos	costaremos
2. costáis	costabais	costaréis
3. cuestan	costaban	costarán

PRETERITE	PERFECT	PLUPERFECT
1. costé	he costado	había costado
2. costaste	has costado	habías costado
3. costó	ha costado	había costado
1. costamos	hemos costado	habíamos costado
2. costasteis	habéis costado	habíais costado
3. costaron	han costado	habían costado

PAST ANTERIOR	FUTURE PERFECT
hube costado *etc*	habré costado *etc*

CONDITIONAL

IMPERATIVE

PRESENT	PAST	
1. costaría	habría costado	
2. costarías	habrías costado	(tú) cuesta
3. costaría	habría costado	(Vd) cueste
1. costaríamos	habríamos costado	(nosotros) costemos
2. costaríais	habríais costado	(vosotros) costad
3. costarían	habrían costado	(Vds) cuesten

SUBJUNCTIVE

PRESENT	IMPERFECT	PLUPERFECT
1. cueste	cost-ara/ase	hubiera costado
2. cuestes	cost-aras/ases	hubieras costado
3. cueste	cost-ara/ase	hubiera costado
1. costemos	cost-áramos/ásemos	hubiéramos costado
2. costéis	cost-arais/aseis	hubierais costado
3. cuesten	cost-aran/asen	hubieran costado
PERFECT	haya costado *etc*	

INFINITIVE

PARTICIPLE

PRESENT	PRESENT
costar	costando

PAST	PAST
haber costado	costado

PRESENT	IMPERFECT	FUTURE
1. crezco	crecía	creceré
2. creces	crecías	crecerás
3. crece	crecía	crecerá
1. crecemos	crecíamos	creceremos
2. crecéis	crecíais	creceréis
3. crecen	crecían	crecerán

PRETERITE	PERFECT	PLUPERFECT
1. crecí	he crecido	había crecido
2. creciste	has crecido	habías crecido
3. creció	ha crecido	había crecido
1. crecimos	hemos crecido	habíamos crecido
2. crecisteis	habéis crecido	habíais crecido
3. crecieron	han crecido	habían crecido

PAST ANTERIOR	FUTURE PERFECT
hube crecido *etc*	habré crecido *etc*

CONDITIONAL

IMPERATIVE

PRESENT	PAST	
1. crecería	habría crecido	
2. crecerías	habrías crecido	(tú) crece
3. crecería	habría crecido	(Vd) crezca
1. creceríamos	habríamos crecido	(nosotros) crezcamos
2. creceríais	habríais crecido	(vosotros) creced
3. crecerían	habrían crecido	(Vds) crezcan

SUBJUNCTIVE

PRESENT	IMPERFECT	PLUPERFECT
1. crezca	crec-iera/iese	hubiera crecido
2. crezcas	crec-ieras/ieses	hubieras crecido
3. crezca	crec-iera/iese	hubiera crecido
1. crezcamos	crec-iéramos/iésemos	hubiéramos crecido
2. crezcáis	crec-ierais/ieseis	hubierais crecido
3. crezcan	crec-ieran/iesen	hubieran crecido

PERFECT	haya crecido *etc*

INFINITIVE

PARTICIPLE

PRESENT	PRESENT
crecer	creciendo

PAST	PAST
haber crecido	crecido

CREER
61 *to believe*

PRESENT	IMPERFECT	FUTURE
1. creo	creía	creeré
2. crees	creías	creerás
3. cree	creía	creerá
1. creemos	creíamos	creeremos
2. creéis	creíais	creeréis
3. creen	creían	creerán

PRETERITE	PERFECT	PLUPERFECT
1. creí	he creído	había creído
2. creíste	has creído	habías creído
3. creyó	ha creído	había creído
1. creímos	hemos creído	habíamos creído
2. creísteis	habéis creído	habíais creído
3. creyeron	han creído	habían creído

PAST ANTERIOR	FUTURE PERFECT
hube creído *etc*	habré creído *etc*

CONDITIONAL

PRESENT	PAST
1. creería	habría creído
2. creerías	habrías creído
3. creería	habría creído
1. creeríamos	habríamos creído
2. creeríais	habríais creído
3. creerían	habrían creído

IMPERATIVE

(tú) cree
(Vd) crea
(nosotros) creamos
(vosotros) creed
(Vds) crean

SUBJUNCTIVE

PRESENT	IMPERFECT	PLUPERFECT
1. crea	cre-yera/yese	hubiera creído
2. creas	cre-yeras/yeses	hubieras creído
3. crea	cre-yera/yese	hubiera creído
1. creamos	cre-yéramos/yésemos	hubiéramos creído
2. creáis	cre-yerais/yeseis	hubierais creído
3. crean	cre-yeran/yesen	hubieran creído

PERFECT haya creído *etc*

INFINITIVE

PRESENT
creer

PAST
haber creído

PARTICIPLE

PRESENT
creyendo

PAST
creído

PRESENT	IMPERFECT	FUTURE
1. cruzo	cruzaba	cruzaré
2. cruzas	cruzabas	cruzarás
3. cruza	cruzaba	cruzará
1. cruzamos	cruzábamos	cruzaremos
2. cruzáis	cruzabais	cruzaréis
3. cruzan	cruzaban	cruzarán

PRETERITE	PERFECT	PLUPERFECT
1. crucé	he cruzado	había cruzado
2. cruzaste	has cruzado	habías cruzado
3. cruzó	ha cruzado	había cruzado
1. cruzamos	hemos cruzado	habíamos cruzado
2. cruzasteis	habéis cruzado	habíais cruzado
3. cruzaron	han cruzado	habían cruzado

PAST ANTERIOR	FUTURE PERFECT
hube cruzado *etc*	habré cruzado *etc*

CONDITIONAL

IMPERATIVE

PRESENT	PAST	
1. cruzaría	habría cruzado	
2. cruzarías	habrías cruzado	(tú) cruza
3. cruzaría	habría cruzado	(Vd) cruce
1. cruzaríamos	habríamos cruzado	(nosotros) crucemos
2. cruzaríais	habríais cruzado	(vosotros) cruzad
3. cruzarían	habrían cruzado	(Vds) crucen

SUBJUNCTIVE

PRESENT	IMPERFECT	PLUPERFECT
1. cruce	cruz-ara/ase	hubiera cruzado
2. cruces	cruz-aras/ases	hubieras cruzado
3. cruce	cruz-ara/ase	hubiera cruzado
1. crucemos	cruz-áramos/ásemos	hubiéramos cruzado
2. crucéis	cruz-arais/aseis	hubierais cruzado
3. crucen	cruz-aran/asen	hubieran cruzado

PERFECT	haya cruzado *etc*

INFINITIVE

PARTICIPLE

PRESENT	PRESENT
cruzar	cruzando

PAST	PAST
haber cruzado	cruzado

PRESENT	IMPERFECT	FUTURE
1. cubro	cubría	cubriré
2. cubres	cubrías	cubrirás
3. cubre	cubría	cubrirá
1. cubrimos	cubríamos	cubriremos
2. cubrís	cubríais	cubriréis
3. cubren	cubrían	cubrirán

PRETERITE	PERFECT	PLUPERFECT
1. cubrí	he cubierto	había cubierto
2. cubriste	has cubierto	habías cubierto
3. cubrió	ha cubierto	había cubierto
1. cubrimos	hemos cubierto	habíamos cubierto
2. cubristeis	habéis cubierto	habíais cubierto
3. cubrieron	han cubierto	habían cubierto

PAST ANTERIOR	FUTURE PERFECT
hube cubierto *etc*	habré cubierto *etc*

CONDITIONAL

IMPERATIVE

PRESENT	PAST	
1. cubriría	habría cubierto	
2. cubrirías	habrías cubierto	(tú) cubre
3. cubriría	habría cubierto	(Vd) cubra
1. cubriríamos	habríamos cubierto	(nosotros) cubramos
2. cubriríais	habríais cubierto	(vosotros) cubrid
3. cubrirían	habrían cubierto	(Vds) cubran

SUBJUNCTIVE

PRESENT	IMPERFECT	PLUPERFECT
1. cubra	cubr-iera/iese	hubiera cubierto
2. cubras	cubr-ieras/ieses	hubieras cubierto
3. cubra	cubr-iera/iese	hubiera cubierto
1. cubramos	cubr-iéramos/iésemos	hubiéramos cubierto
2. cubráis	cubr-ierais/ieseis	hubierais cubierto
3. cubran	cubr-ieran/iesen	hubieran cubierto
PERFECT	haya cubierto *etc*	

INFINITIVE

PARTICIPLE

PRESENT	PRESENT
cubrir	cubriendo
PAST	PAST
haber cubierto	cubierto

PRESENT	**IMPERFECT**	**FUTURE**
1. doy	daba	daré
2. das	dabas	darás
3. da	daba	dará
1. damos	dábamos	daremos
2. dais	dabais	daréis
3. dan	daban	darán

PRETERITE	**PERFECT**	**PLUPERFECT**
1. di	he dado	había dado
2. diste	has dado	habías dado
3. dio	ha dado	había dado
1. dimos	hemos dado	habíamos dado
2. disteis	habéis dado	habíais dado
3. dieron	han dado	habían dado

PAST ANTERIOR	**FUTURE PERFECT**
hube dado *etc*	habré dado *etc*

CONDITIONAL

IMPERATIVE

PRESENT	**PAST**	
1. daría	habría dado	
2. darías	habrías dado	(tú) da
3. daría	habría dado	(Vd) dé
1. daríamos	habríamos dado	(nosotros) demos
2. daríais	habríais dado	(vosotros) dad
3. darían	habrían dado	(Vds) den

SUBJUNCTIVE

PRESENT	**IMPERFECT**	**PLUPERFECT**
1. dé	di-era/ese	hubiera dado
2. des	di-eras/eses	hubieras dado
3. dé	di-era/ese	hubiera dado
1. demos	di-éramos/ésemos	hubiéramos dado
2. deis	di-erais/eseis	hubierais dado
3. den	di-eran/esen	hubieran dado

PERFECT	haya dado *etc*

INFINITIVE

PARTICIPLE

PRESENT	**PRESENT**
dar	dando

PAST	**PAST**
haber dado	dado

DEBER
65 *to owe; to have to*

PRESENT	IMPERFECT	FUTURE
1. debo	debía	deberé
2. debes	debías	deberás
3. debe	debía	deberá
1. debemos	debíamos	deberemos
2. debéis	debíais	deberéis
3. deben	debían	deberán

PRETERITE	PERFECT	PLUPERFECT
1. debí	he debido	había debido
2. debiste	has debido	habías debido
3. debió	ha debido	había debido
1. debimos	hemos debido	habíamos debido
2. debisteis	habéis debido	habíais debido
3. debieron	han debido	habían debido

PAST ANTERIOR		FUTURE PERFECT
hube debido *etc*		habré debido *etc*

CONDITIONAL

PRESENT	PAST
1. debería	habría debido
2. deberías	habrías debido
3. debería	habría debido
1. deberíamos	habríamos debido
2. deberíais	habríais debido
3. deberían	habrían debido

IMPERATIVE

(tú) debe
(Vd) deba
(nosotros) debamos
(vosotros) debed
(Vds) deban

SUBJUNCTIVE

PRESENT	IMPERFECT	PLUPERFECT
1. deba	deb-iera/iese	hubiera debido
2. debas	deb-ieras/ieses	hubieras debido
3. deba	deb-iera/iese	hubiera debido
1. debamos	deb-iéramos/iésemos	hubiéramos debido
2. debáis	deb-ierais/ieseis	hubierais debido
3. deban	deb-ieran/iesen	hubieran debido

PERFECT   haya debido *etc*

INFINITIVE

PRESENT
deber

PAST
haber debido

PARTICIPLE

PRESENT
debiendo

PAST
debido

PRESENT	IMPERFECT	FUTURE
1. decido	decidía	decidiré
2. decides	decidías	decidirás
3. decide	decidía	decidirá
1. decidimos	decidíamos	decidiremos
2. decidís	decidíais	decidiréis
3. deciden	decidían	decidirán

PRETERITE	PERFECT	PLUPERFECT
1. decidí	he decidido	había decidido
2. decidiste	has decidido	habías decidido
3. decidió	ha decidido	había decidido
1. decidimos	hemos decidido	habíamos decidido
2. decidisteis	habéis decidido	habíais decidido
3. decidieron	han decidido	habían decidido

PAST ANTERIOR	FUTURE PERFECT
hube decidido *etc*	habré decidido *etc*

CONDITIONAL

IMPERATIVE

PRESENT	PAST	
1. decidiría	habría decidido	
2. decidirías	habrías decidido	(tú) decide
3. decidiría	habría decidido	(Vd) decida
1. decidiríamos	habríamos decidido	(nosotros) decidamos
2. decidiríais	habríais decidido	(vosotros) decidid
3. decidirían	habrían decidido	(Vds) decidan

SUBJUNCTIVE

PRESENT	IMPERFECT	PLUPERFECT
1. decida	decid-iera/iese	hubiera decidido
2. decidas	decid-ieras/ieses	hubieras decidido
3. decida	decid-iera/iese	hubiera decidido
1. decidamos	decid-iéramos/iésemos	hubiéramos decidido
2. decidáis	decid-ierais/ieseis	hubierais decidido
3. decidan	decid-ieran/iesen	hubieran decidido

PERFECT	haya decidido *etc*

INFINITIVE	PARTICIPLE
PRESENT	**PRESENT**
decidir	decidiendo
PAST	**PAST**
haber decidido	decidido

DECIR
67 *to say*

PRESENT	IMPERFECT	FUTURE
1. digo	decía	diré
2. dices	decías	dirás
3. dice	decía	dirá
1. decimos	decíamos	diremos
2. decís	decíais	diréis
3. dicen	decían	dirán

PRETERITE	PERFECT	PLUPERFECT
1. dije	he dicho	había dicho
2. dijiste	has dicho	habías dicho
3. dijo	ha dicho	había dicho
1. dijimos	hemos dicho	habíamos dicho
2. dijisteis	habéis dicho	habíais dicho
3. dijeron	han dicho	habían dicho

PAST ANTERIOR	FUTURE PERFECT
hube dicho *etc*	habré dicho *etc*

CONDITIONAL

IMPERATIVE

PRESENT	PAST	
1. diría	habría dicho	
2. dirías	habrías dicho	
3. diría	habría dicho	(tú) di
1. diríamos	habríamos dicho	(Vd) diga
2. diríais	habríais dicho	(nosotros) digamos
3. dirían	habrían dicho	(vosotros) decid
		(Vds) digan

SUBJUNCTIVE

PRESENT	IMPERFECT	PLUPERFECT
1. diga	dij-era/ese	hubiera dicho
2. digas	dij-eras/eses	hubieras dicho
3. diga	dij-era/ese	hubiera dicho
1. digamos	dij-éramos/ésemos	hubiéramos dicho
2. digáis	dij-erais/eseis	hubierais dicho
3. digan	dij-eran/esen	hubieran dicho

PERFECT   haya dicho *etc*

INFINITIVE

PARTICIPLE

PRESENT	PRESENT
decir	diciendo

PAST	PAST
haber dicho	dicho

PRESENT
1. degüello
2. degüellas
3. degüella
1. degollamos
2. degolláis
3. degüellan

IMPERFECT
degollaba
degollabas
degollaba
degollábamos
degollabais
degollaban

FUTURE
degollaré
degollarás
degollará
degollaremos
degollaréis
degollarán

PRETERITE
1. degollé
2. degollaste
3. degolló
1. degollamos
2. degollasteis
3. degollaron

PERFECT
he degollado
has degollado
ha degollado
hemos degollado
habéis degollado
han degollado

PLUPERFECT
había degollado
habías degollado
había degollado
habíamos degollado
habíais degollado
habían degollado

PAST ANTERIOR
hube degollado *etc*

FUTURE PERFECT
habré degollado *etc*

CONDITIONAL

PRESENT
1. degollaría
2. degollarías
3. degollaría
1. degollaríamos
2. degollaríais
3. degollarían

PAST
habría degollado
habrías degollado
habría degollado
habríamos degollado
habríais degollado
habrían degollado

IMPERATIVE

(tú) degüella
(Vd) degüelle
(nosotros) degollemos
(vosotros) degollad
(Vds) degüellen

SUBJUNCTIVE

PRESENT
1. degüelle
2. degüelles
3. degüelle
1. degollemos
2. degolléis
3. degüellen

IMPERFECT
degoll-ara/ase
degoll-aras/ases
degoll-ara/ase
degoll-áramos/ásemos
degoll-arais/aseis
degoll-aran/asen

PLUPERFECT
hubiera degollado
hubieras degollado
hubiera degollado
hubiéramos degollado
hubierais degollado
hubieran degollado

PERFECT   haya degollado *etc*

INFINITIVE

PRESENT
degollar

PAST
haber degollado

PARTICIPLE

PRESENT
degollando

PAST
degollado

DEJAR
69 *to leave; to let*

PRESENT	IMPERFECT	FUTURE
1. dejo	dejaba	dejaré
2. dejas	dejabas	dejarás
3. deja	dejaba	dejará
1. dejamos	dejábamos	dejaremos
2. dejáis	dejabais	dejaréis
3. dejan	dejaban	dejarán

PRETERITE	PERFECT	PLUPERFECT
1. dejé	he dejado	había dejado
2. dejaste	has dejado	habías dejado
3. dejó	ha dejado	había dejado
1. dejamos	hemos dejado	habíamos dejado
2. dejasteis	habéis dejado	habíais dejado
3. dejaron	han dejado	habían dejado

PAST ANTERIOR	FUTURE PERFECT
hube dejado *etc*	habré dejado *etc*

CONDITIONAL

PRESENT	PAST	IMPERATIVE
1. dejaría	habría dejado	
2. dejarías	habrías dejado	(tú) deja
3. dejaría	habría dejado	(Vd) deje
1. dejaríamos	habríamos dejado	(nosotros) dejemos
2. dejaríais	habríais dejado	(vosotros) dejad
3. dejarían	habrían dejado	(Vds) dejen

SUBJUNCTIVE

PRESENT	IMPERFECT	PLUPERFECT
1. deje	dej-ara/ase	hubiera dejado
2. dejes	dej-aras/ases	hubieras dejado
3. deje	dej-ara/ase	hubiera dejado
1. dejemos	dej-áramos/ásemos	hubiéramos dejado
2. dejéis	dej-arais/aseis	hubierais dejado
3. dejen	dej-aran/asen	hubieran dejado

PERFECT   haya dejado *etc*

INFINITIVE

PRESENT	PARTICIPLE
dejar	**PRESENT** dejando

PAST	PAST
haber dejado	dejado

PRESENT	IMPERFECT	FUTURE
1. delinco	delinquía	delinquiré
2. delinques	delinquías	delinquirás
3. delinque	delinquía	delinquirá
1. delinquimos	delinquíamos	delinquiremos
2. delinquís	delinquíais	delinquiréis
3. delinquen	delinquían	delinquirán

PRETERITE	PERFECT	PLUPERFECT
1. delinquí	he delinquido	había delinquido
2. delinquiste	has delinquido	habías delinquido
3. delinquió	ha delinquido	había delinquido
1. delinquimos	hemos delinquido	habíamos delinquido
2. delinquisteis	habéis delinquido	habíais delinquido
3. delinquieron	han delinquido	habían delinquido

PAST ANTERIOR		FUTURE PERFECT
hube delinquido *etc*		habré delinquido *etc*

CONDITIONAL

IMPERATIVE

PRESENT	PAST	
1. delinquiría	habría delinquido	
2. delinquirías	habrías delinquido	(tú) delinque
3. delinquiría	habría delinquido	(Vd) delinca
1. delinquiríamos	habríamos delinquido	(nosotros) delincamos
2. delinquiríais	habríais delinquido	(vosotros) delinquid
3. delinquirían	habrían delinquido	(Vds) delincan

SUBJUNCTIVE

PRESENT	IMPERFECT	PLUPERFECT
1. delinca	delinqu-iera/iese	hubiera delinquido
2. delincas	delinqu-ieras/ieses	hubieras delinquido
3. delinca	delinqu-iera/iese	hubiera delinquido
1. delincamos	delinqu-iéramos/iésemos	hubiéramos delinquido
2. delincáis	delinqu-ierais/ieseis	hubierais delinquido
3. delincan	delinqu-ieran/iesen	hubieran delinquido

PERFECT haya delinquido *etc*

INFINITIVE

PARTICIPLE

PRESENT	PRESENT
delinquir	delinquiendo
PAST	**PAST**
haber delinquido	delinquido

DESCENDER

71 *to descend; to get down*

PRESENT	IMPERFECT	FUTURE
1. desciendo	descendía	descenderé
2. desciendes	descendías	descenderás
3. desciende	descendía	descenderá
1. descendemos	descendíamos	descenderemos
2. descendéis	descendíais	descenderéis
3. descienden	descendían	descenderán

PRETERITE	PERFECT	PLUPERFECT
1. descendí	he descendido	había descendido
2. descendiste	has descendido	habías descendido
3. descendió	ha descendido	había descendido
1. descendimos	hemos descendido	habíamos descendido
2. descendisteis	habéis descendido	habíais descendido
3. descendieron	han descendido	habían descendido

PAST ANTERIOR	FUTURE PERFECT
hube descendido *etc*	habré descendido *etc*

CONDITIONAL

IMPERATIVE

PRESENT	PAST	
1. descendería	habría descendido	
2. descenderías	habrías descendido	(tú) desciende
3. descendería	habría descendido	(Vd) descienda
1. descenderíamos	habríamos descendido	(nosotros) descendamos
2. descenderíais	habríais descendido	(vosotros) descended
3. descenderían	habrían descendido	(Vds) desciendan

SUBJUNCTIVE

PRESENT	IMPERFECT	PLUPERFECT
1. descienda	descend-iera/iese	hubiera descendido
2. desciendas	descend-ieras/ieses	hubieras descendido
3. descienda	descend-iera/iese	hubiera descendido
1. descendamos	descend-iéramos/iésemos	hubiéramos descendido
2. descendáis	descend-ierais/ieseis	hubierais descendido
3. desciendan	descend-ieran/iesen	hubieran descendido

PERFECT haya descendido *etc*

INFINITIVE

PARTICIPLE

PRESENT	PRESENT
descender	descendiendo

PAST	PAST
haber descendido	descendido

PRESENT	IMPERFECT	FUTURE
1. descubro	descubría	descubriré
2. descubres	descubrías	descubrirás
3. descubre	descubría	descubrirá
1. descubrimos	descubríamos	descubriremos
2. descubrís	descubríais	descubriréis
3. descubren	descubrían	descubrirán

PRETERITE	PERFECT	PLUPERFECT
1. descubrí	he descubierto	había descubierto
2. descubriste	has descubierto	habías descubierto
3. descubrió	ha descubierto	había descubierto
1. descubrimos	hemos descubierto	habíamos descubierto
2. descubristeis	habéis descubierto	habíais descubierto
3. descubrieron	han descubierto	habían descubierto

PAST ANTERIOR		FUTURE PERFECT
hube descubierto *etc*		habré descubierto *etc*

CONDITIONAL

IMPERATIVE

PRESENT	PAST	
1. descubriría	habría descubierto	
2. descubrirías	habrías descubierto	(tú) descubre
3. descubriría	habría descubierto	(Vd) descubra
1. descubriríamos	habríamos descubierto	(nosotros) descubramos
2. descubriríais	habríais descubierto	(vosotros) descubrid
3. descubrirían	habrían descubierto	(Vds) descubran

SUBJUNCTIVE

PRESENT	IMPERFECT	PLUPERFECT
1. descubra	descubr-iera/iese	hubiera descubierto
2. descubras	descubr-ieras/ieses	hubieras descubierto
3. descubra	descubr-iera/iese	hubiera descubierto
1. descubramos	descubr-iéramos/iésemos	hubiéramos descubierto
2. descubráis	descubr-ierais/ieseis	hubierais descubierto
3. descubran	descubr-ieran/iesen	hubieran descubierto

PERFECT   haya descubierto *etc*

INFINITIVE

PARTICIPLE

PRESENT	PRESENT
descubrir	descubriendo

PAST	PAST
haber descubierto	descubierto

DESPERTARSE
73 *to wake up*

PRESENT	IMPERFECT	FUTURE
1. me despierto	me despertaba	me despertaré
2. te despiertas	te despertabas	te despertarás
3. se despierta	se despertaba	se despertará
1. nos despertamos	nos despertábamos	nos despertaremos
2. os despertáis	os despertabais	os despertaréis
3. se despiertan	se despertaban	se despertarán

PRETERITE	PERFECT	PLUPERFECT
1. me desperté	me he despertado	me había despertado
2. te despertaste	te has despertado	te habías despertado
3. se despertó	se ha despertado	se había despertado
1. nos despertamos	nos hemos despertado	nos habíamos despertado
2. os despertasteis	os habéis despertado	os habíais despertado
3. se despertaron	se han despertado	se habían despertado

PAST ANTERIOR		FUTURE PERFECT
me hube despertado *etc*		me habré despertado *etc*

CONDITIONAL

PRESENT	PAST
1. me despertaría	me habría despertado
2. te despertarías	te habrías despertado
3. se despertaría	se habría despertado
1. nos despertaríamos	nos habríamos despertado
2. os despertaríais	os habríais despertado
3. se despertarían	se habrían despertado

IMPERATIVE

(tú) despiértate
(Vd) despiértese
(nosotros) despertémonos
(vosotros) despertaos
(Vds) despiértense

SUBJUNCTIVE

PRESENT	IMPERFECT	PLUPERFECT
1. me despierte	me despert-ara/ase	me hubiera despertado
2. te despiertes	te despert-aras/ases	te hubieras despertado
3. se despierte	se despert-ara/ase	se hubiera despertado
1. nos despertemos	nos despert-áramos/ásemos	nos hubiéramos despertado
2. os despertéis	os despert-arais/aseis	os hubierais despertado
3. se despierten	se despert-aran/asen	se hubieran despertado

PERFECT   me haya despertado *etc*

INFINITIVE

PRESENT	
despertarse	

PAST
haberse despertado

PARTICIPLE

PRESENT
despertándose

PAST
despertado

PRESENT	IMPERFECT	FUTURE
1. destruyo	destruía	destruiré
2. destruyes	destruías	destruirás
3. destruye	destruía	destruirá
1. destruimos	destruíamos	destruiremos
2. destruís	destruíais	destruiréis
3. destruyen	destruían	destruirán

PRETERITE	PERFECT	PLUPERFECT
1. destruí	he destruido	había destruido
2. destruiste	has destruido	habías destruido
3. destruyó	ha destruido	había destruido
1. destruimos	hemos destruido	habíamos destruido
2. destruisteis	habéis destruido	habíais destruido
3. destruyeron	han destruido	habían destruido

PAST ANTERIOR	FUTURE PERFECT
hube destruido *etc*	habré destruido *etc*

CONDITIONAL

IMPERATIVE

PRESENT	PAST	
1. destruiría	habría destruido	
2. destruirías	habrías destruido	
3. destruiría	habría destruido	(tú) destruye
1. destruiríamos	habríamos destruido	(Vd) destruya
2. destruiríais	habríais destruido	(nosotros) destruyamos
3. destruirían	habrían destruido	(vosotros) destruid
		(Vds) destruyan

SUBJUNCTIVE

PRESENT	IMPERFECT	PLUPERFECT
1. destruya	destru-yera/yese	hubiera destruido
2. destruyas	destru-yeras/yeses	hubieras destruido
3. destruya	destru-yera/yese	hubiera destruido
1. destruyamos	destru-yéramos/yésemos	hubiéramos destruido
2. destruyáis	destru-yerais/yeseis	hubierais destruido
3. destruyan	destru-yeran/yesen	hubieran destruido

PERFECT   haya destruido *etc*

INFINITIVE

PARTICIPLE

PRESENT	PRESENT
destruir	destruyendo

PAST	PAST
haber destruido	destruido

DIGERIR
75 *to digest*

PRESENT	IMPERFECT	FUTURE
1. digiero	digería	digeriré
2. digieres	digerías	digerirás
3. digiere	digería	digerirá
1. digerimos	digeríamos	digeriremos
2. digerís	digeríais	digeriréis
3. digieren	digerían	digerirán

PRETERITE	PERFECT	PLUPERFECT
1. digerí	he digerido	había digerido
2. digeriste	has digerido	habías digerido
3. digjrió	ha digerido	había digerido
1. digerimos	hemos digerido	habíamos digerido
2. digeristeis	habéis digerido	habíais digerido
3. digirieron	han digerido	habían digerido

PAST ANTERIOR	FUTURE PERFECT
hube digerido *etc*	habré digerido *etc*

CONDITIONAL

IMPERATIVE

PRESENT	PAST	
1. digeriría	habría digerido	
2. digerirías	habrías digerido	(tú) digiere
3. digeriría	habría digerido	(Vd) digiera
1. digeriríamos	habríamos digerido	(nosotros) digiramos
2. digeriríais	habríais digerido	(vosotros) digerid
3. digerirían	habrían digerido	(Vds) digieran

SUBJUNCTIVE

PRESENT	IMPERFECT	PLUPERFECT
1. digiera	digir-iera/iese	hubiera digerido
2. digieras	digir-ieras/ieses	hubieras digerido
3. digiera	digir-iera/iese	hubiera digerido
1. digiramos	digir-iéramos/iésemos	hubiéramos digerido
2. digiráis	digir-ierais/ieseis	hubierais digerido
3. digieran	digir-ieran/iesen	hubieran digerido

PERFECT	haya digerido *etc*

INFINITIVE

PARTICIPLE

PRESENT	PRESENT
digerir	digiriendo

PAST	PAST
haber digerido	digerido

PRESENT	IMPERFECT	FUTURE
1. dirijo	dirigía	dirigiré
2. diriges	dirigías	dirigirás
3. dirige	dirigía	dirigirá
1. dirigimos	dirigíamos	dirigiremos
2. dirigís	dirigíais	dirigiréis
3. dirigen	dirigían	dirigirán

PRETERITE	PERFECT	PLUPERFECT
1. dirigí	he dirigido	había dirigido
2. dirigiste	has dirigido	habías dirigido
3. dirigió	ha dirigido	había dirigido
1. dirigimos	hemos dirigido	habíamos dirigido
2. dirigisteis	habéis dirigido	habíais dirigido
3. dirigieron	han dirigido	habían dirigido

PAST ANTERIOR	FUTURE PERFECT
hube dirigido *etc*	habré dirigido *etc*

CONDITIONAL

PRESENT	PAST
1. dirigiría	habría dirigido
2. dirigirías	habrías dirigido
3. dirigiría	habría dirigido
1. dirigiríamos	habríamos dirigido
2. dirigiríais	habríais dirigido
3. dirigirían	habrían dirigido

IMPERATIVE

(tú) dirige
(Vd) dirija
(nosotros) dirijamos
(vosotros) dirigid
(Vds) dirijan

SUBJUNCTIVE

PRESENT	IMPERFECT	PLUPERFECT
1. dirija	dirig-iera/iese	hubiera dirigido
2. dirijas	dirig-ieras/ieses	hubieras dirigido
3. dirija	dirig-iera/iese	hubiera dirigido
1. dirijamos	dirig-iéramos/iésemos	hubiéramos dirigido
2. dirijáis	dirig-ierais/ieseis	hubierais dirigido
3. dirijan	dirig-ieran/iesen	hubieran dirigido

PERFECT   haya dirigido *etc*

INFINITIVE	PARTICIPLE
PRESENT	**PRESENT**
dirigir	dirigiendo
PAST	**PAST**
haber dirigido	dirigido

DISCERNIR
77 to discern

PRESENT	IMPERFECT	FUTURE
1. discierno	discernía	discerniré
2. disciernes	discernías	discernirás
3. discierne	discernía	discernirá
1. discernimos	discerníamos	discerniremos
2. discernís	discerníais	discerniréis
3. disciernen	discernían	discernirán

PRETERITE	PERFECT	PLUPERFECT
1. discerní	he discernido	había discernido
2. discerniste	has discernido	habías discernido
3. discernió	ha discernido	había discernido
1. discernimos	hemos discernido	habíamos discernido
2. discernisteis	habéis discernido	habíais discernido
3. discernieron	han discernido	habían discernido

PAST ANTERIOR	FUTURE PERFECT
hube discernido *etc*	habré discernido *etc*

CONDITIONAL

IMPERATIVE

PRESENT	PAST	
1. discerniría	habría discernido	
2. discernirías	habrías discernido	
3. discerniría	habría discernido	(tú) discierne
1. discerniríamos	habríamos discernido	(Vd) discierna
2. discerniríais	habríais discernido	(nosotros) discirnamos
3. discernirían	habrían discernido	(vosotros) discernid
		(Vds) disciernan

SUBJUNCTIVE

PRESENT	IMPERFECT	PLUPERFECT
1. discierna	discirn-iera/iese	hubiera discernido
2. disciernas	discirn-ieras/ieses	hubieras discernido
3. discierna	discirn-iera/iese	hubiera discernido
1. discirnamos	discirn-iéramos/iésemos	hubiéramos discernido
2. discirnáis	discirn-ierais/ieseis	hubierais discernido
3. disciernan	discirn-ieran/iesen	hubieran discernido

PERFECT   haya discernido *etc*

INFINITIVE

PARTICIPLE

PRESENT	PRESENT
discernir	discirniendo

PAST	PAST
haber discernido	discernido

PRESENT	IMPERFECT	FUTURE
1. distingo	distinguía	distinguiré
2. distingues	distinguías	distinguirás
3. distingue	distinguía	distinguirá
1. distinguimos	distinguíamos	distinguiremos
2. distinguís	distinguíais	distinguiréis
3. distinguen	distinguían	distinguirán

PRETERITE	PERFECT	PLUPERFECT
1. distinguí	he distinguido	había distinguido
2. distinguiste	has distinguido	habías distinguido
3. distinguió	ha distinguido	había distinguido
1. distinguimos	hemos distinguido	habíamos distinguido
2. distinguisteis	habéis distinguido	habíais distinguido
3. distinguieron	han distinguido	habían distinguido

PAST ANTERIOR	FUTURE PERFECT
hube distinguido *etc*	habré distinguido *etc*

CONDITIONAL

IMPERATIVE

PRESENT	PAST	
1. distinguiría	habría distinguido	
2. distinguirías	habrías distinguido	
3. distinguiría	habría distinguido	(tú) distingue
1. distinguiríamos	habríamos distinguido	(Vd) distinga
2. distinguiríais	habríais distinguido	(nosotros) distingamos
3. distinguirían	habrían distinguido	(vosotros) dintinguid
		(Vds) distingan

SUBJUNCTIVE

PRESENT	IMPERFECT	PLUPERFECT
1. distinga	distingu-iera/iese	hubiera distinguido
2. distingas	distingu-ieras/ieses	hubieras distinguido
3. distinga	distingu-iera/iese	hubiera distinguido
1. distingamos	distingu-iéramos/iésemos	hubiéramos distinguido
2. distingáis	distingu-ierais/ieseis	hubierais distinguido
3. distingan	distingu-ieran/iesen	hubieran distinguido

PERFECT   haya distinguido *etc*

INFINITIVE

PARTICIPLE

PRESENT	PRESENT
distinguir	distinguiendo

PAST	PAST
haber distinguido	distinguido

DIVERTIRSE
79 *to have a good time*

PRESENT	IMPERFECT	FUTURE
1. me divierto	me divertía	me divertiré
2. te diviertes	te divertías	te divertirás
3. se divierte	se divertía	se divertirá
1. nos divertimos	nos divertíamos	nos divertiremos
2. os divertís	os divertíais	os divertiréis
3. se divierten	se divertían	se divertirán

PRETERITE	PERFECT	PLUPERFECT
1. me divertí	me he divertido	me había divertido
2. te divertiste	te has divertido	te habías divertido
3. se divirtió	se ha divertido	se había divertido
1. nos divertimos	nos hemos divertido	nos habíamos divertido
2. os divertisteis	os habéis divertido	os habíais divertido
3. se divirtieron	se han divertido	se habían divertido

PAST ANTERIOR		FUTURE PERFECT
me hube divertido *etc*		me habré divertido *etc*

CONDITIONAL

IMPERATIVE

PRESENT	PAST	
1. me divertiría	me habría divertido	
2. te divertirías	te habrías divertido	(tú) diviértete
3. se divertiría	se habría divertido	(Vd) diviértase
1. nos divertiríamos	nos habríamos divertido	(nosotros) divirtámonos
2. os divertiríais	os habríais divertido	(vosotros) divertíos
3. se divertirían	se habrían divertido	(Vds) diviértanse

SUBJUNCTIVE

PRESENT	IMPERFECT	PLUPERFECT
1. me divierta	me divirt-iera/iese	me hubiera divertido
2. te diviertas	te divirt-ieras/ieses	te hubieras divertido
3. se divierta	se divirt-iera/iese	se hubiera divertido
1. nos divirtamos	nos divirt-iéramos/iésemos	nos hubiéramos divertido
2. os divirtáis	os divirt-ierais/ieseis	os hubierais divertido
3. se diviertan	se divirt-ieran/iesen	se hubieran divertido

PERFECT   me haya divertido *etc*

INFINITIVE

PARTICIPLE

PRESENT	PRESENT
divertirse	divirtiéndose

PAST	PAST
haberse divertido	divertido

English

DORMIR
81 *to sleep*

PRESENT	IMPERFECT	FUTURE
1. duermo	dormía	dormiré
2. duermes	dormías	dormirás
3. duerme	dormía	dormirá
1. dormimos	dormíamos	dormiremos
2. dormís	dormíais	dormiréis
3. duermen	dormían	dormirán

PRETERITE	PERFECT	PLUPERFECT
1. dormí	he dormido	había dormido
2. dormiste	has dormido	habías dormido
3. durmió	ha dormido	había dormido
1. dormimos	hemos dormido	habíamos dormido
2. dormisteis	habéis dormido	habíais dormido
3. durmieron	han dormido	habían dormido

PAST ANTERIOR	FUTURE PERFECT
hube dormido *etc*	habré dormido *etc*

CONDITIONAL

IMPERATIVE

PRESENT	PAST	
1. dormiría	habría dormido	
2. dormirías	habrías dormido	(tú) duerme
3. dormiría	habría dormido	(Vd) duerma
1. dormiríamos	habríamos dormido	(nosotros) durmamos
2. dormiríais	habríais dormido	(vosotros) dormid
3. dormirían	habrían dormido	(Vds) duerman

SUBJUNCTIVE

PRESENT	IMPERFECT	PLUPERFECT
1. duerma	durm-iera/iese	hubiera dormido
2. duermas	durm-ieras/ieses	hubieras dormido
3. duerma	durm-iera/iese	hubiera dormido
1. durmamos	durm-iéramos/iésemos	hubiéramos dormido
2. durmáis	durm-ierais/ieseis	hubierais dormido
3. duerman	durm-ieran/iesen	hubieran dormido

PERFECT	haya dormido *etc*

INFINITIVE

PARTICIPLE

PRESENT	PRESENT
dormir	durmiendo

PAST	PAST
haber dormido	dormido

PRESENT	IMPERFECT	FUTURE
1. educo	educaba	educaré
2. educas	educabas	educarás
3. educa	educaba	educará
1. educamos	educábamos	educaremos
2. educáis	educabais	educaréis
3. educan	educaban	educarán

PRETERITE	PERFECT	PLUPERFECT
1. eduqué	he educado	había educado
2. educaste	has educado	habías educado
3. educó	ha educado	había educado
1. educamos	hemos educado	habíamos educado
2. educasteis	habéis educado	habíais educado
3. educaron	han educado	habían educado

PAST ANTERIOR	FUTURE PERFECT
hube educado *etc*	habré educado *etc*

CONDITIONAL

IMPERATIVE

PRESENT	PAST	
1. educaría	habría educado	
2. educarías	habrías educado	(tú) educa
3. educaría	habría educado	(Vd) eduque
1. educaríamos	habríamos educado	(nosotros) eduquemos
2. educaríais	habríais educado	(vosotros) educad
3. educarían	habrían educado	(Vds) eduquen

SUBJUNCTIVE

PRESENT	IMPERFECT	PLUPERFECT
1. eduque	educ-ara/ase	hubiera educado
2. eduques	educ-aras/ases	hubieras educado
3. eduque	educ-ara/ase	hubiera educado
1. eduquemos	educ-áramos/ásemos	hubiéramos educado
2. eduquéis	educ-arais/aseis	hubierais educado
3. eduquen	educ-aran/asen	hubieran educado
PERFECT	haya educado *etc*	

INFINITIVE

PARTICIPLE

PRESENT	PRESENT
educar	educando

PAST	PAST
haber educado	educado

ELEGIR

83 *to choose*

PRESENT	IMPERFECT	FUTURE
1. elijo	elegía	elegiré
2. eliges	elegías	elegirás
3. elige	elegía	elegirá
1. elegimos	elegíamos	elegiremos
2. elegís	elegíais	elegiréis
3. eligen	elegían	elegirán

PRETERITE	PERFECT	PLUPERFECT
1. elegí	he elegido	había elegido
2. elegiste	has elegido	habías elegido
3. eligió	ha elegido	había elegido
1. elegimos	hemos elegido	habíamos elegido
2. elegisteis	habéis elegido	habíais elegido
3. eligieron	han elegido	habían elegido

PAST ANTERIOR		FUTURE PERFECT
hube elegido *etc*		habré elegido *etc*

CONDITIONAL | IMPERATIVE

PRESENT	PAST	
1. elegiría	habría elegido	
2. elegirías	habrías elegido	
3. elegiría	habría elegido	(tú) elige
1. elegiríamos	habríamos elegido	(Vd) elija
2. elegiríais	habríais elegido	(nosotros) elijamos
3. elegirían	habrían elegido	(vosotros) elegid
		(Vds) elijan

SUBJUNCTIVE

PRESENT	IMPERFECT	PLUPERFECT
1. elija	elig-iera/iese	hubiera elegido
2. elijas	elig-ieras/ieses	hubieras elegido
3. elija	elig-iera/iese	hubiera elegido
1. elijamos	elig-iéramos/iésemos	hubiéramos elegido
2. elijáis	elig-ierais/ieseis	hubierais elegido
3. elijan	elig-ieran/iesen	hubieran elegido

PERFECT	haya elegido *etc*	

INFINITIVE | PARTICIPLE

PRESENT	PRESENT
elegir	eligiendo

PAST	PAST
haber elegido	elegido

PRESENT	**IMPERFECT**	**FUTURE**
1. embarco	embarcaba	embarcaré
2. embarcas	embarcabas	embarcarás
3. embarca	embarcaba	embarcará
1. embarcamos	embarcábamos	embarcaremos
2. embarcáis	embarcabais	embarcaréis
3. embarcan	embarcaban	embarcarán

PRETERITE	**PERFECT**	**PLUPERFECT**
1. embarqué	he embarcado	había embarcado
2. embarcaste	has embarcado	habías embarcado
3. embarcó	ha embarcado	había embarcado
1. embarcamos	hemos embarcado	habíamos embarcado
2. embarcasteis	habéis embarcado	habíais embarcado
3. embarcaron	han embarcado	habían embarcado

PAST ANTERIOR	**FUTURE PERFECT**
hube embarcado *etc*	habré embarcado *etc*

CONDITIONAL

IMPERATIVE

PRESENT	**PAST**	
1. embarcaría	habría embarcado	
2. embarcarías	habrías embarcado	(tú) embarca
3. embarcaría	habría embarcado	(Vd) embarque
1. embarcaríamos	habríamos embarcado	(nosotros) embarquemos
2. embarcaríais	habríais embarcado	(vosotros) embarcad
3. embarcarían	habrían embarcado	(Vds) embarquen

SUBJUNCTIVE

PRESENT	**IMPERFECT**	**PLUPERFECT**
1. embarque	embarc-ara/ase	hubiera embarcado
2. embarques	embarc-aras/ases	hubieras embarcado
3. embarque	embarc-ara/ase	hubiera embarcado
1. embarquemos	embarc-áramos/ásemos	hubiéramos embarcado
2. embarquéis	embarc-arais/aseis	hubierais embarcado
3. embarquen	embarc-aran/asen	hubieran embarcado

PERFECT haya embarcado *etc*

INFINITIVE

PARTICIPLE

PRESENT	**PRESENT**
embarcar	embarcando

PAST	**PAST**
haber embarcado	embarcado

EMPEZAR
85 to start

PRESENT	IMPERFECT	FUTURE
1. empiezo	empezaba	empezaré
2. empiezas	empezabas	empezarás
3. empieza	empezaba	empezará
1. empezamos	empezábamos	empezaremos
2. empezáis	empezabais	empezaréis
3. empiezan	empezaban	empezarán

PRETERITE	PERFECT	PLUPERFECT
1. empecé	he empezado	había empezado
2. empezaste	has empezado	habías empezado
3. empezó	ha empezado	había empezado
1. empezamos	hemos empezado	habíamos empezado
2. empezasteis	habéis empezado	habíais empezado
3. empezaron	han empezado	habían empezado

PAST ANTERIOR		FUTURE PERFECT
hube empezado *etc*		habré empezado *etc*

CONDITIONAL

IMPERATIVE

PRESENT	PAST	
1. empezaría	habría empezado	
2. empezarías	habrías empezado	
3. empezaría	habría empezado	(tú) empieza
1. empezaríamos	habríamos empezado	(Vd) empiece
2. empezaríais	habríais empezado	(nosotros) empecemos
3. empezarían	habrían empezado	(vosotros) empezad
		(Vds) empiecen

SUBJUNCTIVE

PRESENT	IMPERFECT	PLUPERFECT
1. empiece	empez-ara/ase	hubiera empezado
2. empieces	empez-aras/ases	hubieras empezado
3. empiece	empez-ara/ase	hubiera empezado
1. empecemos	empez-áramos/ásemos	hubiéramos empezado
2. empecéis	empez-arais/aseis	hubierais empezado
3. empiecen	empez-aran/asen	hubieran empezado

PERFECT   haya empezado *etc*

INFINITIVE

PARTICIPLE

PRESENT	PRESENT
empezar	empezando

PAST	PAST
haber empezado	empezado

PRESENT	IMPERFECT	FUTURE
1. empujo	empujaba	empujaré
2. empujas	empujabas	empujarás
3. empuja	empujaba	empujará
1. empujamos	empujábamos	empujaremos
2. empujáis	empujabais	empujaréis
3. empujan	empujaban	empujarán

PRETERITE	PERFECT	PLUPERFECT
1. empujé	he empujado	había empujado
2. empujaste	has empujado	habías empujado
3. empujó	ha empujado	había empujado
1. empujamos	hemos empujado	habíamos empujado
2. empujasteis	habéis empujado	habíais empujado
3. empujaron	han empujado	habían empujado

PAST ANTERIOR		FUTURE PERFECT
hube empujado *etc*		habré empujado *etc*

CONDITIONAL

PRESENT	PAST
1. empujaría	habría empujado
2. empujarías	habrías empujado
3. empujaría	habría empujado
1. empujaríamos	habríamos empujado
2. empujaríais	habríais empujado
3. empujarían	habrían empujado

IMPERATIVE

(tú) empuja
(Vd) empuje
(nosotros) empujemos
(vosotros) empujad
(Vds) empujen

SUBJUNCTIVE

PRESENT	IMPERFECT	PLUPERFECT
1. empuje	empuj-ara/ase	hubiera empujado
2. empujes	empuj-aras/ases	hubieras empujado
3. empuje	empuj-ara/ase	hubiera empujado
1. empujemos	empuj-áramos/ásemos	hubiéramos empujado
2. empujéis	empuj-arais/aseis	hubierais empujado
3. empujen	empuj-aran/asen	hubieran empujado

PERFECT	haya empujado *etc*

INFINITIVE

PRESENT
empujar

PAST
haber empujado

PARTICIPLE

PRESENT
empujando

PAST
empujado

ENCENDER
87 *to light; to switch on*

PRESENT	IMPERFECT	FUTURE
1. enciendo	encendía	encenderé
2. enciendes	encendías	encenderás
3. enciende	encendía	encenderá
1. encendemos	encendíamos	encenderemos
2. encendéis	encendíais	encenderéis
3. encienden	encendían	encenderán

PRETERITE	PERFECT	PLUPERFECT
1. encendí	he encendido	había encendido
2. encendiste	has encendido	habías encendido
3. encendió	ha encendido	había encendido
1. encendimos	hemos encendido	habíamos encendido
2. encendisteis	habéis encendido	habíais encendido
3. encendieron	han encendido	habían encendido

PAST ANTERIOR
hube encendido *etc*

FUTURE PERFECT
habré encendido *etc*

CONDITIONAL

IMPERATIVE

PRESENT	PAST
1. encendería	habría encendido
2. encenderías	habrías encendido
3. encendería	habría encendido
1. encenderíamos	habríamos encendido
2. encenderíais	habríais encendido
3. encenderían	habrían encendido

(tú) enciende
(Vd) encienda
(nosotros) encendamos
(vosotros) encended
(Vds) enciendan

SUBJUNCTIVE

PRESENT	IMPERFECT	PLUPERFECT
1. encienda	encend-iera/iese	hubiera encendido
2. enciendas	encend-ieras/ieses	hubieras encendido
3. encienda	encend-iera/iese	hubiera encendido
1. encendamos	encend-iéramos/iésemos	hubiéramos encendido
2. encendáis	encend-ierais/ieseis	hubierais encendido
3. enciendan	encend-ieran/iesen	hubieran encendido

PERFECT haya encendido *etc*

INFINITIVE

PARTICIPLE

PRESENT	PRESENT
encender	encendiendo

PAST	PAST
haber encendido	encendido

PRESENT
1. encuentro
2. encuentras
3. encuentra
1. encontramos
2. encontráis
3. encuentran

IMPERFECT
encontraba
encontrabas
encontraba
encontrábamos
encontrabais
encontraban

FUTURE
encontraré
encontrarás
encontrará
encontraremos
encontraréis
encontrarán

PRETERITE
1. encontré
2. encontraste
3. encontró
1. encontramos
2. encontrasteis
3. encontraron

PERFECT
he encontrado
has encontrado
ha encontrado
hemos encontrado
habéis encontrado
han encontrado

PLUPERFECT
había encontrado
habías encontrado
había encontrado
habíamos encontrado
habíais encontrado
habían encontrado

PAST ANTERIOR
hube encontrado *etc*

FUTURE PERFECT
habré encontrado *etc*

CONDITIONAL

PRESENT
1. encontraría
2. encontrarías
3. encontraría
1. encontraríamos
2. encontraríais
3. encontrarían

PAST
habría encontrado
habrías encontrado
habría encontrado
habríamos encontrado
habríais encontrado
habrían encontrado

IMPERATIVE

(tú) encuentra
(Vd) encuentre
(nosotros) encontremos
(vosotros) encontrad
(Vds) encuentren

SUBJUNCTIVE

PRESENT
1. encuentre
2. encuentres
3. encuentre
1. encontremos
2. encontréis
3. encuentren

IMPERFECT
encontr-ara/ase
encontr-aras/ases
encontr-ara/ase
encontr-áramos/ásemos
encontr-arais/aseis
encontr-aran/asen

PLUPERFECT
hubiera encontrado
hubieras encontrado
hubiera encontrado
hubiéramos encontrado
hubierais encontrado
hubieran encontrado

PERFECT   haya encontrado *etc*

INFINITIVE

PRESENT
encontrar

PAST
haber encontrado

PARTICIPLE

PRESENT
encontrando

PAST
encontrado

ENFRIAR
89 *to cool (down)*

PRESENT	IMPERFECT	FUTURE
1. enfrío	enfriaba	enfriaré
2. enfrías	enfriabas	enfriarás
3. enfría	enfriaba	enfriará
1. enfriamos	enfriábamos	enfriaremos
2. enfriáis	enfriabais	enfriaréis
3. enfrían	enfriaban	enfriarán

PRETERITE	PERFECT	PLUPERFECT
1. enfrié	he enfriado	había enfriado
2. enfriaste	has enfriado	habías enfriado
3. enfrió	ha enfriado	había enfriado
1. enfriamos	hemos enfriado	habíamos enfriado
2. enfriasteis	habéis enfriado	habíais enfriado
3. enfriaron	han enfriado	habían enfriado

PAST ANTERIOR		FUTURE PERFECT
hube enfriado *etc*		habré enfriado *etc*

CONDITIONAL

IMPERATIVE

PRESENT	PAST
1. enfriaría	habría enfriado
2. enfriarías	habrías enfriado
3. enfriaría	habría enfriado
1. enfriaríamos	habríamos enfriado
2. enfriaríais	habríais enfriado
3. enfriarían	habrían enfriado

(tú) enfría
(Vd) enfríe
(nosotros) enfriemos
(vosotros) enfriad
(Vds) enfríen

SUBJUNCTIVE

PRESENT	IMPERFECT	PLUPERFECT
1. enfríe	enfri-ara/ase	hubiera enfriado
2. enfríes	enfri-aras/ases	hubieras enfriado
3. enfríe	enfri-ara/ase	hubiera enfriado
1. enfriemos	enfri-áramos/ásemos	hubiéramos enfriado
2. enfriéis	enfri-arais/aseis	hubierais enfriado
3. enfríen	enfri-aran/asen	hubieran enfriado

PERFECT	haya enfriado *etc*

INFINITIVE

PARTICIPLE

PRESENT	PRESENT
enfriar	enfriando

PAST	PAST
haber enfriado	enfriado

PRESENT	**IMPERFECT**	**FUTURE**
1. me enfurezco	me enfurecía	me enfureceré
2. te enfureces	te enfurecías	te enfurecerás
3. se enfurece	se enfurecía	se enfurecerá
1. nos enfurecemos	nos enfurecíamos	nos enfureceremos
2. os enfurecéis	os enfurecíais	os enfureceréis
3. se enfurecen	se enfurecían	se enfurecerán

PRETERITE	**PERFECT**	**PLUPERFECT**
1. me enfurecí	me he enfurecido	me había enfurecido
2. te enfureciste	te has enfurecido	te habías enfurecido
3. se enfureció	se ha enfurecido	se había enfurecido
1. nos enfurecimos	nos hemos enfurecido	nos habíamos enfurecido
2. os enfurecisteis	os habéis enfurecido	os habíais enfurecido
3. se enfurecieron	se han enfurecido	se habían enfurecido

PAST ANTERIOR	**FUTURE PERFECT**
me hube enfurecido *etc*	me habré enfurecido *etc*

CONDITIONAL

IMPERATIVE

PRESENT	**PAST**	
1. me enfurecería	me habría enfurecido	
2. te enfurecerías	te habrías enfurecido	(tú) enfurécete
3. se enfurecería	se habría enfurecido	(Vd) enfurézcase
1. nos enfureceríamos	nos habríamos enfurecido	(nosotros) enfurezcámonos
2. os enfureceríais	os habríais enfurecido	(vosotros) enfureceos
3. se enfurecerían	se habrían enfurecido	(Vds) enfurézcanse

SUBJUNCTIVE

PRESENT	**IMPERFECT**	**PLUPERFECT**
1. me enfurezca	me enfurec-iera/iese	me hubiera enfurecido
2. te enfurezcas	te enfurec-ieras/ieses	te hubieras enfurecido
3. se enfurezca	se enfurec-iera/iese	se hubiera enfurecido
1. nos enfurezcamos	nos enfurec-iéramos/iésemos	nos hubiéramos enfurecido
2. os enfurezcáis	os enfurec-ierais/ieseis	os hubierais enfurecido
3. se enfurezcan	se enfurec-ieran/iesen	se hubieran enfurecido

PERFECT   me haya enfurecido *etc*

INFINITIVE

PARTICIPLE

PRESENT	**PRESENT**
enfurecerse	enfureciéndose

PAST	**PAST**
haberse enfurecido	enfurecido

ENMUDECER
91 to go silent

PRESENT	IMPERFECT	FUTURE
1. enmudezco	enmudecía	enmudeceré
2. enmudeces	enmudecías	enmudecerás
3. enmudece	enmudecía	enmudecerá
1. enmudecemos	enmudecíamos	enmudeceremos
2. enmudecéis	enmudecíais	enmudeceréis
3. enmudecen	enmudecían	enmudecerán

PRETERITE	PERFECT	PLUPERFECT
1. enmudecí	he enmudecido	había enmudecido
2. enmudeciste	has enmudecido	habías enmudecido
3. enmudeció	ha enmudecido	había enmudecido
1. enmudecimos	hemos enmudecido	habíamos enmudecido
2. enmudecisteis	habéis enmudecido	habíais enmudecido
3. enmudecieron	han enmudecido	habían enmudecido

PAST ANTERIOR		FUTURE PERFECT
hube enmudecido *etc*		habré enmudecido *etc*

CONDITIONAL

IMPERATIVE

PRESENT	PAST	
1. enmudecería	habría enmudecido	
2. enmudecerías	habrías enmudecido	(tú) enmudece
3. enmudecería	habría enmudecido	(Vd) enmudezca
1. enmudeceríamos	habríamos enmudecido	(nosotros) enmudezcamos
2. enmudeceríais	habríais enmudecido	(vosotros) enmudeced
3. enmudecerían	habrían enmudecido	(Vds) enmudezcan

SUBJUNCTIVE

PRESENT	IMPERFECT	PLUPERFECT
1. enmudezca	enmudec-iera/iese	hubiera enmudecido
2. enmudezcas	enmudec-ieras/ieses	hubieras enmudecido
3. enmudezca	enmudec-iera/iese	hubiera enmudecido
1. enmudezcamos	enmudec-iéramos/iésemos	hubiéramos enmudecido
2. enmudezcáis	enmudec-ierais/ieseis	hubierais enmudecido
3. enmudezcan	enmudec-ieran/iesen	hubieran enmudecido

PERFECT	haya enmudecido *etc*

INFINITIVE

PARTICIPLE

PRESENT	PRESENT
enmudecer	enmudeciendo

PAST	PAST
haber enmudecido	enmudecido

PRESENT	IMPERFECT	FUTURE
1. enraízo	enraizaba	enraizaré
2. enraízas	enraizabas	enraizarás
3. enraíza	enraizaba	enraizará
1. enraizamos	enraizábamos	enraizaremos
2. enraizais	enraizabais	enraizaréis
3. enraízan	enraizaban	enraizarán

PRETERITE	PERFECT	PLUPERFECT
1. enraicé	he enraizado	había enraizado
2. enraizaste	has enraizado	habías enraizado
3. enraizó	ha enraizado	había enraizado
1. enraizamos	hemos enraizado	habíamos enraizado
2. enraizasteis	habéis enraizado	habíais enraizado
3. enraizaron	han enraizado	habían enraizado

PAST ANTERIOR	FUTURE PERFECT
hube enraizado *etc*	habré enraizado *etc*

CONDITIONAL

IMPERATIVE

PRESENT	PAST	
1. enraizaría	habría enraizado	
2. enraizarías	habrías enraizado	(tú) enraíza
3. enraizaría	habría enraizado	(Vd) enraíce
1. enraizaríamos	habríamos enraizado	(nosotros) enraicemos
2. enraizaríais	habríais enraizado	(vosotros) enraizad
3. enraizarían	habrían enraizado	(Vds) enraícen

SUBJUNCTIVE

PRESENT	IMPERFECT	PLUPERFECT
1. enraíce	enraiz-ara/ase	hubiera enraizado
2. enraíces	enraiz-aras/ases	hubieras enraizado
3. enraíce	enraiz-ara/ase	hubiera enraizado
1. enraicemos	enraiz-áramos/ásemos	hubiéramos enraizado
2. enraicéis	enraiz-arais/aseis	hubierais enraizado
3. enraícen	enraiz-aran/asen	hubieran enraizado

PERFECT	haya enraizado *etc*

INFINITIVE

PARTICIPLE

PRESENT	PRESENT
enraizar	enraizando

PAST	PAST
haber enraizado	enraizado

ENTENDER
93 to understand

PRESENT	IMPERFECT	FUTURE
1. entiendo	entendía	entenderé
2. entiendes	entendías	entenderás
3. entiende	entendía	entenderá
1. entendemos	entendíamos	entenderemos
2. entendéis	entendíais	entenderéis
3. entienden	entendían	entenderán

PRETERITE	PERFECT	PLUPERFECT
1. entendí	he entendido	había entendido
2. entendiste	has entendido	habías entendido
3. entendió	ha entendido	había entendido
1. entendimos	hemos entendido	habíamos entendido
2. entendisteis	habéis entendido	habíais entendido
3. entendieron	han entendido	habían entendido

PAST ANTERIOR	FUTURE PERFECT
hube entendido *etc*	habré entendido *etc*

CONDITIONAL

PRESENT	PAST
1. entendería	habría entendido
2. entenderías	habrías entendido
3. entendería	habría entendido
1. entenderíamos	habríamos entendido
2. entenderíais	habríais entendido
3. entenderían	habrían entendido

IMPERATIVE

(tú) entiende
(Vd) entienda
(nosotros) entendamos
(vosotros) entended
(Vds) entiendan

SUBJUNCTIVE

PRESENT	IMPERFECT	PLUPERFECT
1. entienda	entend-iera/iese	hubiera entendido
2. entiendas	entend-ieras/ieses	hubieras entendido
3. entienda	entend-iera/iese	hubiera entendido
1. entendamos	entend-iéramos/iésemos	hubiéramos entendido
2. entendáis	entend-ierais/ieseis	hubierais entendido
3. entiendan	entend-ieran/iesen	hubieran entendido

PERFECT	haya entendido *etc*

INFINITIVE

| PARTICIPLE |

PRESENT	PRESENT
entender	entendiendo

PAST	PAST
haber entendido	entendido

PRESENT	IMPERFECT	FUTURE
1. entro	entraba	entraré
2. entras	entrabas	entrarás
3. entra	entraba	entrará
1. entramos	entrábamos	entraremos
2. entráis	entrabais	entraréis
3. entran	entraban	entrarán

PRETERITE	PERFECT	PLUPERFECT
1. entré	he entrado	había entrado
2. entraste	has entrado	habías entrado
3. entró	ha entrado	había entrado
1. entramos	hemos entrado	habíamos entrado
2. entrasteis	habéis entrado	habíais entrado
3. entraron	han entrado	habían entrado

PAST ANTERIOR		FUTURE PERFECT
hube entrado *etc*		habré entrado *etc*

CONDITIONAL

IMPERATIVE

PRESENT	PAST	
1. entraría	habría entrado	
2. entrarías	habrías entrado	(tú) entra
3. entraría	habría entrado	(Vd) entre
1. entraríamos	habríamos entrado	(nosotros) entremos
2. entraríais	habríais entrado	(vosotros) entrad
3. entrarían	habrían entrado	(Vds) entren

SUBJUNCTIVE

PRESENT	IMPERFECT	PLUPERFECT
1. entre	entr-ara/ase	hubiera entrado
2. entres	entr-aras/ases	hubieras entrado
3. entre	entr-ara/ase	hubiera entrado
1. entremos	entr-áramos/ásemos	hubiéramos entrado
2. entréis	entr-arais/aseis	hubierais entrado
3. entren	entr-aran/asen	hubieran entrado
PERFECT	haya entrado *etc*	

INFINITIVE

PARTICIPLE

PRESENT	PRESENT
entrar	entrando
PAST	PAST
haber entrado	entrado

ENVIAR
95 *to send*

PRESENT	IMPERFECT	FUTURE
1. envío	enviaba	enviaré
2. envías	enviabas	enviarás
3. envía	enviaba	enviará
1. enviamos	enviábamos	enviaremos
2. enviáis	enviabais	enviaréis
3. envían	enviaban	enviarán

PRETERITE	PERFECT	PLUPERFECT
1. envié	he enviado	había enviado
2. enviaste	has enviado	habías enviado
3. envió	ha enviado	había enviado
1. enviamos	hemos enviado	habíamos enviado
2. enviasteis	habéis enviado	habíais enviado
3. enviaron	han enviado	habían enviado

PAST ANTERIOR	FUTURE PERFECT
hube enviado *etc*	habré enviado *etc*

CONDITIONAL

IMPERATIVE

PRESENT	PAST	
1. enviaría	habría enviado	
2. enviarías	habrías enviado	(tú) envía
3. enviaría	habría enviado	(Vd) envíe
1. enviaríamos	habríamos enviado	(nosotros) enviemos
2. enviaríais	habríais enviado	(vosotros) enviad
3. enviarían	habrían enviado	(Vds) envíen

SUBJUNCTIVE

PRESENT	IMPERFECT	PLUPERFECT
1. envíe	envi-ara/ase	hubiera enviado
2. envíes	envi-aras/ases	hubieras enviado
3. envíe	envi-ara/ase	hubiera enviado
1. enviemos	envi-áramos/ásemos	hubiéramos enviado
2. enviéis	envi-arais/aseis	hubierais enviado
3. envíen	envi-aran/asen	hubieran enviado

PERFECT	haya enviado *etc*

INFINITIVE

PARTICIPLE

PRESENT	PRESENT
enviar	enviando

PAST	PAST
haber enviado	enviado

PRESENT	**IMPERFECT**	**FUTURE**
1. me equivoco	me equivocaba	me equivocaré
2. te equivocas	te equivocabas	te equivocarás
3. se equivoca	se equivocaba	se equivocará
1. nos equivocamos	nos equivocábamos	nos equivocaremos
2. os equivocáis	os equivocabais	os equivocaréis
3. se equivocan	se equivocaban	se equivocarán

PRETERITE	**PERFECT**	**PLUPERFECT**
1. me equivoqué	me he equivocado	me había equivocado
2. te equivocaste	te has equivocado	te habías equivocado
3. se equivocó	se ha equivocado	se había equivocado
1. nos equivocamos	nos hemos equivocado	nos habíamos equivocado
2. os equivocasteis	os habéis equivocado	os habíais equivocado
3. se equivocaron	se han equivocado	se habían equivocado

PAST ANTERIOR
me hube equivocado *etc*

FUTURE PERFECT
me habré equivocado *etc*

CONDITIONAL

PRESENT	**PAST**
1. me equivocaría	me habría equivocado
2. te equivocarías	te habrías equivocado
3. se equivocaría	se habría equivocado
1. nos equivocaríamos	nos habríamos equivocado
2. os equivocaríais	os habríais equivocado
3. se equivocarían	se habrían equivocado

IMPERATIVE

(tú) equivócate
(Vd) equivóquese
(nosotros) equivoquémonos
(vosotros) equivocaos
(Vds) equivóquense

SUBJUNCTIVE

PRESENT	**IMPERFECT**	**PLUPERFECT**
1. me equivoque	me equivoc-ara/ase	me hubiera equivocado
2. te equivoques	te equivoc-aras/ases	te hubieras equivocado
3. se equivoque	se equivoc-ara/ase	se hubiera equivocado
1. nos equivoquemos	nos equivoc-áramos/ásemos	nos hubiéramos equivocado
2. os equivoquéis	os equivoc-arais/aseis	os hubierais equivocado
3. se equivoquen	se equivoc-aran/asen	se hubieran equivocado

PERFECT   me haya equivocado *etc*

INFINITIVE

PRESENT
equivocarse

PAST
haberse equivocado

PARTICIPLE

PRESENT
equivocándose

PAST
equivocado

ERGUIR
97 to erect

PRESENT	IMPERFECT	FUTURE
1. yergo/irgo	erguía	erguiré
2. yergues/irgues	erguías	erguirás
3. yergue/irgue	erguía	erguirá
1. erguimos	erguíamos	erguiremos
2. erguís	erguíais	erguiréis
3. yerguen/irguen	erguían	erguirán

PRETERITE	PERFECT	PLUPERFECT
1. erguí	he erguido	había erguido
2. erguiste	has erguido	habías erguido
3. irguió	ha erguido	había erguido
1. erguimos	hemos erguido	habíamos erguido
2. erguisteis	habéis erguido	habíais erguido
3. irguieron	han erguido	habían erguido

PAST ANTERIOR	FUTURE PERFECT
hube erguido *etc*	habré erguido *etc*

CONDITIONAL		IMPERATIVE

PRESENT	PAST	
1. erguiría	habría erguido	
2. erguirías	habrías erguido	(tú) yergue/irgue
3. erguiría	habría erguido	(Vd) yerga/irga
1. erguiríamos	habríamos erguido	(nosotros) yergamos/irgamos
2. erguiríais	habríais erguido	(vosotros) erguid
3. erguirían	habrían erguido	(Vds) yergan/irgan

SUBJUNCTIVE

PRESENT	IMPERFECT	PLUPERFECT
1. yerga/irga	irgu-iera/iese	hubiera erguido
2. yergas/irgas	irgu-ieras/ieses	hubieras erguido
3. yerga/irga	irgu-iera/iese	hubiera erguido
1. yergamos/irgamos	irgu-iéramos/iésemos	hubiéramos erguido
2. yergáis/irgáis	irgu-ierais/ieseis	hubierais erguido
3. yergan/irgan	irgu-ieran/iesen	hubieran erguido
PERFECT	haya erguido *etc*	

INFINITIVE	PARTICIPLE	NOTE
PRESENT	**PRESENT**	The yer- forms are
erguir	irguiendo	more common than the
		ir- forms.
PAST	**PAST**	
haber erguido	erguido	

PRESENT	IMPERFECT	FUTURE
1. yerro	erraba	erraré
2. yerras	errabas	errarás
3. yerra	erraba	errará
1. erramos	errábamos	erraremos
2. erráis	errabais	erraréis
3. yerran	erraban	errarán

PRETERITE	PERFECT	PLUPERFECT
1. erré	he errado	había errado
2. erraste	has errado	habías errado
3. erró	ha errado	había errado
1. erramos	hemos errado	habíamos errado
2. errasteis	habéis errado	habíais errado
3. erraron	han errado	habían errado

PAST ANTERIOR	FUTURE PERFECT
hube errado *etc*	habré errado *etc*

CONDITIONAL

IMPERATIVE

PRESENT	PAST	
1. erraría	habría errado	
2. errarías	habrías errado	(tú) yerra
3. erraría	habría errado	(Vd) yerre
1. erraríamos	habríamos errado	(nosotros) erremos
2. erraríais	habíais errado	(vosotros) errad
3. errarían	habrían errado	(Vds) yerren

SUBJUNCTIVE

PRESENT	IMPERFECT	PLUPERFECT
1. yerre	err-ara/ase	hubiera errado
2. yerres	err-aras/ases	hubieras errado
3. yerre	err-ara/ase	hubiera errado
1. erremos	err-áramos/ásemos	hubiéramos errado
2. erréis	err-arais/aseis	hubierais errado
3. yerren	err-aran/asen	hubieran errado

PERFECT   haya errado *etc*

INFINITIVE

PARTICIPLE

PRESENT	PRESENT
errar	errando

PAST	PAST
haber errado	errado

ESCRIBIR
99 *to write*

PRESENT	IMPERFECT	FUTURE
1. escribo	escribía	escribiré
2. escribes	escribías	escribirás
3. escribe	escribía	escribirá
1. escribimos	escribíamos	escribiremos
2. escribís	escribíais	escribiréis
3. escriben	escribían	escribirán

PRETERITE	PERFECT	PLUPERFECT
1. escribí	he escrito	había escrito
2. escribiste	has escrito	habías escrito
3. escribió	ha escrito	había escrito
1. escribimos	hemos escrito	habíamos escrito
2. escribisteis	habéis escrito	habíais escrito
3. escribieron	han escrito	habían escrito

PAST ANTERIOR		FUTURE PERFECT
hube escrito *etc*		habré escrito *etc*

CONDITIONAL

IMPERATIVE

PRESENT	PAST	
1. escribiría	habría escrito	
2. escribirías	habrías escrito	(tú) escribe
3. escribiría	habría escrito	(Vd) escriba
1. escribiríamos	habríamos escrito	(nosotros) escribamos
2. escribiríais	habríais escrito	(vosotros) escribid
3. escribirían	habrían escrito	(Vds) escriban

SUBJUNCTIVE

PRESENT	IMPERFECT	PLUPERFECT
1. escriba	escrib-iera/iese	hubiera escrito
2. escribas	escrib-ieras/ieses	hubieras escrito
3. escriba	escrib-iera/iese	hubiera escrito
1. escribamos	escrib-iéramos/iésemos	hubiéramos escrito
2. escribáis	escrib-ierais/ieseis	hubierais escrito
3. escriban	escrib-ieran/iesen	hubieran escrito
PERFECT	haya escrito *etc*	

INFINITIVE

PARTICIPLE

PRESENT	PRESENT
escribir	escribiendo

PAST	PAST
haber escrito	escrito

PRESENT	**IMPERFECT**	**FUTURE**
1. me esfuerzo	me esforzaba	me esforzaré
2. te esfuerzas	te esforzabas	te esforzarás
3. se esfuerza	se esforzaba	se esforzará
1. nos esforzamos	nos esforzábamos	nos esforzaremos
2. os esforzáis	os esforzabais	os esforzaréis
3. se esfuerzan	se esforzaban	se esforzarán

PRETERITE	**PERFECT**	**PLUPERFECT**
1. me esforcé	me he esforzado	me había esforzado
2. te esforzaste	te has esforzado	te habías esforzado
3. se esforzó	se ha esforzado	se había esforzado
1. nos esforzamos	nos hemos esforzado	nos habíamos esforzado
2. os esforzasteis	os habéis esforzado	os habíais esforzado
3. se esforzaron	se han esforzado	se habían esforzado

PAST ANTERIOR	**FUTURE PERFECT**
me hube esforzado *etc*	me habré esforzado *etc*

CONDITIONAL		*IMPERATIVE*

PRESENT	**PAST**	
1. me esforzaría	me habría esforzado	
2. te esforzarías	te habrías esforzado	(tú) esfuérzate
3. se esforzaría	se habría esforzado	(Vd) esfuércese
1. nos esforzaríamos	nos habríamos esforzado	(nosotros) esforcémonos
2. os esforzaríais	os habríais esforzado	(vosotros) esforzaos
3. se esforzarían	se habrían esforzado	(Vds) esfuércense

SUBJUNCTIVE		

PRESENT	**IMPERFECT**	**PLUPERFECT**
1. me esfuerce	me esforz-ara/ase	me hubiera esforzado
2. te esfuerces	te esforz-aras/ases	te hubieras esforzado
3. se esfuerce	se esforz-ara/ase	se hubiera esforzado
1. nos esforcemos	nos esforz-áramos/ásemos	nos hubiéramos esforzado
2. os esforcéis	os esforz-arais/aseis	os hubierais esforzado
3. se esfuercen	se esforz-aran/asen	se hubieran esforzado
PERFECT	me haya esforzado *etc*	

INFINITIVE	*PARTICIPLE*

PRESENT	**PRESENT**
esforzarse	esforzándose

PAST	**PAST**
haberse esforzado	esforzado

ESPERAR
101 *to wait; to hope*

PRESENT	IMPERFECT	FUTURE
1. espero	esperaba	esperaré
2. esperas	esperabas	esperarás
3. espera	esperaba	esperará
1. esperamos	esperábamos	esperaremos
2. esperáis	esperabais	esperaréis
3. esperan	esperaban	esperarán

PRETERITE	PERFECT	PLUPERFECT
1. esperé	he esperado	había esperado
2. esperaste	has esperado	habías esperado
3. esperó	ha esperado	había esperado
1. esperamos	hemos esperado	habíamos esperado
2. esperasteis	habéis esperado	habíais esperado
3. esperaron	han esperado	habían esperado

PAST ANTERIOR		FUTURE PERFECT
hube esperado *etc*		habré esperado *etc*

CONDITIONAL

IMPERATIVE

PRESENT	PAST	
1. esperaría	habría esperado	
2. esperarías	habrías esperado	(tú) espera
3. esperaría	habría esperado	(Vd) espere
1. esperaríamos	habríamos esperado	(nosotros) esperemos
2. esperaríais	habríais esperado	(vosotros) esperad
3. esperarían	habrían esperado	(Vds) esperen

SUBJUNCTIVE

PRESENT	IMPERFECT	PLUPERFECT
1. espere	esper-ara/ase	hubiera esperado
2. esperes	esper-aras/ases	hubieras esperado
3. espere	esper-ara/ase	hubiera esperado
1. esperemos	esper-áramos/ásemos	hubiéramos esperado
2. esperéis	esper-arais/aseis	hubierais esperado
3. esperen	esper-aran/asen	hubieran esperado
PERFECT	haya esperado *etc*	

INFINITIVE

PARTICIPLE

PRESENT	PRESENT
esperar	esperando
PAST	PAST
haber esperado	esperado

PRESENT	IMPERFECT	FUTURE
1. estoy	estaba	estaré
2. estás	estabas	estarás
3. está	estaba	estará
1. estamos	estábamos	estaremos
2. estáis	estabais	estaréis
3. están	estaban	estarán

PRETERITE	PERFECT	PLUPERFECT
1. estuve	he estado	había estado
2. estuviste	has estado	habías estado
3. estuvo	ha estado	había estado
1. estuvimos	hemos estado	habíamos estado
2. estuvisteis	habéis estado	habíais estado
3. estuvieron	han estado	habían estado

PAST ANTERIOR		FUTURE PERFECT
hube estado *etc*		habré estado *etc*

CONDITIONAL

IMPERATIVE

PRESENT	PAST	
1. estaría	habría estado	
2. estarías	habrías estado	(tú) está
3. estaría	habría estado	(Vd) esté
1. estaríamos	habríamos estado	(nosotros) estemos
2. estaríais	habríais estado	(vosotros) estad
3. estarían	habrían estado	(Vds) estén

SUBJUNCTIVE

PRESENT	IMPERFECT	PLUPERFECT
1. esté	estuv-iera/iese	hubiera estado
2. estés	estuv-ieras/ieses	hubieras estado
3. esté	estuv-iera/iese	hubiera estado
1. estemos	estuv-iéramos/iésemos	hubiéramos estado
2. estéis	estuv-ierais/ieseis	hubierais estado
3. estén	estuv-ieran/iesen	hubieran estado
PERFECT	haya estado *etc*	

INFINITIVE

PARTICIPLE

PRESENT	PRESENT
estar	estando
PAST	PAST
haber estado	estado

PRESENT	IMPERFECT	FUTURE
1. evacuo	evacuaba	evacuaré
2. evacuas	evacuabas	evacuarás
3. evacua	evacuaba	evacuará
1. evacuamos	evacuábamos	evacuaremos
2. evacuáis	evacuabais	evacuaréis
3. evacuan	evacuaban	evacuarán

PRETERITE	PERFECT	PLUPERFECT
1. evacué	he evacuado	había evacuado
2. evacuaste	has evacuado	habías evacuado
3. evacuó	ha evacuado	había evacuado
1. evacuamos	hemos evacuado	habíamos evacuado
2. evacuasteis	habéis evacuado	habíais evacuado
3. evacuaron	han evacuado	habían evacuado

PAST ANTERIOR	FUTURE PERFECT
hube evacuado *etc*	habré evacuado *etc*

CONDITIONAL

IMPERATIVE

PRESENT	PAST	
1. evacuaría	habría evacuado	
2. evacuarías	habrías evacuado	(tú) evacua
3. evacuaría	habría evacuado	(Vd) evacue
1. evacuaríamos	habríamos evacuado	(nosotros) evacuemos
2. evacuaríais	habríais evacuado	(vosotros) evacuad
3. evacuarían	habrían evacuado	(Vds) evacuen

SUBJUNCTIVE

PRESENT	IMPERFECT	PLUPERFECT
1. evacue	evacu-ara/ase	hubiera evacuado
2. evacues	evacu-aras/ases	hubieras evacuado
3. evacue	evacu-ara/ase	hubiera evacuado
1. evacuemos	evacu-áramos/ásemos	hubiéramos evacuado
2. evacuéis	evacu-arais/aseis	hubierais evacuado
3. evacuen	evacu-aran/asen	hubieran evacuado

PERFECT	haya evacuado *etc*

INFINITIVE

PARTICIPLE

PRESENT	PRESENT
evacuar	evacuando

PAST	PAST
haber evacuado	evacuado

PRESENT	IMPERFECT	FUTURE
1. exijo	exigía	exigiré
2. exiges	exigías	exigirás
3. exige	exigía	exigirá
1. exigimos	exigíamos	exigiremos
2. exigís	exigíais	exigiréis
3. exigen	exigían	exigirán

PRETERITE	PERFECT	PLUPERFECT
1. exigí	he exigido	había exigido
2. exigiste	has exigido	habías exigido
3. exigió	ha exigido	había exigido
1. exigimos	hemos exigido	habíamos exigido
2. exigisteis	habéis exigido	habíais exigido
3. exigieron	han exigido	habían exigido

PAST ANTERIOR		FUTURE PERFECT
hube exigido *etc*		habré exigido *etc*

CONDITIONAL

IMPERATIVE

PRESENT	PAST	
1. exigiría	habría exigido	
2. exigirías	habrías exigido	(tú) exige
3. exigiría	habría exigido	(Vd) exija
1. exigiríamos	habríamos exigido	(nosotros) exijamos
2. exigiríais	habríais exigido	(vosotros) exigid
3. exigirían	habrían exigido	(Vds) exijan

SUBJUNCTIVE

PRESENT	IMPERFECT	PLUPERFECT
1. exija	exig-iera/iese	hubiera exigido
2. exijas	exig-ieras/ieses	hubieras exigido
3. exija	exig-iera/iese	hubiera exigido
1. exijamos	exig-iéramos/iésemos	hubiéramos exigido
2. exijáis	exig-ierais/ieseis	hubierais exigido
3. exijan	exig-ieran/iesen	hubieran exigido

PERFECT	haya exigido *etc*	

INFINITIVE	PARTICIPLE
PRESENT	**PRESENT**
exigir	exigiendo
PAST	**PAST**
haber exigido	exigido

EXPLICAR
105 _to explain_

PRESENT	IMPERFECT	FUTURE
1. explico	explicaba	explicaré
2. explicas	explicabas	explicarás
3. explica	explicaba	explicará
1. explicamos	explicábamos	explicaremos
2. explicáis	explicabais	explicaréis
3. explican	explicaban	explicarán

PRETERITE	PERFECT	PLUPERFECT
1. expliqué	he explicado	había explicado
2. explicaste	has explicado	habías explicado
3. explicó	ha explicado	había explicado
1. explicamos	hemos explicado	habíamos explicado
2. explicasteis	habéis explicado	habíais explicado
3. explicaron	han explicado	habían explicado

PAST ANTERIOR		FUTURE PERFECT
hube explicado _etc_		habré explicado _etc_

CONDITIONAL | IMPERATIVE

PRESENT	PAST	
1. explicaría	habría explicado	
2. explicarías	habrías explicado	
3. explicaría	habría explicado	(tú) explica
1. explicaríamos	habríamos explicado	(Vd) explique
2. explicaríais	habríais explicado	(nosotros) expliquemos
3. explicarían	habrían explicado	(vosotros) explicad
		(Vds) expliquen

SUBJUNCTIVE

PRESENT	IMPERFECT	PLUPERFECT
1. explique	explic-ara/ase	hubiera explicado
2. expliques	explic-aras/ases	hubieras explicado
3. explique	explic-ara/ase	hubiera explicado
1. expliquemos	explic-áramos/ásemos	hubiéramos explicado
2. expliquéis	explic-arais/aseis	hubierais explicado
3. expliquen	explic-aran/asen	hubieran explicado

PERFECT   haya explicado _etc_

INFINITIVE | PARTICIPLE

PRESENT	PRESENT
explicar	explicando

PAST	PAST
haber explicado	explicado

PRESENT	IMPERFECT	FUTURE
1. friego	fregaba	fregaré
2. friegas	fregabas	fregarás
3. friega	fregaba	fregará
1. fregamos	fregábamos	fregaremos
2. fregáis	fregabais	fregaréis
3. friegan	fregaban	fregarán

PRETERITE	PERFECT	PLUPERFECT
1. fregué	he fregado	había fregado
2. fregaste	has fregado	habías fregado
3. fregó	ha fregado	había fregado
1. fregamos	hemos fregado	habíamos fregado
2. fregasteis	habéis fregado	habíais fregado
3. fregaron	han fregado	habían fregado

PAST ANTERIOR		FUTURE PERFECT
hube fregado *etc*		habré fregado *etc*

CONDITIONAL

IMPERATIVE

PRESENT	PAST	
1. fregaría	habría fregado	
2. fregarías	habrías fregado	(tú) friega
3. fregaría	habría fregado	(Vd) friegue
1. fregaríamos	habríamos fregado	(nosotros) freguemos
2. fregaríais	habríais fregado	(vosotros) fregad
3. fregarían	habrían fregado	(Vds) frieguen

SUBJUNCTIVE

PRESENT	IMPERFECT	PLUPERFECT
1. friegue	freg-ara/ase	hubiera fregado
2. friegues	freg-aras/ases	hubieras fregado
3. friegue	freg-ara/ase	hubiera fregado
1. freguemos	freg-áramos/ásemos	hubiéramos fregado
2. freguéis	freg-arais/aseis	hubierais fregado
3. frieguen	freg-aran/asen	hubieran fregado
PERFECT	haya fregado *etc*	

INFINITIVE

PARTICIPLE

PRESENT	PRESENT
fregar	fregando
PAST	PAST
haber fregado	fregado

FREÍR
to fry

PRESENT	IMPERFECT	FUTURE
1. frío	freía	freiré
2. fríes	freías	freirás
3. fríe	freía	freirá
1. freímos	freíamos	freiremos
2. freís	freíais	freiréis
3. fríen	freían	freirán

PRETERITE	PERFECT	PLUPERFECT
1. freí	he frito	había frito
2. freíste	has frito	habías frito
3. frió	ha frito	había frito
1. freímos	hemos frito	habíamos frito
2. freísteis	habéis frito	habíais frito
3. frieron	han frito	habían frito

PAST ANTERIOR		FUTURE PERFECT
hube frito *etc*		habré frito *etc*

CONDITIONAL

IMPERATIVE

PRESENT	PAST	
1. freiría	habría frito	
2. freirías	habrías frito	(tú) fríe
3. freiría	habría frito	(Vd) fría
1. freiríamos	habríamos frito	(nosotros) friamos
2. freiríais	habríais frito	(vosotros) freíd
3. freirían	habrían frito	(Vds) frían

SUBJUNCTIVE

PRESENT	IMPERFECT	PLUPERFECT
1. fría	fr-iera/iese	hubiera frito
2. frías	fr-ieras/ieses	hubieras frito
3. fría	fr-iera/iese	hubiera frito
1. friamos	fr-iéramos/iésemos	hubiéramos frito
2. friáis	fr-ierais/ieseis	hubierais frito
3. frían	fr-ieran/iesen	hubieran frito
PERFECT	haya frito *etc*	

INFINITIVE

PARTICIPLE

PRESENT	PRESENT
freír	friendo

PAST	PAST
haber frito	frito

PRESENT	IMPERFECT	FUTURE
1. gimo	gemía	gemiré
2. gimes	gemías	gemirás
3. gime	gemía	gemirá
1. gemimos	gemíamos	gemiremos
2. gemís	gemíais	gemiréis
3. gimen	gemían	gemirán

PRETERITE	PERFECT	PLUPERFECT
1. gemí	he gemido	había gemido
2. gemiste	has gemido	habías gemido
3. gimió	ha gemido	había gemido
1. gemimos	hemos gemido	habíamos gemido
2. gemisteis	habéis gemido	habíais gemido
3. gimieron	han gemido	habían gemido

PAST ANTERIOR	FUTURE PERFECT
hube gemido *etc*	habré gemido *etc*

CONDITIONAL

IMPERATIVE

PRESENT	PAST	
1. gemiría	habría gemido	
2. gemirías	habrías gemido	(tú) gime
3. gemiría	habría gemido	(Vd) gima
1. gemiríamos	habríamos gemido	(nosotros) gimamos
2. gemiríais	habríais gemido	(vosotros) gemid
3. gemirían	habrían gemido	(Vds) giman

SUBJUNCTIVE

PRESENT	IMPERFECT	PLUPERFECT
1. gima	gim-iera/iese	hubiera gemido
2. gimas	gim-ieras/ieses	hubieras gemido
3. gima	gim-iera/iese	hubiera gemido
1. gimamos	gim-iéramos/iésemos	hubiéramos gemido
2. gimáis	gim-ierais/ieseis	hubierais gemido
3. giman	gim-ieran/iesen	hubieran gemido

PERFECT	haya gemido *etc*

INFINITIVE

PARTICIPLE

PRESENT	PRESENT
gemir	gimiendo

PAST	PAST
haber gemido	gemido

GRUÑIR
109 *to grunt*

PRESENT	IMPERFECT	FUTURE
1. gruño	gruñía	gruñiré
2. gruñes	gruñías	gruñirás
3. gruñe	gruñía	gruñirá
1. gruñimos	gruñíamos	gruñiremos
2. gruñís	gruñíais	gruñiréis
3. gruñen	gruñían	gruñirán

PRETERITE	PERFECT	PLUPERFECT
1. gruñí	he gruñido	había gruñido
2. gruñiste	has gruñido	habías gruñido
3. gruñó	ha gruñido	había gruñido
1. gruñimos	hemos gruñido	habíamos gruñido
2. gruñisteis	habéis gruñido	habíais gruñido
3. gruñeron	han gruñido	habían gruñido

PAST ANTERIOR	FUTURE PERFECT
hube gruñido *etc*	habré gruñido *etc*

CONDITIONAL

IMPERATIVE

PRESENT	PAST	
1. gruñiría	habría gruñido	
2. gruñirías	habrías gruñido	
3. gruñiría	habría gruñido	(tú) gruñe
1. gruñiríamos	habríamos gruñido	(Vd) gruña
2. gruñiríais	habríais gruñido	(nosotros) gruñamos
3. gruñirían	habrían gruñido	(vosotros) gruñid
		(Vds) gruñan

SUBJUNCTIVE

PRESENT	IMPERFECT	PLUPERFECT
1. gruña	gruñ-era/ese	hubiera gruñido
2. gruñas	gruñ-eras/eses	hubieras gruñido
3. gruña	gruñ-era/ese	hubiera gruñido
1. gruñamos	gruñ-éramos/ésemos	hubiéramos gruñido
2. gruñáis	gruñ-erais/eseis	hubierais gruñido
3. gruñan	gruñ-eran/esen	hubieran gruñido

PERFECT	haya gruñido *etc*

INFINITIVE

PARTICIPLE

PRESENT	PRESENT
gruñir	gruñendo

PAST	PAST
haber gruñido	gruñido

PRESENT	IMPERFECT	FUTURE
1. gusto	gustaba	gustaré
2. gustas	gustabas	gustarás
3. gusta	gustaba	gustará
1. gustamos	gustábamos	gustaremos
2. gustáis	gustabais	gustaréis
3. gustan	gustaban	gustarán

PRETERITE	PERFECT	PLUPERFECT
1. gusté	he gustado	había gustado
2. gustaste	has gustado	habías gustado
3. gustó	ha gustado	había gustado
1. gustamos	hemos gustado	habíamos gustado
2. gustasteis	habéis gustado	habíais gustado
3. gustaron	han gustado	habían gustado

PAST ANTERIOR		FUTURE PERFECT
hube gustado *etc*		habré gustado *etc*

CONDITIONAL

IMPERATIVE

PRESENT	PAST	
1. gustaría	habría gustado	
2. gustarías	habrías gustado	(tú) gusta
3. gustaría	habría gustado	(Vd) guste
1. gustaríamos	habríamos gustado	(nosotros) gustemos
2. gustaríais	habríais gustado	(vosotros) gustad
3. gustarían	habrían gustado	(Vds) gusten

SUBJUNCTIVE

PRESENT	IMPERFECT	PLUPERFECT
1. guste	gust-ara/ase	hubiera gustado
2. gustes	gust-aras/ases	hubieras gustado
3. guste	gust-ara/ase	hubiera gustado
1. gustemos	gust-áramos/ásemos	hubiéramos gustado
2. gustéis	gust-arais/aseis	hubierais gustado
3. gusten	gust-aran/asen	hubieran gustado
PERFECT	haya gustado *etc*	

INFINITIVE	PARTICIPLE	NOTE
PRESENT	**PRESENT**	Normally used only in
gustar	gustando	third person;
		I like = me gusta
PAST	**PAST**	
haber gustado	gustado	

HABER
111 *to have (auxiliary)*

PRESENT	IMPERFECT	FUTURE
1. he	había	habré
2. has	habías	habrás
3. ha/hay*	había	habrá
1. hemos	habíamos	habremos
2. habéis	habíais	habréis
3. han	habían	habrán

PRETERITE	PERFECT	PLUPERFECT
1. hube		
2. hubiste		
3. hubo	ha habido	había habido
1. hubimos		
2. hubisteis		
3. hubieron		

PAST ANTERIOR	FUTURE PERFECT
hubo habido *etc*	habrá habido *etc*

CONDITIONAL

PRESENT	PAST
1. habría	
2. habrías	
3. habría	habría habido
1. habríamos	
2. habríais	
3. habrían	

IMPERATIVE

SUBJUNCTIVE

PRESENT	IMPERFECT	PLUPERFECT
1. haya	hub-iera/iese	
2. hayas	hub-ieras/ieses	
3. haya	hub-iera/iese	hubiera habido
1. hayamos	hub-iéramos/iésemos	
2. hayáis	hub-ierais/ieseis	
3. hayan	hub-ieran/iesen	

PERFECT	haya habido *etc*

INFINITIVE

PRESENT
haber

PAST
haber habido

PARTICIPLE

PRESENT
habiendo

PAST
habido

NOTE

This verb is an auxiliary used for compound tenses (eg **he bebido** – I have drunk)

*hay means 'there is/are'.

PRESENT	IMPERFECT	FUTURE
1. hablo	hablaba	hablaré
2. hablas	hablabas	hablarás
3. habla	hablaba	hablará
1. hablamos	hablábamos	hablaremos
2. habláis	hablabais	hablaréis
3. hablan	hablaban	hablarán

PRETERITE	PERFECT	PLUPERFECT
1. hablé	he hablado	había hablado
2. hablaste	has hablado	habías hablado
3. habló	ha hablado	había hablado
1. hablamos	hemos hablado	habíamos hablado
2. hablasteis	habéis hablado	habíais hablado
3. hablaron	han hablado	habían hablado

PAST ANTERIOR	FUTURE PERFECT
hube hablado *etc*	habré hablado *etc*

CONDITIONAL

IMPERATIVE

PRESENT	PAST	
1. hablaría	habría hablado	
2. hablarías	habrías hablado	(tú) habla
3. hablaría	habría hablado	(Vd) hable
1. hablaríamos	habríamos hablado	(nosotros) hablemos
2. hablaríais	habríais hablado	(vosotros) hablad
3. hablarían	habrían hablado	(Vds) hablen

SUBJUNCTIVE

PRESENT	IMPERFECT	PLUPERFECT
1. hable	habl-ara/ase	hubiera hablado
2. hables	habl-aras/ases	hubieras hablado
3. hable	habl-ara/ase	hubiera hablado
1. hablemos	habl-áramos/ásemos	hubiéramos hablado
2. habléis	habl-arais/aseis	hubierais hablado
3. hablen	habl-aran/asen	hubieran hablado

PERFECT	haya hablado *etc*

INFINITIVE

PARTICIPLE

PRESENT	PRESENT
hablar	hablando

PAST	PAST
haber hablado	hablado

HACER
113 to make; to do

PRESENT	IMPERFECT	FUTURE
1. hago	hacía	haré
2. haces	hacías	harás
3. hace	hacía	hará
1. hacemos	hacíamos	haremos
2. hacéis	hacíais	haréis
3. hacen	hacían	harán

PRETERITE	PERFECT	PLUPERFECT
1. hice	he hecho	había hecho
2. hiciste	has hecho	habías hecho
3. hizo	ha hecho	había hecho
1. hicimos	hemos hecho	habíamos hecho
2. hicisteis	habéis hecho	habíais hecho
3. hicieron	han hecho	habían hecho

PAST ANTERIOR		FUTURE PERFECT
hube hecho *etc*		habré hecho *etc*

CONDITIONAL

PRESENT	PAST
1. haría	habría hecho
2. harías	habrías hecho
3. haría	habría hecho
1. haríamos	habríamos hecho
2. haríais	habríais hecho
3. harían	habrían hecho

IMPERATIVE

(tú) haz
(Vd) haga
(nosotros) hagamos
(vosotros) haced
(Vds) hagan

SUBJUNCTIVE

PRESENT	IMPERFECT	PLUPERFECT
1. haga	hic-iera/iese	hubiera hecho
2. hagas	hic-ieras/ieses	hubieras hecho
3. haga	hic-iera/iese	hubiera hecho
1. hagamos	hic-iéramos/iésemos	hubiéramos hecho
2. hagáis	hic-ierais/ieseis	hubierais hecho
3. hagan	hic-ieran/iesen	hubieran hecho

PERFECT	haya hecho *etc*

INFINITIVE

PRESENT
hacer

PAST
haber hecho

PARTICIPLE

PRESENT
haciendo

PAST
hecho

PRESENT	IMPERFECT	FUTURE
1. me hallo	me hallaba	me hallaré
2. te hallas	te hallabas	te hallarás
3. se halla	se hallaba	se hallará
1. nos hallamos	nos hallábamos	nos hallaremos
2. os halláis	os hallabais	os hallaréis
3. se hallan	se hallaban	se hallarán

PRETERITE	PERFECT	PLUPERFECT
1. me hallé	me he hallado	me había hallado
2. te hallaste	te has hallado	te habías hallado
3. se halló	se ha hallado	se había hallado
1. nos hallamos	nos hemos hallado	nos habíamos hallado
2. os hallasteis	os habéis hallado	os habíais hallado
3. se hallaron	se han hallado	se habían hallado

PAST ANTERIOR		FUTURE PERFECT
me hube hallado *etc*		me habré hallado *etc*

CONDITIONAL

IMPERATIVE

PRESENT	PAST	
1. me hallaría	me habría hallado	
2. te hallarías	te habrías hallado	
3. se hallaría	se habría hallado	(tú) hállate
1. nos hallaríamos	nos habríamos hallado	(Vd) hállese
2. os hallaríais	os habríais hallado	(nosotros) hallémonos
3. se hallarían	se habrían hallado	(vosotros) hallaos
		(Vds) hállense

SUBJUNCTIVE

PRESENT	IMPERFECT	PLUPERFECT
1. me halle	me hall-ara/ase	me hubiera hallado
2. te halles	te hall-aras/ases	te hubieras hallado
3. se halle	se hall-ara/ase	se hubiera hallado
1. nos hallemos	nos hall-áramos/ásemos	nos hubiéramos hallado
2. os halléis	os hall-arais/aseis	os hubierais hallado
3. se hallen	se hall-aran/asen	se hubieran hallado

PERFECT	me haya hallado *etc*

INFINITIVE

PARTICIPLE

PRESENT	PRESENT
hallarse	hallándose

PAST	PAST
haberse hallado	hallado

PRESENT 3. hiela	**IMPERFECT** helaba	**FUTURE** helará
PRETERITE 3. heló	**PERFECT** ha helado	**PLUPERFECT** había helado
PAST ANTERIOR hubo helado		**FUTURE PERFECT** habrá helado

CONDITIONAL

		IMPERATIVE
PRESENT 3. helaría	**PAST** habría helado	

SUBJUNCTIVE

PRESENT 3. hiele	**IMPERFECT** hel-ara/ase	**PLUPERFECT** hubiera helado
PERFECT haya helado		

INFINITIVE

	PARTICIPLE
PRESENT helar	**PRESENT** helando
PAST haber helado	**PAST** helado

PRESENT	IMPERFECT	FUTURE
1. hiero	hería	heriré
2. hieres	herías	herirás
3. hiere	hería	herirá
1. herimos	heríamos	heriremos
2. herís	heríais	heriréis
3. hieren	herían	herirán

PRETERITE	PERFECT	PLUPERFECT
1. herí	he herido	había herido
2. heriste	has herido	habías herido
3. hirió	ha herido	había herido
1. herimos	hemos herido	habíamos herido
2. heristeis	habéis herido	habíais herido
3. hirieron	han herido	habían herido

PAST ANTERIOR	FUTURE PERFECT
hube herido *etc*	habré herido *etc*

CONDITIONAL

IMPERATIVE

PRESENT	PAST	
1. heriría	habría herido	
2. herirías	habrías herido	
3. heriría	habría herido	(tú) hiere
1. heriríamos	habríamos herido	(Vd) hiera
2. heriríais	habríais herido	(nosotros) hiramos
3. herirían	habrían herido	(vosotros) herid
		(Vds) hieran

SUBJUNCTIVE

PRESENT	IMPERFECT	PLUPERFECT
1. hiera	hir-iera/iese	hubiera herido
2. hieras	hir-ieras/ieses	hubieras herido
3. hiera	hir-iera/iese	hubiera herido
1. hiramos	hir-iéramos/iésemos	hubiéramos herido
2. hiráis	hir-ierais/ieseis	hubierais herido
3. hieran	hir-ieran/iesen	hubieran herido

PERFECT	haya herido *etc*

INFINITIVE

PARTICIPLE

PRESENT	PRESENT
herir	hiriendo

PAST	PAST
haber herido	herido

PRESENT	IMPERFECT	FUTURE
1. huyo	huía	huiré
2. huyes	huías	huirás
3. huye	huía	huirá
1. huimos	huíamos	huiremos
2. huís	huíais	huiréis
3. huyen	huían	huirán

PRETERITE	PERFECT	PLUPERFECT
1. huí	he huido	había huido
2. huiste	has huido	habías huido
3. huyó	ha huido	había huido
1. huimos	hemos huido	habíamos huido
2. huisteis	habéis huido	habíais huido
3. huyeron	han huido	habían huido

PAST ANTERIOR	FUTURE PERFECT
hube huido *etc*	habré huido *etc*

CONDITIONAL

IMPERATIVE

PRESENT	PAST	
1. huiría	habría huido	
2. huirías	habrías huido	(tú) huye
3. huiría	habría huido	(Vd) huya
1. huiríamos	habríamos huido	(nosotros) huyamos
2. huiríais	habríais huido	(vosotros) huid
3. huirían	habrían huido	(Vds) huyan

SUBJUNCTIVE

PRESENT	IMPERFECT	PLUPERFECT
1. huya	hu-yera/yese	hubiera huido
2. huyas	hu-yeras/yeses	hubieras huido
3. huya	hu-yera/yese	hubiera huido
1. huyamos	hu-yéramos/yésemos	hubiéramos huido
2. huyáis	hu-yerais/yeseis	hubierais huido
3. huyan	hu-yeran/yesen	hubieran huido
PERFECT	haya huido *etc*	

INFINITIVE

PARTICIPLE

PRESENT	PRESENT
huir	huyendo

PAST	PAST
haber huido	huido

PRESENT	IMPERFECT	FUTURE
1. indico	indicaba	indicaré
2. indicas	indicabas	indicarás
3. indica	indicaba	indicará
1. indicamos	indicábamos	indicaremos
2. indicáis	indicabais	indicaréis
3. indican	indicaban	indicarán

PRETERITE	PERFECT	PLUPERFECT
1. indiqué	he indicado	había indicado
2. indicaste	has indicado	habías indicado
3. indicó	ha indicado	había indicado
1. indicamos	hemos indicado	habíamos indicado
2. indicasteis	habéis indicado	habíais indicado
3. indicaron	han indicado	habían indicado

PAST ANTERIOR		FUTURE PERFECT
hube indicado *etc*		habré indicado *etc*

CONDITIONAL

		IMPERATIVE

PRESENT	PAST	
1. indicaría	habría indicado	
2. indicarías	habrías indicado	(tú) indica
3. indicaría	habría indicado	(Vd) indique
1. indicaríamos	habríamos indicado	(nosotros) indiquemos
2. indicaríais	habríais indicado	(vosotros) indicad
3. indicarían	habrían indicado	(Vds) indiquen

SUBJUNCTIVE

PRESENT	IMPERFECT	PLUPERFECT
1. indique	indic-ara/ase	hubiera indicado
2. indiques	indic-aras/ases	hubieras indicado
3. indique	indic-ara/ase	hubiera indicado
1. indiquemos	indic-áramos/ásemos	hubiéramos indicado
2. indiquéis	indic-arais/aseis	hubierais indicado
3. indiquen	indic-aran/asen	hubieran indicado
PERFECT	haya indicado *etc*	

INFINITIVE	PARTICIPLE
PRESENT	PRESENT
indicar	indicando
PAST	PAST
haber indicado	indicado

PRESENT	**IMPERFECT**	**FUTURE**
1. intento	intentaba	intentaré
2. intentas	intentabas	intentarás
3. intenta	intentaba	intentará
1. intentamos	intentábamos	intentaremos
2. intentáis	intentabais	intentaréis
3. intentan	intentaban	intentarán

PRETERITE	**PERFECT**	**PLUPERFECT**
1. intenté	he intentado	había intentado
2. intentaste	has intentado	habías intentado
3. intentó	ha intentado	había intentado
1. intentamos	hemos intentado	habíamos intentado
2. intentasteis	habéis intentado	habíais intentado
3. intentaron	han intentado	habían intentado

PAST ANTERIOR		**FUTURE PERFECT**
hube intentado *etc*		habré intentado *etc*

CONDITIONAL

IMPERATIVE

PRESENT	**PAST**	
1. intentaría	habría intentado	
2. intentarías	habrías intentado	(tú) intenta
3. intentaría	habría intentado	(Vd) intente
1. intentaríamos	habríamos intentado	(nosotros) intentemos
2. intentaríais	habríais intentado	(vosotros) intentad
3. intentarían	habrían intentado	(Vds) intenten

SUBJUNCTIVE

PRESENT	**IMPERFECT**	**PLUPERFECT**
1. intente	intent-ara/ase	hubiera intentado
2. intentes	intent-aras/ases	hubieras intentado
3. intente	intent-ara/ase	hubiera intentado
1. intentemos	intent-áramos/ásemos	hubiéramos intentado
2. intentéis	intent-arais/aseis	hubierais intentado
3. intenten	intent-aran/asen	hubieran intentado

PERFECT   haya intentado *etc*

INFINITIVE

PARTICIPLE

PRESENT	**PRESENT**
intentar	intentando
PAST	**PAST**
haber intentado	intentado

PRESENT	**IMPERFECT**	**FUTURE**
1. introduzco	introducía	introduciré
2. introduces	introducías	introducirás
3. introduce	introducía	introducirá
1. introducimos	introducíamos	introduciremos
2. introducís	introducíais	introduciréis
3. introducen	introducían	introducirán

PRETERITE	**PERFECT**	**PLUPERFECT**
1. introduje	he introducido	había introducido
2. introdujiste	has introducido	habías introducido
3. introdujo	ha introducido	había introducido
1. introdujimos	hemos introducido	habíamos introducido
2. introdujisteis	habéis introducido	habíais introducido
3. introdujeron	han introducido	habían introducido

PAST ANTERIOR		**FUTURE PERFECT**
hube introducido *etc*		habré introducido *etc*

CONDITIONAL

IMPERATIVE

PRESENT	**PAST**	
1. introduciría	habría introducido	
2. introducirías	habrías introducido	(tú) introduce
3. introduciría	habría introducido	(Vd) introduzca
1. introduciríamos	habríamos introducido	(nosotros) introduzcamos
2. introduciríais	habríais introducido	(vosotros) introducid
3. introducirían	habrían introducido	(Vds) introduzcan

SUBJUNCTIVE

PRESENT	**IMPERFECT**	**PLUPERFECT**
1. introduzca	introduj-era/ese	hubiera introducido
2. introduzcas	introduj-eras/eses	hubieras introducido
3. introduzca	introduj-era/ese	hubiera introducido
1. introduzcamos	introduj-éramos/ésemos	hubiéramos introducido
2. introduzcáis	introduj-erais/eseis	hubierais introducido
3. introduzcan	introduj-eran/esen	hubieran introducido
PERFECT haya introducido *etc*		

INFINITIVE

PARTICIPLE

PRESENT	**PRESENT**
introducir	introduciendo
PAST	**PAST**
haber introducido	introducido

PRESENT	IMPERFECT	FUTURE
1. voy	iba	iré
2. vas	ibas	irás
3. va	iba	irá
1. vamos	íbamos	iremos
2. vais	ibais	iréis
3. van	iban	irán

PRETERITE	PERFECT	PLUPERFECT
1. fui	he ido	había ido
2. fuiste	has ido	habías ido
3. fue	ha ido	había ido
1. fuimos	hemos ido	habíamos ido
2. fuisteis	habéis ido	habíais ido
3. fueron	han ido	habían ido

PAST ANTERIOR	FUTURE PERFECT
hube ido *etc*	habré ido *etc*

CONDITIONAL

IMPERATIVE

PRESENT	PAST	
1. iría	habría ido	
2. irías	habrías ido	
3. iría	habría ido	(tú) ve
1. iríamos	habríamos ido	(Vd) vaya
2. iríais	habríais ido	(nosotros) vamos
3. irían	habrían ido	(vosotros) id
		(Vds) vayan

SUBJUNCTIVE

PRESENT	IMPERFECT	PLUPERFECT
1. vaya	fu-era/ese	hubiera ido
2. vayas	fu-eras/eses	hubieras ido
3. vaya	fu-era/ese	hubiera ido
1. vayamos	fu-éramos/ésemos	hubiéramos ido
2. vayáis	fu-erais/eseis	hubierais ido
3. vayan	fu-eran/esen	hubieran ido
PERFECT	haya ido *etc*	

INFINITIVE

PARTICIPLE

PRESENT	PRESENT
ir	yendo

PAST	PAST
haber ido	ido

PRESENT	IMPERFECT	FUTURE
1. juego	jugaba	jugaré
2. juegas	jugabas	jugarás
3. juega	jugaba	jugará
1. jugamos	jugábamos	jugaremos
2. jugáis	jugabais	jugaréis
3. juegan	jugaban	jugarán

PRETERITE	PERFECT	PLUPERFECT
1. jugué	he jugado	había jugado
2. jugaste	has jugado	habías jugado
3. jugó	ha jugado	había jugado
1. jugamos	hemos jugado	habíamos jugado
2. jugasteis	habéis jugado	habíais jugado
3. jugaron	han jugado	habían jugado

PAST ANTERIOR	FUTURE PERFECT
hube jugado *etc*	habré jugado *etc*

CONDITIONAL

IMPERATIVE

PRESENT	PAST	
1. jugaría	habría jugado	
2. jugarías	habrías jugado	(tú) juega
3. jugaría	habría jugado	(Vd) juegue
1. jugaríamos	habríamos jugado	(nosotros) juguemos
2. jugaríais	habríais jugado	(vosotros) jugad
3. jugarían	habrían jugado	(Vds) jueguen

SUBJUNCTIVE

PRESENT	IMPERFECT	PLUPERFECT
1. juegue	jug-ara/ase	hubiera jugado
2. juegues	jug-aras/ases	hubieras jugado
3. juegue	jug-ara/ase	hubiera jugado
1. juguemos	jug-áramos/ásemos	hubiéramos jugado
2. juguéis	jug-arais/aseis	hubierais jugado
3. jueguen	jug-aran/asen	hubieran jugado

PERFECT   haya jugado *etc*

INFINITIVE

PARTICIPLE

PRESENT	PRESENT
jugar	jugando

PAST	PAST
haber jugado	jugado

PRESENT	IMPERFECT	FUTURE
1. juzgo	juzgaba	juzgaré
2. juzgas	juzgabas	juzgarás
3. juzga	juzgaba	juzgará
1. juzgamos	juzgábamos	juzgaremos
2. juzgáis	juzgabais	juzgaréis
3. juzgan	juzgaban	juzgarán

PRETERITE	PERFECT	PLUPERFECT
1. juzgué	he juzgado	había juzgado
2. juzgaste	has juzgado	habías juzgado
3. juzgó	ha juzgado	había juzgado
1. juzgamos	hemos juzgado	habíamos juzgado
2. juzgasteis	habéis juzgado	habíais juzgado
3. juzgaron	han juzgado	habían juzgado

PAST ANTERIOR	FUTURE PERFECT
hube juzgado _etc_	habré juzgado _etc_

CONDITIONAL

IMPERATIVE

PRESENT	PAST	
1. juzgaría	habría juzgado	
2. juzgarías	habrías juzgado	(tú) juzga
3. juzgaría	habría juzgado	(Vd) juzgue
1. juzgaríamos	habríamos juzgado	(nosotros) juzguemos
2. juzgaríais	habríais juzgado	(vosotros) juzgad
3. juzgarían	habrían juzgado	(Vds) juzguen

SUBJUNCTIVE

PRESENT	IMPERFECT	PLUPERFECT
1. juzgue	juzg-ara/ase	hubiera juzgado
2. juzgues	juzg-aras/ases	hubieras juzgado
3. juzgue	juzg-ara/ase	hubiera juzgado
1. juzguemos	juzg-áramos/ásemos	hubiéramos juzgado
2. juzguéis	juzg-arais/aseis	hubierais juzgado
3. juzguen	juzg-aran/asen	hubieran juzgado
PERFECT	haya juzgado _etc_	

INFINITIVE

PARTICIPLE

PRESENT	PRESENT
juzgar	juzgando

PAST	PAST
haber juzgado	juzgado

PRESENT	IMPERFECT	FUTURE
1. lavo	lavaba	lavaré
2. lavas	lavabas	lavarás
3. lava	lavaba	lavará
1. lavamos	lavábamos	lavaremos
2. laváis	lavabais	lavaréis
3. lavan	lavaban	lavarán

PRETERITE	PERFECT	PLUPERFECT
1. lavé	he lavado	había lavado
2. lavaste	has lavado	habías lavado
3. lavó	ha lavado	había lavado
1. lavamos	hemos lavado	habíamos lavado
2. lavasteis	habéis lavado	habíais lavado
3. lavaron	han lavado	habían lavado

PAST ANTERIOR	FUTURE PERFECT
hube lavado *etc*	habré lavado *etc*

CONDITIONAL		IMPERATIVE

PRESENT	PAST	
1. lavaría	habría lavado	
2. lavarías	habrías lavado	(tú) lava
3. lavaría	habría lavado	(Vd) lave
1. lavaríamos	habríamos lavado	(nosotros) lavemos
2. lavaríais	habríais lavado	(vosotros) lavad
3. lavarían	habrían lavado	(Vds) laven

SUBJUNCTIVE

PRESENT	IMPERFECT	PLUPERFECT
1. lave	lav-ara/ase	hubiera lavado
2. laves	lav-aras/ases	hubieras lavado
3. lave	lav-ara/ase	hubiera lavado
1. lavemos	lav-áramos/ásemos	hubiéramos lavado
2. lavéis	lav-arais/aseis	hubierais lavado
3. laven	lav-aran/asen	hubieran lavado

PERFECT   haya lavado *etc*

INFINITIVE	PARTICIPLE
PRESENT	PRESENT
lavar	lavando
PAST	PAST
haber lavado	lavado

LEER
125 *to read*

PRESENT	IMPERFECT	FUTURE
1. leo	leía	leeré
2. lees	leías	leerás
3. lee	leía	leerá
1. leemos	leíamos	leeremos
2. leéis	leíais	leeréis
3. leen	leían	leerán

PRETERITE	PERFECT	PLUPERFECT
1. leí	he leído	había leído
2. leíste	has leído	habías leído
3. leyó	ha leído	había leído
1. leímos	hemos leído	habíamos leído
2. leísteis	habéis leído	habíais leído
3. leyeron	han leído	habían leído

PAST ANTERIOR	FUTURE PERFECT
hube leído *etc*	habré leído *etc*

CONDITIONAL

IMPERATIVE

PRESENT	PAST	
1. leería	habría leído	
2. leerías	habrías leído	(tú) lee
3. leería	habría leído	(Vd) lea
1. leeríamos	habríamos leído	(nosotros) leamos
2. leeríais	habríais leído	(vosotros) leed
3. leerían	habrían leído	(Vds) lean

SUBJUNCTIVE

PRESENT	IMPERFECT	PLUPERFECT
1. lea	le-yera/yese	hubiera leído
2. leas	le-yeras/yeses	hubieras leído
3. lea	le-yera/yese	hubiera leído
1. leamos	le-yéramos/yésemos	hubiéramos leído
2. leáis	le-yerais/yeseis	hubierais leído
3. lean	le-yeran/yesen	hubieran leído

PERFECT	haya leído *etc*

INFINITIVE

PARTICIPLE

PRESENT	PRESENT
leer	leyendo

PAST	PAST
haber leído	leído

PRESENT	**IMPERFECT**	**FUTURE**
1. llamo	llamaba	llamaré
2. llamas	llamabas	llamarás
3. llama	llamaba	llamará
1. llamamos	llamábamos	llamaremos
2. llamáis	llamabais	llamaréis
3. llaman	llamaban	llamarán

PRETERITE	**PERFECT**	**PLUPERFECT**
1. llamé	he llamado	había llamado
2. llamaste	has llamado	habías llamado
3. llamó	ha llamado	había llamado
1. llamamos	hemos llamado	habíamos llamado
2. llamasteis	habéis llamado	habíais llamado
3. llamaron	han llamado	habían llamado

PAST ANTERIOR	**FUTURE PERFECT**
hube llamado *etc*	habré llamado *etc*

CONDITIONAL

IMPERATIVE

PRESENT	**PAST**	
1. llamaría	habría llamado	
2. llamarías	habrías llamado	(tú) llama
3. llamaría	habría llamado	(Vd) llame
1. llamaríamos	habríamos llamado	(nosotros) llamemos
2. llamaríais	habríais llamado	(vosotros) llamad
3. llamarían	habrían llamado	(Vds) llamen

SUBJUNCTIVE

PRESENT	**IMPERFECT**	**PLUPERFECT**
1. llame	llam-ara/ase	hubiera llamado
2. llames	llam-aras/ases	hubieras llamado
3. llame	llam-ara/ase	hubiera llamado
1. llamemos	llam-áramos/ásemos	hubiéramos llamado
2. llaméis	llam-arais/aseis	hubierais llamado
3. llamen	llam-aran/asen	hubieran llamado
PERFECT	haya llamado *etc*	

INFINITIVE

PARTICIPLE

PRESENT	**PRESENT**
llamar	llamando
PAST	**PAST**
haber llamado	llamado

PRESENT	IMPERFECT	FUTURE
1. llego	llegaba	llegaré
2. llegas	llegabas	llegarás
3. llega	llegaba	llegará
1. llegamos	llegábamos	llegaremos
2. llegáis	llegabais	llegaréis
3. llegan	llegaban	llegarán

PRETERITE	PERFECT	PLUPERFECT
1. llegué	he llegado	había llegado
2. llegaste	has llegado	habías llegado
3. llegó	ha llegado	había llegado
1. llegamos	hemos llegado	habíamos llegado
2. llegasteis	habéis llegado	habíais llegado
3. llegaron	han llegado	habían llegado

PAST ANTERIOR	FUTURE PERFECT
hube llegado *etc*	habré llegado *etc*

CONDITIONAL

IMPERATIVE

PRESENT	PAST	
1. llegaría	habría llegado	
2. llegarías	habrías llegado	(tú) llega
3. llegaría	habría llegado	(Vd) llegue
1. llegaríamos	habríamos llegado	(nosotros) lleguemos
2. llegaríais	habríais llegado	(vosotros) llegad
3. llegarían	habrían llegado	(Vds) lleguen

SUBJUNCTIVE

PRESENT	IMPERFECT	PLUPERFECT
1. llegue	lleg-ara/ase	hubiera llegado
2. llegues	lleg-aras/ases	hubieras llegado
3. llegue	lleg-ara/ase	hubiera llegado
1. lleguemos	lleg-áramos/ásemos	hubiéramos llegado
2. lleguéis	lleg-arais/aseis	hubierais llegado
3. lleguen	lleg-aran/asen	hubieran llegado
PERFECT	haya llegado *etc*	

INFINITIVE

PARTICIPLE

PRESENT	PRESENT
llegar	llegando
PAST	PAST
haber llegado	llegado

PRESENT	IMPERFECT	FUTURE
3. llueve	llovía	lloverá

PRETERITE	PERFECT	PLUPERFECT
3. llovió	ha llovido	había llovido

PAST ANTERIOR		FUTURE PERFECT
hubo llovido		habrá llovido

CONDITIONAL   IMPERATIVE

PRESENT	PAST
3. llovería	habría llovido

SUBJUNCTIVE

PRESENT	IMPERFECT	PLUPERFECT
3. llueva	llov-iera/iese	hubiera llovido
PERFECT haya llovido		

INFINITIVE   PARTICIPLE

PRESENT	PRESENT
llover	lloviendo

PAST	PAST
haber llovido	llovido

LUCIR
129 *to shine*

PRESENT	IMPERFECT	FUTURE
1. luzco	lucía	luciré
2. luces	lucías	lucirás
3. luce	lucía	lucirá
1. lucimos	lucíamos	luciremos
2. lucís	lucíais	luciréis
3. lucen	lucían	lucirán

PRETERITE	PERFECT	PLUPERFECT
1. lucí	he lucido	había lucido
2. luciste	has lucido	habías lucido
3. lució	ha lucido	había lucido
1. lucimos	hemos lucido	habíamos lucido
2. lucisteis	habéis lucido	habíais lucido
3. lucieron	han lucido	habían lucido

PAST ANTERIOR	FUTURE PERFECT
hube lucido *etc*	habré lucido *etc*

CONDITIONAL

IMPERATIVE

PRESENT	PAST
1. luciría	habría lucido
2. lucirías	habrías lucido
3. luciría	habría lucido
1. luciríamos	habríamos lucido
2. luciríais	habríais lucido
3. lucirían	habrían lucido

(tú) luce
(Vd) luzca
(nosotros) luzcamos
(vosotros) lucid
(Vds) luzcan

SUBJUNCTIVE

PRESENT	IMPERFECT	PLUPERFECT
1. luzca	luc-iera/iese	hubiera lucido
2. luzcas	luc-ieras/ieses	hubieras lucido
3. luzca	luc-iera/iese	hubiera lucido
1. luzcamos	luc-iéramos/iésemos	hubiéramos lucido
2. luzcáis	luc-ierais/ieseis	hubierais lucido
3. luzcan	luc-ieran/iesen	hubieran lucido

PERFECT	haya lucido *etc*

INFINITIVE

PARTICIPLE

PRESENT	PRESENT
lucir	luciendo

PAST	PAST
haber lucido	lucido

PRESENT	IMPERFECT	FUTURE
1. miento	mentía	mentiré
2. mientes	mentías	mentirás
3. miente	mentía	mentirá
1. mentimos	mentíamos	mentiremos
2. mentís	mentíais	mentiréis
3. mienten	mentían	mentirán

PRETERITE	PERFECT	PLUPERFECT
1. mentí	he mentido	había mentido
2. mentiste	has mentido	habías mentido
3. mintió	ha mentido	había mentido
1. mentimos	hemos mentido	habíamos mentido
2. mentisteis	habéis mentido	habíais mentido
3. mintieron	han mentido	habían mentido

PAST ANTERIOR	FUTURE PERFECT
hube mentido *etc*	habré mentido *etc*

CONDITIONAL

IMPERATIVE

PRESENT	PAST	
1. mentiría	habría mentido	
2. mentirías	habrías mentido	
3. mentiría	habría mentido	(tú) miente
1. mentiríamos	habríamos mentido	(Vd) mienta
2. mentiríais	habríais mentido	(nosotros) mintamos
3. mentirían	habrían mentido	(vosotros) mentid
		(Vds) mientan

SUBJUNCTIVE

PRESENT	IMPERFECT	PLUPERFECT
1. mienta	mint-iera/iese	hubiera mentido
2. mientas	mint-ieras/ieses	hubieras mentido
3. mienta	mint-iera/iese	hubiera mentido
1. mintamos	mint-iéramos/iésemos	hubiéramos mentido
2. mintáis	mint-ierais/ieseis	hubierais mentido
3. mientan	mint-ieran/iesen	hubieran mentido

PERFECT   haya mentido *etc*

INFINITIVE

PARTICIPLE

PRESENT	PRESENT
mentir	mintiendo

PAST	PAST
haber mentido	mentido

MERECER
131 *to deserve*

PRESENT	IMPERFECT	FUTURE
1. merezco	merecía	mereceré
2. mereces	merecías	merecerás
3. merece	merecía	merecerá
1. merecemos	merecíamos	mereceremos
2. merecéis	merecíais	mereceréis
3. merecen	merecían	merecerán

PRETERITE	PERFECT	PLUPERFECT
1. merecí	he merecido	había merecido
2. mereciste	has merecido	habías merecido
3. mereció	ha merecido	había merecido
1. merecimos	hemos merecido	habíamos merecido
2. merecisteis	habéis merecido	habíais merecido
3. merecieron	han merecido	habían merecido

PAST ANTERIOR		FUTURE PERFECT
hube merecido *etc*		habré merecido *etc*

CONDITIONAL

IMPERATIVE

PRESENT	PAST
1. merecería	habría merecido
2. merecerías	habrías merecido
3. merecería	habría merecido
1. mereceríamos	habríamos merecido
2. mereceríais	habríais merecido
3. merecerían	habrían merecido

(tú) merece
(Vd) merezca
(nosotros) merezcamos
(vosotros) mereced
(Vds) merezcan

SUBJUNCTIVE

PRESENT	IMPERFECT	PLUPERFECT
1. merezca	merec-iera/iese	hubiera merecido
2. merezcas	merec-ieras/ieses	hubieras merecido
3. merezca	merec-iera/iese	hubiera merecido
1. merezcamos	merec-iéramos/iésemos	hubiéramos merecido
2. merezcáis	merec-ierais/ieseis	hubierais merecido
3. merezcan	merec-ieran/iesen	hubieran merecido

PERFECT	haya merecido *etc*

INFINITIVE

PARTICIPLE

PRESENT	PRESENT
merecer	mereciendo

PAST	PAST
haber merecido	merecido

PRESENT	IMPERFECT	FUTURE
1. muerdo	mordía	morderé
2. muerdes	mordías	morderás
3. muerde	mordía	morderá
1. mordemos	mordíamos	morderemos
2. mordéis	mordíais	morderéis
3. muerden	mordían	morderán

PRETERITE	PERFECT	PLUPERFECT
1. mordí	he mordido	había mordido
2. mordiste	has mordido	habías mordido
3. mordió	ha mordido	había mordido
1. mordimos	hemos mordido	habíamos mordido
2. mordisteis	habéis mordido	habíais mordido
3. mordieron	han mordido	habían mordido

PAST ANTERIOR		FUTURE PERFECT
hube mordido *etc*		habré mordido *etc*

CONDITIONAL		IMPERATIVE

PRESENT	PAST	
1. mordería	habría mordido	
2. morderías	habrías mordido	
3. mordería	habría mordido	(tú) muerde
1. morderíamos	habríamos mordido	(Vd) muerda
2. morderíais	habríais mordido	(nosotros) mordamos
3. morderían	habrían mordido	(vosotros) morded
		(Vds) muerdan

SUBJUNCTIVE		

PRESENT	IMPERFECT	PLUPERFECT
1. muerda	mord-iera/iese	hubiera mordido
2. muerdas	mord-ieras/ieses	hubieras mordido
3. muerda	mord-iera/iese	hubiera mordido
1. mordamos	mord-iéramos/iésemos	hubiéramos mordido
2. mordáis	mord-ierais/ieseis	hubierais mordido
3. muerdan	mord-ieran/iesen	hubieran mordido
PERFECT	haya mordido *etc*	

INFINITIVE	PARTICIPLE

PRESENT	PRESENT
morder	mordiendo

PAST	PAST
haber mordido	mordido

MORIR
133 to die

PRESENT	IMPERFECT	FUTURE
1. muero	moría	moriré
2. mueres	morías	morirás
3. muere	moría	morirá
1. morimos	moríamos	moriremos
2. morís	moríais	moriréis
3. mueren	morían	morirán

PRETERITE	PERFECT	PLUPERFECT
1. morí	he muerto	había muerto
2. moriste	has muerto	habías muerto
3. murió	ha muerto	había muerto
1. morimos	hemos muerto	habíamos muerto
2. moristeis	habéis muerto	habíais muerto
3. murieron	han muerto	habían muerto

PAST ANTERIOR	FUTURE PERFECT
hube muerto *etc*	habré muerto *etc*

CONDITIONAL

IMPERATIVE

PRESENT	PAST	
1. moriría	habría muerto	
2. morirías	habrías muerto	
3. moriría	habría muerto	(tú) muere
1. moriríamos	habríamos muerto	(Vd) muera
2. moriríais	habríais muerto	(nosotros) muramos
3. morirían	habrían muerto	(vosotros) morid
		(Vds) mueran

SUBJUNCTIVE

PRESENT	IMPERFECT	PLUPERFECT
1. muera	mur-iera/iese	hubiera muerto
2. mueras	mur-ieras/ieses	hubieras muerto
3. muera	mur-iera/iese	hubiera muerto
1. muramos	mur-iéramos/iésemos	hubiéramos muerto
2. muráis	mur-ierais/ieseis	hubierais muerto
3. mueran	mur-ieran/iesen	hubieran muerto

PERFECT   haya muerto *etc*

INFINITIVE

PARTICIPLE

PRESENT	PRESENT
morir	muriendo

PAST	PAST
haber muerto	muerto

PRESENT	IMPERFECT	FUTURE
1. muevo	movía	moveré
2. mueves	movías	moverás
3. mueve	movía	moverá
1. movemos	movíamos	moveremos
2. movéis	movíais	moveréis
3. mueven	movían	moverán

PRETERITE	PERFECT	PLUPERFECT
1. moví	he movido	había movido
2. moviste	has movido	habías movido
3. movió	ha movido	había movido
1. movimos	hemos movido	habíamos movido
2. movisteis	habéis movido	habíais movido
3. movieron	han movido	habían movido

PAST ANTERIOR	FUTURE PERFECT
hube movido *etc*	habré movido *etc*

CONDITIONAL

IMPERATIVE

PRESENT	PAST	
1. movería	habría movido	
2. moverías	habrías movido	(tú) mueve
3. movería	habría movido	(Vd) mueva
1. moveríamos	habríamos movido	(nosotros) movamos
2. moveríais	habríais movido	(vosotros) moved
3. moverían	habrían movido	(Vds) muevan

SUBJUNCTIVE

PRESENT	IMPERFECT	PLUPERFECT
1. mueva	mov-iera/iese	hubiera movido
2. muevas	mov-ieras/ieses	hubieras movido
3. mueva	mov-iera/iese	hubiera movido
1. movamos	mov-iéramos/iésemos	hubiéramos movido
2. mováis	mov-ierais/ieseis	hubierais movido
3. muevan	mov-ieran/iesen	hubieran movido

PERFECT   haya movido *etc*

INFINITIVE

PARTICIPLE

PRESENT	PRESENT
mover	moviendo

PAST	PAST
haber movido	movido

PRESENT	IMPERFECT	FUTURE
1. nazco	nacía	naceré
2. naces	nacías	nacerás
3. nace	nacía	nacerá
1. nacemos	nacíamos	naceremos
2. nacéis	nacíais	naceréis
3. nacen	nacían	nacerán

PRETERITE	PERFECT	PLUPERFECT
1. nací	he nacido	había nacido
2. naciste	has nacido	habías nacido
3. nació	ha nacido	había nacido
1. nacimos	hemos nacido	habíamos nacido
2. nacisteis	habéis nacido	habíais nacido
3. nacieron	han nacido	habían nacido

PAST ANTERIOR	FUTURE PERFECT
hube nacido *etc*	habré nacido *etc*

CONDITIONAL

IMPERATIVE

PRESENT	PAST	
1. nacería	habría nacido	
2. nacerías	habrías nacido	
3. nacería	habría nacido	(tú) nace
1. naceríamos	habríamos nacido	(Vd) nazca
2. naceríais	habríais nacido	(nosotros) nazcamos
3. nacerían	habrían nacido	(vosotros) naced
		(Vds) nazcan

SUBJUNCTIVE

PRESENT	IMPERFECT	PLUPERFECT
1. nazca	nac-iera/iese	hubiera nacido
2. nazcas	nac-ieras/ieses	hubieras nacido
3. nazca	nac-iera/iese	hubiera nacido
1. nazcamos	nac-iéramos/iésemos	hubiéramos nacido
2. nazcáis	nac-ierais/ieseis	hubierais nacido
3. nazcan	nac-ieran/iesen	hubieran nacido

PERFECT	haya nacido *etc*

INFINITIVE

PARTICIPLE

PRESENT	PRESENT
nacer	naciendo

PAST	PAST
haber nacido	nacido

PRESENT	IMPERFECT	FUTURE
1. nado	nadaba	nadaré
2. nadas	nadabas	nadarás
3. nada	nadaba	nadará
1. nadamos	nadábamos	nadaremos
2. nadáis	nadabais	nadaréis
3. nadan	nadaban	nadarán

PRETERITE	PERFECT	PLUPERFECT
1. nadé	he nadado	había nadado
2. nadaste	has nadado	habías nadado
3. nadó	ha nadado	había nadado
1. nadamos	hemos nadado	habíamos nadado
2. nadasteis	habéis nadado	habíais nadado
3. nadaron	han nadado	habían nadado

PAST ANTERIOR	FUTURE PERFECT
hube nadado *etc*	habré nadado *etc*

CONDITIONAL

IMPERATIVE

PRESENT	PAST	
1. nadaría	habría nadado	
2. nadarías	habrías nadado	(tú) nada
3. nadaría	habría nadado	(Vd) nade
1. nadaríamos	habríamos nadado	(nosotros) nademos
2. nadaríais	habríais nadado	(vosotros) nadad
3. nadarían	habrían nadado	(Vds) naden

SUBJUNCTIVE

PRESENT	IMPERFECT	PLUPERFECT
1. nade	nad-ara/ase	hubiera nadado
2. nades	nad-aras/ases	hubieras nadado
3. nade	nad-ara/ase	hubiera nadado
1. nademos	nad-áramos/ásemos	hubiéramos nadado
2. nadéis	nad-arais/aseis	hubierais nadado
3. naden	nad-aran/asen	hubieran nadado

PERFECT   haya nadado *etc*

INFINITIVE

PARTICIPLE

PRESENT	PRESENT
nadar	nadando

PAST	PAST
haber nadado	nadado

NECESITAR
137 *to need*

PRESENT	IMPERFECT	FUTURE
1. necesito	necesitaba	necesitaré
2. necesitas	necesitabas	necesitarás
3. necesita	necesitaba	necesitará
1. necesitamos	necesitábamos	necesitaremos
2. necesitáis	necesitabais	necesitaréis
3. necesitan	necesitaban	necesitarán

PRETERITE	PERFECT	PLUPERFECT
1. necesité	he necesitado	había necesitado
2. necesitaste	has necesitado	habías necesitado
3. necesitó	ha necesitado	había necesitado
1. necesitamos	hemos necesitado	habíamos necesitado
2. necesitasteis	habéis necesitado	habíais necesitado
3. necesitaron	han necesitado	habían necesitado

PAST ANTERIOR	FUTURE PERFECT
hube necesitado *etc*	habré necesitado *etc*

CONDITIONAL

IMPERATIVE

PRESENT	PAST	
1. necesitaría	habría necesitado	
2. necesitarías	habrías necesitado	(tú) necesita
3. necesitaría	habría necesitado	(Vd) necesite
1. necesitaríamos	habríamos necesitado	(nosotros) necesitemos
2. necesitaríais	habríais necesitado	(vosotros) necesitad
3. necesitarían	habrían necesitado	(Vds) necesiten

SUBJUNCTIVE

PRESENT	IMPERFECT	PLUPERFECT
1. necesite	necesit-ara/ase	hubiera necesitado
2. necesites	necesit-aras/ases	hubieras necesitado
3. necesite	necesit-ara/ase	hubiera necesitado
1. necesitemos	necesit-áramos/ásemos	hubiéramos necesitado
2. necesitéis	necesit-arais/aseis	hubierais necesitado
3. necesiten	necesit-aran/asen	hubieran necesitado

PERFECT	haya necesitado *etc*

INFINITIVE

PARTICIPLE

PRESENT	PRESENT
necesitar	necesitando

PAST	PAST
haber necesitado	necesitado

PRESENT	IMPERFECT	FUTURE
1. niego	negaba	negaré
2. niegas	negabas	negarás
3. niega	negaba	negará
1. negamos	negábamos	negaremos
2. negáis	negabais	negaréis
3. niegan	negaban	negarán

PRETERITE	PERFECT	PLUPERFECT
1. negué	he negado	había negado
2. negaste	has negado	habías negado
3. negó	ha negado	había negado
1. negamos	hemos negado	habíamos negado
2. negasteis	habéis negado	habíais negado
3. negaron	han negado	habían negado

PAST ANTERIOR	FUTURE PERFECT
hube negado *etc*	habré negado *etc*

CONDITIONAL

IMPERATIVE

PRESENT	PAST	
1. negaría	habría negado	
2. negarías	habrías negado	(tú) niega
3. negaría	habría negado	(Vd) niegue
1. negaríamos	habríamos negado	(nosotros) neguemos
2. negaríais	habríais negado	(vosotros) negad
3. negarían	habrían negado	(Vds) nieguen

SUBJUNCTIVE

PRESENT	IMPERFECT	PLUPERFECT
1. niegue	neg-ara/ase	hubiera negado
2. niegues	neg-aras/ases	hubieras negado
3. niegue	neg-ara/ase	hubiera negado
1. neguemos	neg-áramos/ásemos	hubiéramos negado
2. neguéis	neg-arais/aseis	hubierais negado
3. nieguen	neg-aran/asen	hubieran negado

PERFECT	haya negado *etc*

INFINITIVE

PARTICIPLE

PRESENT	PRESENT
negar	negando

PAST	PAST
haber negado	negado

NEVAR
139 *to snow*

PRESENT	IMPERFECT	FUTURE
3. nieva	nevaba	nevará

PRETERITE	PERFECT	PLUPERFECT
3. nevó	ha nevado	había nevado

PAST ANTERIOR		FUTURE PERFECT
hubo nevado		habrá nevado

CONDITIONAL

PRESENT	PAST
3. nevaría	habría nevado

IMPERATIVE

SUBJUNCTIVE

PRESENT	IMPERFECT	PLUPERFECT
3. nieve	nev-ara/ase	hubiera nevado
PERFECT	haya nevado	

INFINITIVE

PRESENT
nevar

PAST
haber nevado

PARTICIPLE

PRESENT
nevando

PAST
nevado

PRESENT	IMPERFECT	FUTURE
1. obedezco	obedecía	obedeceré
2. obedeces	obedecías	obedecerás
3. obedece	obedecía	obedecerá
1. obedecemos	obedecíamos	obedeceremos
2. obedecéis	obedecíais	obedeceréis
3. obedecen	obedecían	obedecerán

PRETERITE	PERFECT	PLUPERFECT
1. obedecí	he obedecido	había obedecido
2. obedeciste	has obedecido	habías obedecido
3. obedeció	ha obedecido	había obedecido
1. obedecimos	hemos obedecido	habíamos obedecido
2. obedecisteis	habéis obedecido	habíais obedecido
3. obedecieron	han obedecido	habían obedecido

PAST ANTERIOR	FUTURE PERFECT
hube obedecido *etc*	habré obedecido *etc*

CONDITIONAL

IMPERATIVE

PRESENT	PAST	
1. obedecería	habría obedecido	
2. obedecerías	habrías obedecido	(tú) obedece
3. obedecería	habría obedecido	(Vd) obedezca
1. obedeceríamos	habríamos obedecido	(nosotros) obedezcamos
2. obedeceríais	habríais obedecido	(vosotros) obedeced
3. obedecerían	habrían obedecido	(Vds) obedezcan

SUBJUNCTIVE

PRESENT	IMPERFECT	PLUPERFECT
1. obedezca	obedec-iera/iese	hubiera obedecido
2. obedezcas	obedec-ieras/ieses	hubieras obedecido
3. obedezca	obedec-iera/iese	hubiera obedecido
1. obedezcamos	obedec-iéramos/iésemos	hubiéramos obedecido
2. obedezcáis	obedec-ierais/ieseis	hubierais obedecido
3. obedezcan	obedec-ieran/iesen	hubieran obedecido

PERFECT   haya obedecido *etc*

INFINITIVE	PARTICIPLE
PRESENT	**PRESENT**
obedecer	obedeciendo
PAST	**PAST**
haber obedecido	obedecido

OBLIGAR

141 *to compel, to force*

PRESENT	IMPERFECT	FUTURE
1. obligo	obligaba	obligaré
2. obligas	obligabas	obligarás
3. obliga	obligaba	obligará
1. obligamos	obligábamos	obligaremos
2. obligáis	obligabais	obligaréis
3. obligan	obligaban	obligarán

PRETERITE	PERFECT	PLUPERFECT
1. obligué	he obligado	había obligado
2. obligaste	has obligado	habías obligado
3. obligó	ha obligado	había obligado
1. obligamos	hemos obligado	habíamos obligado
2. obligasteis	habéis obligado	habíais obligado
3. obligaron	han obligado	habían obligado

PAST ANTERIOR	FUTURE PERFECT
hube obligado *etc*	habré obligado *etc*

CONDITIONAL

IMPERATIVE

PRESENT	PAST	
1. obligaría	habría obligado	
2. obligarías	habrías obligado	
3. obligaría	habría obligado	(tú) obliga
1. obligaríamos	habríamos obligado	(Vd) obligue
2. obligaríais	habríais obligado	(nosotros) obliguemos
3. obligarían	habrían obligado	(vosotros) obligad
		(Vds) obliguen

SUBJUNCTIVE

PRESENT	IMPERFECT	PLUPERFECT
1. obligue	oblig-ara/ase	hubiera obligado
2. obligues	oblig-aras/ases	hubieras obligado
3. obligue	oblig-ara/ase	hubiera obligado
1. obliguemos	oblig-áramos/ásemos	hubiéramos obligado
2. obliguéis	oblig-arais/aseis	hubierais obligado
3. obliguen	oblig-aran/asen	hubieran obligado

PERFECT   haya obligado *etc*

INFINITIVE

PARTICIPLE

PRESENT	PRESENT
obligar	obligando

PAST	PAST
haber obligado	obligado

PRESENT	IMPERFECT	FUTURE
1. ofrezco	ofrecía	ofreceré
2. ofreces	ofrecías	ofrecerás
3. ofrece	ofrecía	ofrecerá
1. ofrecemos	ofrecíamos	ofreceremos
2. ofrecéis	ofrecíais	ofreceréis
3. ofrecen	ofrecían	ofrecerán

PRETERITE	PERFECT	PLUPERFECT
1. ofrecí	he ofrecido	había ofrecido
2. ofreciste	has ofrecido	habías ofrecido
3. ofreció	ha ofrecido	había ofrecido
1. ofrecimos	hemos ofrecido	habíamos ofrecido
2. ofrecisteis	habéis ofrecido	habíais ofrecido
3. ofrecieron	han ofrecido	habían ofrecido

PAST ANTERIOR		FUTURE PERFECT
hube ofrecido *etc*		habré ofrecido *etc*

CONDITIONAL

IMPERATIVE

PRESENT	PAST	
1. ofrecería	habría ofrecido	
2. ofrecerías	habrías ofrecido	(tú) ofrece
3. ofrecería	habría ofrecido	(Vd) ofrezca
1. ofreceríamos	habríamos ofrecido	(nosotros) ofrezcamos
2. ofreceríais	habríais ofrecido	(vosotros) ofreced
3. ofrecerían	habrían ofrecido	(Vds) ofrezcan

SUBJUNCTIVE

PRESENT	IMPERFECT	PLUPERFECT
1. ofrezca	ofrec-iera/iese	hubiera ofrecido
2. ofrezcas	ofrec-ieras/ieses	hubieras ofrecido
3. ofrezca	ofrec-iera/iese	hubiera ofrecido
1. ofrezcamos	ofrec-iéramos/iésemos	hubiéramos ofrecido
2. ofrezcáis	ofrec-ierais/ieseis	hubierais ofrecido
3. ofrezcan	ofrec-ieran/iesen	hubieran ofrecido

PERFECT haya ofrecido *etc*

INFINITIVE

PARTICIPLE

PRESENT	PRESENT
ofrecer	ofreciendo

PAST	PAST
haber ofrecido	ofrecido

PRESENT	IMPERFECT	FUTURE
1. oigo	oía	oiré
2. oyes	oías	oirás
3. oye	oía	oirá
1. oímos	oíamos	oiremos
2. oís	oíais	oiréis
3. oyen	oían	oirán

PRETERITE	PERFECT	PLUPERFECT
1. oí	he oído	había oído
2. oíste	has oído	habías oído
3. oyó	ha oído	había oído
1. oímos	hemos oído	habíamos oído
2. oísteis	habéis oído	habíais oído
3. oyeron	han oído	habían oído

PAST ANTERIOR	FUTURE PERFECT
hube oído *etc*	habré oído *etc*

CONDITIONAL

IMPERATIVE

PRESENT	PAST	
1. oiría	habría oído	
2. oirías	habrías oído	(tú) oye
3. oiría	habría oído	(Vd) oiga
1. oiríamos	habríamos oído	(nosotros) oigamos
2. oiríais	habríais oído	(vosotros) oíd
3. oirían	habrían oído	(Vds) oigan

SUBJUNCTIVE

PRESENT	IMPERFECT	PLUPERFECT
1. oiga	o-yera/yese	hubiera oído
2. oigas	o-yeras/yeses	hubieras oído
3. oiga	o-yera/yese	hubiera oído
1. oigamos	o-yéramos/yésemos	hubiéramos oído
2. oigáis	o-yerais/yeseis	hubierais oído
3. oigan	o-yeran/yesen	hubieran oído

PERFECT   haya oído *etc*

INFINITIVE

PARTICIPLE

PRESENT	PRESENT
oír	oyendo

PAST	PAST
haber oído	oído

PRESENT	IMPERFECT	FUTURE
1. huelo	olía	oleré
2. hueles	olías	olerás
3. huele	olía	olerá
1. olemos	olíamos	oleremos
2. oléis	olíais	oleréis
3. huelen	olían	olerán

PRETERITE	PERFECT	PLUPERFECT
1. olí	he olido	había olido
2. oliste	has olido	habías olido
3. olió	ha olido	había olido
1. olimos	hemos olido	habíamos olido
2. olisteis	habéis olido	habíais olido
3. olieron	han olido	habían olido

PAST ANTERIOR	FUTURE PERFECT
hube olido *etc*	habré olido *etc*

CONDITIONAL

IMPERATIVE

PRESENT	PAST	
1. olería	habría olido	
2. olerías	habrías olido	
3. olería	habría olido	(tú) huele
1. oleríamos	habríamos olido	(Vd) huela
2. oleríais	habríais olido	(nosotros) olamos
3. olerían	habrían olido	(vosotros) oled
		(Vds) huelan

SUBJUNCTIVE

PRESENT	IMPERFECT	PLUPERFECT
1. huela	ol-iera/iese	hubiera olido
2. huelas	ol-ieras/ieses	hubieras olido
3. huela	ol-iera/iese	hubiera olido
1. olamos	ol-iéramos/iésemos	hubiéramos olido
2. oláis	ol-ierais/ieseis	hubierais olido
3. huelan	ol-ieran/iesen	hubieran olido

PERFECT   haya olido *etc*

INFINITIVE

PARTICIPLE

PRESENT	PRESENT
oler	oliendo

PAST	PAST
haber olido	olido

PRESENT	IMPERFECT	FUTURE
1. pago	pagaba	pagaré
2. pagas	pagabas	pagarás
3. paga	pagaba	pagará
1. pagamos	pagábamos	pagaremos
2. pagáis	pagabais	pagaréis
3. pagan	pagaban	pagarán

PRETERITE	PERFECT	PLUPERFECT
1. pagué	he pagado	había pagado
2. pagaste	has pagado	habías pagado
3. pagó	ha pagado	había pagado
1. pagamos	hemos pagado	habíamos pagado
2. pagasteis	habéis pagado	habíais pagado
3. pagaron	han pagado	habían pagado

PAST ANTERIOR	FUTURE PERFECT
hube pagado *etc*	habré pagado *etc*

CONDITIONAL

IMPERATIVE

PRESENT	PAST	
1. pagaría	habría pagado	
2. pagarías	habrías pagado	(tú) paga
3. pagaría	habría pagado	(Vd) pague
1. pagaríamos	habríamos pagado	(nosotros) paguemos
2. pagaríais	habríais pagado	(vosotros) pagad
3. pagarían	habrían pagado	(Vds) paguen

SUBJUNCTIVE

PRESENT	IMPERFECT	PLUPERFECT
1. pague	pag-ara/ase	hubiera pagado
2. pagues	pag-aras/ases	hubieras pagado
3. pague	pag-ara/ase	hubiera pagado
1. paguemos	pag-áramos/ásemos	hubiéramos pagado
2. paguéis	pag-arais/aseis	hubierais pagado
3. paguen	pag-aran/asen	hubieran pagado

PERFECT	haya pagado *etc*

INFINITIVE

PARTICIPLE

PRESENT	PRESENT
pagar	pagando

PAST	PAST
haber pagado	pagado

PRESENT	**IMPERFECT**	**FUTURE**
1. parezco	parecía	pareceré
2. pareces	parecías	parecerás
3. parece	parecía	parecerá
1. parecemos	parecíamos	pareceremos
2. parecéis	parecíais	pareceréis
3. parecen	parecían	parecerán

PRETERITE	**PERFECT**	**PLUPERFECT**
1. parecí	he parecido	había parecido
2. pareciste	has parecido	habías parecido
3. pareció	ha parecido	había parecido
1. parecimos	hemos parecido	habíamos parecido
2. parecisteis	habéis parecido	habíais parecido
3. parecieron	han parecido	habían parecido

PAST ANTERIOR	**FUTURE PERFECT**
hube parecido *etc*	habré parecido *etc*

CONDITIONAL

IMPERATIVE

PRESENT	**PAST**	
1. parecería	habría parecido	
2. parecerías	habrías parecido	(tú) parece
3. parecería	habría parecido	(Vd) parezca
1. pareceríamos	habríamos parecido	(nosotros) parezcamos
2. pareceríais	habríais parecido	(vosotros) pareced
3. parecerían	habrían parecido	(Vds) parezcan

SUBJUNCTIVE

PRESENT	**IMPERFECT**	**PLUPERFECT**
1. parezca	parec-iera/iese	hubiera parecido
2. parezcas	parec-ieras/ieses	hubieras parecido
3. parezca	parec-iera/iese	hubiera parecido
1. parezcamos	parec-iéramos/iésemos	hubiéramos parecido
2. parezcáis	parec-ierais/ieseis	hubierais parecido
3. parezcan	parec-ieran/iesen	hubieran parecido
PERFECT	haya parecido *etc*	

INFINITIVE

PARTICIPLE

PRESENT	**PRESENT**
parecer	pareciendo
PAST	**PAST**
haber parecido	parecido

PRESENT	IMPERFECT	FUTURE
1. paseo	paseaba	pasearé
2. paseas	paseabas	pasearás
3. pasea	paseaba	paseará
1. paseamos	paseábamos	pasearemos
2. paseáis	paseabais	pasearéis
3. pasean	paseaban	pasearán

PRETERITE	PERFECT	PLUPERFECT
1. paseé	he paseado	había paseado
2. paseaste	has paseado	habías paseado
3. paseó	ha paseado	había paseado
1. paseamos	hemos paseado	habíamos paseado
2. paseasteis	habéis paseado	habíais paseado
3. pasearon	han paseado	habían paseado

PAST ANTERIOR	FUTURE PERFECT
hube paseado *etc*	habré paseado *etc*

CONDITIONAL

IMPERATIVE

PRESENT	PAST	
1. pasearía	habría paseado	
2. pasearías	habrías paseado	(tú) pasea
3. pasearía	habría paseado	(Vd) pasee
1. pasearíamos	habríamos paseado	(nosotros) paseemos
2. pasearíais	habríais paseado	(vosotros) pasead
3. pasearían	habrían paseado	(Vds) paseen

SUBJUNCTIVE

PRESENT	IMPERFECT	PLUPERFECT
1. pasee	pase-ara/ase	hubiera paseado
2. pasees	pase-aras/ases	hubieras paseado
3. pasee	pase-ara/ase	hubiera paseado
1. paseemos	pase-áramos/ásemos	hubiéramos paseado
2. paseéis	pase-arais/aseis	hubierais paseado
3. paseen	pase-aran/asen	hubieran paseado

PERFECT haya paseado *etc*

INFINITIVE

PARTICIPLE

PRESENT	PRESENT
pasear	paseando

PAST	PAST
haber paseado	paseado

PRESENT	IMPERFECT	FUTURE
1. pido	pedía	pediré
2. pides	pedías	pedirás
3. pide	pedía	pedirá
1. pedimos	pedíamos	pediremos
2. pedís	pedíais	pediréis
3. piden	pedían	pedirán

PRETERITE	PERFECT	PLUPERFECT
1. pedí	he pedido	había pedido
2. pediste	has pedido	habías pedido
3. pidió	ha pedido	había pedido
1. pedimos	hemos pedido	habíamos pedido
2. pedisteis	habéis pedido	habíais pedido
3. pidieron	han pedido	habían pedido

PAST ANTERIOR		FUTURE PERFECT
hube pedido *etc*		habré pedido *etc*

CONDITIONAL

IMPERATIVE

PRESENT	PAST	
1. pediría	habría pedido	
2. pedirías	habrías pedido	
3. pediría	habría pedido	(tú) pide
1. pediríamos	habríamos pedido	(Vd) pida
2. pediríais	habríais pedido	(nosotros) pidamos
3. pedirían	habrían pedido	(vosotros) pedid
		(Vds) pidan

SUBJUNCTIVE

PRESENT	IMPERFECT	PLUPERFECT
1. pida	pid-iera/iese	hubiera pedido
2. pidas	pid-ieras/ieses	hubieras pedido
3. pida	pid-iera/iese	hubiera pedido
1. pidamos	pid-iéramos/iésemos	hubiéramos pedido
2. pidáis	pid-ierais/ieseis	hubierais pedido
3. pidan	pid-ieran/iesen	hubieran pedido
PERFECT	haya pedido *etc*	

INFINITIVE

PARTICIPLE

PRESENT	PRESENT
pedir	pidiendo
PAST	PAST
haber pedido	pedido

PRESENT	**IMPERFECT**	**FUTURE**
1. pienso	pensaba	pensaré
2. piensas	pensabas	pensarás
3. piensa	pensaba	pensará
1. pensamos	pensábamos	pensaremos
2. pensáis	pensabais	pensaréis
3. piensan	pensaban	pensarán

PRETERITE	**PERFECT**	**PLUPERFECT**
1. pensé	he pensado	había pensado
2. pensaste	has pensado	habías pensado
3. pensó	ha pensado	había pensado
1. pensamos	hemos pensado	habíamos pensado
2. pensasteis	habéis pensado	habíais pensado
3. pensaron	han pensado	habían pensado

PAST ANTERIOR	**FUTURE PERFECT**
hube pensado *etc*	habré pensado *etc*

CONDITIONAL

IMPERATIVE

PRESENT	**PAST**
1. pensaría	habría pensado
2. pensarías	habrías pensado
3. pensaría	habría pensado
1. pensaríamos	habríamos pensado
2. pensaríais	habríais pensado
3. pensarían	habrían pensado

(tú) piensa
(Vd) piense
(nosotros) pensemos
(vosotros) pensad
(Vds) piensen

SUBJUNCTIVE

PRESENT	**IMPERFECT**	**PLUPERFECT**
1. piense	pens-ara/ase	hubiera pensado
2. pienses	pens-ara/ases	hubieras pensado
3. piense	pens-ara/ase	hubiera pensado
1. pensemos	pens-áramos/ásemos	hubiéramos pensado
2. penséis	pens-arais/aseis	hubierais pensado
3. piensen	pens-aran/asen	hubieran pensado

PERFECT   haya pensado *etc*

INFINITIVE

PARTICIPLE

PRESENT	**PRESENT**
pensar	pensando

PAST	**PAST**
haber pensado	pensado

PRESENT	IMPERFECT	FUTURE
1. pierdo	perdía	perderé
2. pierdes	perdías	perderás
3. pierde	perdía	perderá
1. perdemos	perdíamos	perderemos
2. perdéis	perdíais	perderéis
3. pierden	perdían	perderán

PRETERITE	PERFECT	PLUPERFECT
1. perdí	he perdido	había perdido
2. perdiste	has perdido	habías perdido
3. perdió	ha perdido	había perdido
1. perdimos	hemos perdido	habíamos perdido
2. perdisteis	habéis perdido	habíais perdido
3. perdieron	han perdido	habían perdido

PAST ANTERIOR	FUTURE PERFECT
hube perdido *etc*	habré perdido *etc*

CONDITIONAL

IMPERATIVE

PRESENT	PAST	
1. perdería	habría perdido	
2. perderías	habrías perdido	(tú) pierde
3. perdería	habría perdido	(Vd) pierda
1. perderíamos	habríamos perdido	(nosotros) perdamos
2. perderíais	habríais perdido	(vosotros) perded
3. perderían	habrían perdido	(Vds) pierdan

SUBJUNCTIVE

PRESENT	IMPERFECT	PLUPERFECT
1. pierda	perd-iera/iese	hubiera perdido
2. pierdas	perd-ieras/ieses	hubieras perdido
3. pierda	perd-iera/iese	hubiera perdido
1. perdamos	perd-iéramos/iésemos	hubiéramos perdido
2. perdáis	perd-ierais/ieseis	hubierais perdido
3. pierdan	perd-ieran/iesen	hubieran perdido

PERFECT	haya perdido *etc*

INFINITIVE

PARTICIPLE

PRESENT	PRESENT
perder	perdiendo

PAST	PAST
haber perdido	perdido

PERTENECER
151 *to belong*

PRESENT	IMPERFECT	FUTURE
1. pertenezco	pertenecía	perteneceré
2. perteneces	pertenecías	pertenecerás
3. pertenece	pertenecía	pertenecerá
1. pertenecemos	pertenecíamos	perteneceremos
2. pertenecéis	pertenecíais	perteneceréis
3. pertenecen	pertenecían	pertenecerán

PRETERITE	PERFECT	PLUPERFECT
1. pertenecí	he pertenecido	había pertenecido
2. perteneciste	has pertenecido	habías pertenecido
3. perteneció	ha pertenecido	había pertenecido
1. pertenecimos	hemos pertenecido	habíamos pertenecido
2. pertenecisteis	habéis pertenecido	habíais pertenecido
3. pertenecieron	han pertenecido	habían pertenecido

PAST ANTERIOR
hube pertenecido *etc*

FUTURE PERFECT
habré pertenecido *etc*

CONDITIONAL

PRESENT	PAST
1. pertenecería	habría pertenecido
2. pertenecerías	habrías pertenecido
3. pertenecería	habría pertenecido
1. perteneceríamos	habríamos pertenecido
2. perteneceríais	habíais pertenecido
3. pertenecerían	habrían pertenecido

IMPERATIVE

(tú) pertenece
(Vd) pertenezca
(nosotros) pertenezcamos
(vosotros) perteneced
(Vds) pertenezcan

SUBJUNCTIVE

PRESENT	IMPERFECT	PLUPERFECT
1. pertenezca	pertenec-iera/iese	hubiera pertenecido
2. pertenezcas	pertenec-ieras/ieses	hubieras pertenecido
3. pertenezca	pertenec-iera/iese	hubiera pertenecido
1. pertenezcamos	pertenec-iéramos/iésemos	hubiéramos pertenecido
2. pertenezcáis	pertenec-ierais/ieseis	hubierais pertenecido
3. pertenezcan	pertenec-ieran/iesen	hubieran pertenecido

PERFECT   haya pertenecido *etc*

INFINITIVE

PRESENT
pertenecer

PAST
haber pertenecido

PARTICIPLE

PRESENT
perteneciendo

PAST
pertenecido

PRESENT	IMPERFECT	FUTURE
1. puedo	podía	podré
2. puedes	podías	podrás
3. puede	podía	podrá
1. podemos	podíamos	podremos
2. podéis	podíais	podréis
3. pueden	podían	podrán

PRETERITE	PERFECT	PLUPERFECT
1. pude	he podido	había podido
2. pudiste	has podido	habías podido
3. pudo	ha podido	había podido
1. pudimos	hemos podido	habíamos podido
2. pudisteis	habéis podido	habíais podido
3. pudieron	han podido	habían podido

PAST ANTERIOR	FUTURE PERFECT
hube podido *etc*	habré podido *etc*

CONDITIONAL

IMPERATIVE

PRESENT	PAST	
1. podría	habría podido	
2. podrías	habrías podido	(tú) puede
3. podría	habría podido	(Vd) pueda
1. podríamos	habríamos podido	(nosotros) podamos
2. podríais	habríais podido	(vosotros) poded
3. podrían	habrían podido	(Vds) puedan

SUBJUNCTIVE

PRESENT	IMPERFECT	PLUPERFECT
1. pueda	pud-iera/iese	hubiera podido
2. puedas	pud-ieras/ieses	hubieras podido
3. pueda	pud-iera/iese	hubiera podido
1. podamos	pud-iéramos/iésemos	hubiéramos podido
2. podáis	pud-ierais/ieseis	hubierais podido
3. puedan	pud-ieran/iesen	hubieran podido

PERFECT haya podido *etc*

INFINITIVE

PARTICIPLE

PRESENT	PRESENT
poder	pudiendo

PAST	PAST
haber podido	podido

PONER
153 to put

PRESENT	IMPERFECT	FUTURE
1. pongo	ponía	pondré
2. pones	ponías	pondrás
3. pone	ponía	pondrá
1. ponemos	poníamos	pondremos
2. ponéis	poníais	pondréis
3. ponen	ponían	pondrán

PRETERITE	PERFECT	PLUPERFECT
1. puse	he puesto	había puesto
2. pusiste	has puesto	habías puesto
3. puso	ha puesto	había puesto
1. pusimos	hemos puesto	habíamos puesto
2. pusisteis	habéis puesto	habíais puesto
3. pusieron	han puesto	habían puesto

PAST ANTERIOR
hube puesto *etc*

FUTURE PERFECT
habré puesto *etc*

CONDITIONAL

PRESENT	PAST
1. pondría	habría puesto
2. pondrías	habrías puesto
3. pondría	habría puesto
1. pondríamos	habríamos puesto
2. pondríais	habríais puesto
3. pondrían	habrían puesto

IMPERATIVE

(tú) pon
(Vd) ponga
(nosotros) pongamos
(vosotros) poned
(Vds) pongan

SUBJUNCTIVE

PRESENT	IMPERFECT	PLUPERFECT
1. ponga	pus-iera/iese	hubiera puesto
2. pongas	pus-ieras/ieses	hubieras puesto
3. ponga	pus-iera/iese	hubiera puesto
1. pongamos	pus-iéramos/iésemos	hubiéramos puesto
2. pongáis	pus-ierais/ieseis	hubierais puesto
3. pongan	pus-ieran/iesen	hubieran puesto

PERFECT   haya puesto *etc*

INFINITIVE

PRESENT
poner

PAST
haber puesto

PARTICIPLE

PRESENT
poniendo

PAST
puesto

PRESENT	IMPERFECT	FUTURE
1. prefiero	prefería	preferiré
2. prefieres	preferías	preferirás
3. prefiere	prefería	preferirá
1. preferimos	preferíamos	preferiremos
2. preferís	preferíais	preferiréis
3. prefieren	preferían	preferirán

PRETERITE	PERFECT	PLUPERFECT
1. preferí	he preferido	había preferido
2. preferiste	has preferido	habías preferido
3. prefirió	ha preferido	había preferido
1. preferimos	hemos preferido	habíamos preferido
2. preferisteis	habéis preferido	habíais preferido
3. prefirieron	han preferido	habían preferido

PAST ANTERIOR		FUTURE PERFECT
hube preferido *etc*		habré preferido *etc*

CONDITIONAL

IMPERATIVE

PRESENT	PAST	
1. preferiría	habría preferido	
2. preferirías	habrías preferido	
3. preferiría	habría preferido	(tú) prefiere
1. preferiríamos	habríamos preferido	(Vd) prefiera
2. preferiríais	habríais preferido	(nosotros) prefiramos
3. preferirían	habrían preferido	(vosotros) preferid
		(Vds) prefieran

SUBJUNCTIVE

PRESENT	IMPERFECT	PLUPERFECT
1. prefiera	prefir-iera/iese	hubiera preferido
2. prefieras	prefir-ieras/ieses	hubieras preferido
3. prefiera	prefir-iera/iese	hubiera preferido
1. prefiramos	prefir-iéramos/iésemos	hubiéramos preferido
2. prefiráis	prefir-ierais/ieseis	hubierais preferido
3. prefieran	prefir-ieran/iesen	hubieran preferido

PERFECT   haya preferido *etc*

INFINITIVE

PARTICIPLE

PRESENT	PRESENT
preferir	prefiriendo

PAST	PAST
haber preferido	preferido

PROBAR
155 *to try, to taste*

PRESENT	IMPERFECT	FUTURE
1. pruebo	probaba	probaré
2. pruebas	probabas	probarás
3. prueba	probaba	probará
1. probamos	probábamos	probaremos
2. probáis	probabais	probaréis
3. prueban	probaban	probarán

PRETERITE	PERFECT	PLUPERFECT
1. probé	he probado	había probado
2. probaste	has probado	habías probado
3. probó	ha probado	había probado
1. probamos	hemos probado	habíamos probado
2. probasteis	habéis probado	habíais probado
3. probaron	han probado	habían probado

PAST ANTERIOR	FUTURE PERFECT
hube probado *etc*	habré probado *etc*

CONDITIONAL

IMPERATIVE

PRESENT	PAST	
1. probaría	habría probado	
2. probarías	habrías probado	(tú) prueba
3. probaría	habría probado	(Vd) pruebe
1. probaríamos	habríamos probado	(nosotros) probemos
2. probaríais	habríais probado	(vosotros) probad
3. probarían	habrían probado	(Vds) prueben

SUBJUNCTIVE

PRESENT	IMPERFECT	PLUPERFECT
1. pruebe	prob-ara/ase	hubiera probado
2. pruebes	prob-aras/ases	hubieras probado
3. pruebe	prob-ara/ase	hubiera probado
1. probemos	prob-áramos/ásemos	hubiéramos probado
2. probéis	prob-arais/aseis	hubierais probado
3. prueben	prob-aran/asen	hubieran probado

PERFECT   haya probado *etc*

INFINITIVE

PARTICIPLE

PRESENT	PRESENT
probar	probando

PAST	PAST
haber probado	probado

PRESENT	IMPERFECT	FUTURE
1. prohíbo	prohibía	prohibiré
2. prohíbes	prohibías	prohibirás
3. prohíbe	prohibía	prohibirá
1. prohibimos	prohibíamos	prohibiremos
2. prohibís	prohibíais	prohibiréis
3. prohíben	prohibían	prohibirán

PRETERITE	PERFECT	PLUPERFECT
1. prohibí	he prohibido	había prohibido
2. prohibiste	has prohibido	habías prohibido
3. prohibió	ha prohibido	había prohibido
1. prohibimos	hemos prohibido	habíamos prohibido
2. prohibisteis	habéis prohibido	habíais prohibido
3. prohibieron	han prohibido	habían prohibido

PAST ANTERIOR
hube prohibido *etc*

FUTURE PERFECT
habré prohibido *etc*

CONDITIONAL

IMPERATIVE

PRESENT	PAST	
1. prohibiría	habría prohibido	
2. prohibirías	habrías prohibido	(tú) prohíbe
3. prohibiría	habría prohibido	(Vd) prohíba
1. prohibiríamos	habríamos prohibido	(nosotros) prohibamos
2. prohibiríais	habríais prohibido	(vosotros) prohibid
3. prohibirían	habrían prohibido	(Vds) prohíban

SUBJUNCTIVE

PRESENT	IMPERFECT	PLUPERFECT
1. prohíba	prohib-iera/iese	hubiera prohibido
2. prohíbas	prohib-ieras/ieses	hubieras prohibido
3. prohíba	prohib-iera/iese	hubiera prohibido
1. prohibamos	prohib-iéramos/iésemos	hubiéramos prohibido
2. prohibáis	prohib-ierais/ieseis	hubierais prohibido
3. prohíban	prohib-ieran/iesen	hubieran prohibido

PERFECT   haya prohibido *etc*

INFINITIVE

PARTICIPLE

PRESENT	PRESENT
prohibir	prohibiendo
PAST	**PAST**
haber prohibido	prohibido

PROTEGER
157 *to protect*

PRESENT	IMPERFECT	FUTURE
1. protejo	protegía	protegeré
2. proteges	protegías	protegerás
3. protege	protegía	protegerá
1. protegemos	protegíamos	protegeremos
2. protegéis	protegíais	protegeréis
3. protegen	protegían	protegerán

PRETERITE	PERFECT	PLUPERFECT
1. protegí	he protegido	había protegido
2. protegiste	has protegido	habías protegido
3. protegió	ha protegido	había protegido
1. protegimos	hemos protegido	habíamos protegido
2. protegisteis	habéis protegido	habíais protegido
3. protegieron	han protegido	habían protegido

PAST ANTERIOR	FUTURE PERFECT
hube protegido *etc*	habré protegido *etc*

CONDITIONAL

IMPERATIVE

PRESENT	PAST	
1. protegería	habría protegido	
2. protegerías	habrías protegido	(tú) protege
3. protegería	habría protegido	(Vd) proteja
1. protegeríamos	habríamos protegido	(nosotros) protejamos
2. protegeríais	habríais protegido	(vosotros) proteged
3. protegerían	habrían protegido	(Vds) protejan

SUBJUNCTIVE

PRESENT	IMPERFECT	PLUPERFECT
1. proteja	proteg-iera/iese	hubiera protegido
2. protejas	proteg-ieras/ieses	hubieras protegido
3. proteja	proteg-iera/iese	hubiera protegido
1. protejamos	proteg-iéramos/iésemos	hubiéramos protegido
2. protejáis	proteg-ierais/ieseis	hubierais protegido
3. protejan	proteg-ieran/iesen	hubieran protegido

PERFECT   haya protegido *etc*

INFINITIVE

PARTICIPLE

PRESENT	PRESENT
proteger	protegiendo

PAST	PAST
haber protegido	protegido

PRESENT	IMPERFECT	FUTURE
1. pudro	pudría	pudriré
2. pudres	pudrías	pudrirás
3. pudre	pudría	pudrirá
1. pudrimos	pudríamos	pudriremos
2. pudrís	pudríais	pudriréis
3. pudren	pudrían	pudrirán

PRETERITE	PERFECT	PLUPERFECT
1. pudrí	he podrido	había podrido
2. pudriste	has podrido	habías podrido
3. pudrió	ha podrido	había podrido
1. pudrimos	hemos podrido	habíamos podrido
2. pudristeis	habéis podrido	habíais podrido
3. pudrieron	han podrido	habían podrido

PAST ANTERIOR	FUTURE PERFECT
hube podrido *etc*	habré podrido *etc*

CONDITIONAL

IMPERATIVE

PRESENT	PAST	
1. pudriría	habría podrido	
2. pudrirías	habrías podrido	(tú) pudre
3. pudriría	habría podrido	(Vd) pudra
1. pudriríamos	habríamos podrido	(nosotros) pudramos
2. pudriríais	habríais podrido	(vosotros) pudrid
3. pudrirían	habrían podrido	(Vds) pudran

SUBJUNCTIVE

PRESENT	IMPERFECT	PLUPERFECT
1. pudra	pudr-iera/iese	hubiera podrido
2. pudras	pudr-ieras/ieses	hubieras podrido
3. pudra	pudr-iera/iese	hubiera podrido
1. pudramos	pudr-iéramos/iésemos	hubiéramos podrido
2. pudráis	pudr-ierais/ieseis	hubierais podrido
3. pudran	pudr-ieran/iesen	hubieran podrido

PERFECT   haya podrido *etc*

INFINITIVE

PARTICIPLE

PRESENT	PRESENT
pudrir	pudriendo
PAST	**PAST**
haber podrido	podrido

QUERER
159 *to want; to love*

PRESENT	IMPERFECT	FUTURE
1. quiero	quería	querré
2. quieres	querías	querrás
3. quiere	quería	querrá
1. queremos	queríamos	querremos
2. queréis	queríais	querréis
3. quieren	querían	querrán

PRETERITE	PERFECT	PLUPERFECT
1. quise	he querido	había querido
2. quisiste	has querido	habías querido
3. quiso	ha querido	había querido
1. quisimos	hemos querido	habíamos querido
2. quisisteis	habéis querido	habíais querido
3. quisieron	han querido	habían querido

PAST ANTERIOR		FUTURE PERFECT
hube querido *etc*		habré querido *etc*

CONDITIONAL

IMPERATIVE

PRESENT	PAST	
1. querría	habría querido	
2. querrías	habrías querido	(tú) quiere
3. querría	habría querido	(Vd) quiera
1. querríamos	habríamos querido	(nosotros) queramos
2. querríais	habríais querido	(vosotros) quered
3. querrían	habrían querido	(Vds) quieran

SUBJUNCTIVE

PRESENT	IMPERFECT	PLUPERFECT
1. quiera	quis-iera/iese	hubiera querido
2. quieras	quis-ieras/ieses	hubieras querido
3. quiera	quis-iera/iese	hubiera querido
1. queramos	quis-iéramos/iésemos	hubiéramos querido
2. queráis	quis-ierais/ieseis	hubierais querido
3. quieran	quis-ieran/iesen	hubieran querido

PERFECT   haya querido *etc*

INFINITIVE

PARTICIPLE

PRESENT	PRESENT
querer	queriendo

PAST	PAST
haber querido	querido

PRESENT	IMPERFECT	FUTURE
1. recibo	recibía	recibiré
2. recibes	recibías	recibirás
3. recibe	recibía	recibirá
1. recibimos	recibíamos	recibiremos
2. recibís	recibíais	recibiréis
3. reciben	recibían	recibirán

PRETERITE	PERFECT	PLUPERFECT
1. recibí	he recibido	había recibido
2. recibiste	has recibido	habías recibido
3. recibió	ha recibido	había recibido
1. recibimos	hemos recibido	habíamos recibido
2. recibisteis	habéis recibido	habíais recibido
3. recibieron	han recibido	habían recibido

PAST ANTERIOR
hube recibido *etc*

FUTURE PERFECT
habré recibido *etc*

CONDITIONAL

IMPERATIVE

PRESENT	PAST	
1. recibiría	habría recibido	
2. recibirías	habrías recibido	(tú) recibe
3. recibiría	habría recibido	(Vd) reciba
1. recibiríamos	habríamos recibido	(nosotros) recibamos
2. recibiríais	habríais recibido	(vosotros) recibid
3. recibirían	habrían recibido	(Vds) reciban

SUBJUNCTIVE

PRESENT	IMPERFECT	PLUPERFECT
1. reciba	recib-iera/iese	hubiera recibido
2. recibas	recib-ieras/ieses	hubieras recibido
3. reciba	recib-iera/iese	hubiera recibido
1. recibamos	recib-iéramos/iésemos	hubiéramos recibido
2. recibáis	recib-ierais/ieseis	hubierais recibido
3. reciban	recib-ieran/iesen	hubieran recibido

PERFECT   haya recibido *etc*

INFINITIVE

PARTICIPLE

PRESENT	PRESENT
recibir	recibiendo

PAST	PAST
haber recibido	recibido

RECORDAR
161 to remember

PRESENT	IMPERFECT	FUTURE
1. recuerdo	recordaba	recordaré
2. recuerdas	recordabas	recordarás
3. recuerda	recordaba	recordará
1. recordamos	recordábamos	recordaremos
2. recordáis	recordabais	recordaréis
3. recuerdan	recordaban	recordarán

PRETERITE	PERFECT	PLUPERFECT
1. recordé	he recordado	había recordado
2. recordaste	has recordado	habías recordado
3. recordó	ha recordado	había recordado
1. recordamos	hemos recordado	habíamos recordado
2. recordasteis	habéis recordado	habíais recordado
3. recordaron	han recordado	habían recordado

PAST ANTERIOR	FUTURE PERFECT
hube recordado *etc*	habré recordado *etc*

CONDITIONAL

IMPERATIVE

PRESENT	PAST	
1. recordaría	habría recordado	
2. recordarías	habrías recordado	(tú) recuerda
3. recordaría	habría recordado	(Vd) recuerde
1. recordaríamos	habríamos recordado	(nosotros) recordemos
2. recordaríais	habríais recordado	(vosotros) recordad
3. recordarían	habrían recordado	(Vds) recuerden

SUBJUNCTIVE

PRESENT	IMPERFECT	PLUPERFECT
1. recuerde	record-ara/ase	hubiera recordado
2. recuerdes	record-aras/ases	hubieras recordado
3. recuerde	record-ara/ase	hubiera recordado
1. recordemos	record-áramos/ásemos	hubiéramos recordado
2. recordéis	record-arais/aseis	hubierais recordado
3. recuerden	record-aran/asen	hubieran recordado

PERFECT   haya recordado *etc*

INFINITIVE

PARTICIPLE

PRESENT	PRESENT
recordar	recordando

PAST	PAST
haber recordado	recordado

PRESENT
1. reduzco
2. reduces
3. reduce
1. reducimos
2. reducís
3. reducen

IMPERFECT
reducía
reducías
reducía
reducíamos
reducíais
reducían

FUTURE
reduciré
reducirás
reducirá
reduciremos
reduciréis
reducirán

PRETERITE
1. reduje
2. redujiste
3. redujo
1. redujimos
2. redujisteis
3. redujeron

PERFECT
he reducido
has reducido
ha reducido
hemos reducido
habéis reducido
han reducido

PLUPERFECT
había reducido
habías reducido
había reducido
habíamos reducido
habíais reducido
habían reducido

PAST ANTERIOR
hube reducido *etc*

FUTURE PERFECT
habré reducido *etc*

CONDITIONAL

PRESENT
1. reduciría
2. reducirías
3. reduciría
1. reduciríamos
2. reduciríais
3. reducirían

PAST
habría reducido
habrías reducido
habría reducido
habríamos reducido
habríais reducido
habrían reducido

IMPERATIVE

(tú) reduce
(Vd) reduzca
(nosotros) reduzcamos
(vosotros) reducid
(Vds) reduzcan

SUBJUNCTIVE

PRESENT
1. reduzca
2. reduzcas
3. reduzca
1. reduzcamos
2. reduzcáis
3. reduzcan

IMPERFECT
reduj-era/ese
reduj-eras/eses
reduj-era/ese
reduj-éramos/ésemos
reduj-erais/eseis
reduj-eran/esen

PLUPERFECT
hubiera reducido
hubieras reducido
hubiera reducido
hubiéramos reducido
hubierais reducido
hubieran reducido

PERFECT   haya reducido *etc*

INFINITIVE

PRESENT
reducir

PAST
haber reducido

PARTICIPLE

PRESENT
reduciendo

PAST
reducido

REHUIR
163 *to shun, to avoid*

PRESENT	IMPERFECT	FUTURE
1. rehúyo	rehuía	rehuiré
2. rehúyes	rehuías	rehuirás
3. rehúye	rehuía	rehuirá
1. rehuimos	rehuíamos	rehuiremos
2. rehuís	rehuíais	rehuiréis
3. rehúyen	rehuían	rehuirán

PRETERITE	PERFECT	PLUPERFECT
1. rehuí	he rehuido	había rehuido
2. rehuiste	has rehuido	habías rehuido
3. rehuyó	ha rehuido	había rehuido
1. rehuimos	hemos rehuido	habíamos rehuido
2. rehuisteis	habéis rehuido	habíais rehuido
3. rehuyeron	han rehuido	habían rehuido

PAST ANTERIOR	FUTURE PERFECT
hube rehuido *etc*	habré rehuido *etc*

CONDITIONAL

IMPERATIVE

PRESENT	PAST	
1. rehuiría	habría rehuido	
2. rehuirías	habrías rehuido	(tú) rehúye
3. rehuiría	habría rehuido	(Vd) rehúya
1. rehuiríamos	habríamos rehuido	(nosotros) rehuyamos
2. rehuiríais	habríais rehuido	(vosotros) rehuid
3. rehuirían	habrían rehuido	(Vds) rehúyan

SUBJUNCTIVE

PRESENT	IMPERFECT	PLUPERFECT
1. rehúya	rehu-yera/yese	hubiera rehuido
2. rehúyas	rehu-yeras/yeses	hubieras rehuido
3. rehúya	rehu-yera/yese	hubiera rehuido
1. rehuyamos	rehu-yéramos/yésemos	hubiéramos rehuido
2. rehuyáis	rehu-yerais/yeseis	hubierais rehuido
3. rehúyan	rehu-yeran/yesen	hubieran rehuido

PERFECT haya rehuido *etc*

INFINITIVE

PARTICIPLE

PRESENT	PRESENT
rehuir	rehuyendo

PAST	PAST
haber rehuido	rehuido

PRESENT	IMPERFECT	FUTURE
1. rehúso	rehusaba	rehusaré
2. rehúsas	rehusabas	rehusarás
3. rehúsa	rehusaba	rehusará
1. rehusamos	rehusábamos	rehusaremos
2. rehusáis	rehusabais	rehusaréis
3. rehúsan	rehusaban	rehusarán

PRETERITE	PERFECT	PLUPERFECT
1. rehusé	he rehusado	había rehusado
2. rehusaste	has rehusado	habías rehusado
3. rehusó	ha rehusado	había rehusado
1. rehusamos	hemos rehusado	habíamos rehusado
2. rehusasteis	habéis rehusado	habíais rehusado
3. rehusaron	han rehusado	habían rehusado

PAST ANTERIOR
hube rehusado *etc*

FUTURE PERFECT
habré rehusado *etc*

CONDITIONAL

IMPERATIVE

PRESENT	PAST	
1. rehusaría	habría rehusado	
2. rehusarías	habrías rehusado	(tú) rehúsa
3. rehusaría	habría rehusado	(Vd) rehúse
1. rehusaríamos	habríamos rehusado	(nosotros) rehusemos
2. rehusaríais	habríais rehusado	(vosotros) rehusad
3. rehusarían	habrían rehusado	(Vds) rehúsen

SUBJUNCTIVE

PRESENT	IMPERFECT	PLUPERFECT
1. rehúse	rehus-ara/ase	hubiera rehusado
2. rehúses	rehus-aras/ases	hubieras rehusado
3. rehúse	rehus-ara/ase	hubiera rehusado
1. rehusemos	rehus-áramos/ásemos	hubiéramos rehusado
2. rehuséis	rehus-arais/aseis	hubierais rehusado
3. rehúsen	rehus-aran/asen	hubieran rehusado

PERFECT   haya rehusado *etc*

INFINITIVE

PARTICIPLE

PRESENT	PRESENT
rehusar	rehusando

PAST	PAST
haber rehusado	rehusado

PRESENT	IMPERFECT	FUTURE
1. río	reía	reiré
2. ríes	reías	reirás
3. ríe	reía	reirá
1. reímos	reíamos	reiremos
2. reís	reíais	reiréis
3. ríen	reían	reirán

PRETERITE	PERFECT	PLUPERFECT
1. reí	he reído	había reído
2. reíste	has reído	habías reído
3. rió	ha reído	había reído
1. reímos	hemos reído	habíamos reído
2. reísteis	habéis reído	habíais reído
3. rieron	han reído	habían reído

PAST ANTERIOR	FUTURE PERFECT
hube reído *etc*	habré reído *etc*

CONDITIONAL

IMPERATIVE

PRESENT	PAST	
1. reiría	habría reído	
2. reirías	habrías reído	(tú) ríe
3. reiría	habría reído	(Vd) ría
1. reiríamos	habríamos reído	(nosotros) riamos
2. reiríais	habríais reído	(vosotros) reíd
3. reirían	habrían reído	(Vds) rían

SUBJUNCTIVE

PRESENT	IMPERFECT	PLUPERFECT
1. ría	ri-era/ese	hubiera reído
2. rías	ri-eras/eses	hubieras reído
3. ría	ri-era/ese	hubiera reído
1. riamos	ri-éramos/ésemos	hubiéramos reído
2. riáis	ri-erais/eseis	hubierais reído
3. rían	ri-eran/esen	hubieran reído

PERFECT	haya reído *etc*

INFINITIVE

PARTICIPLE

PRESENT	PRESENT
reír	riendo

PAST	PAST
haber reído	reído

PRESENT	IMPERFECT	FUTURE
1. renuevo	renovaba	renovaré
2. renuevas	renovabas	renovarás
3. renueva	renovaba	renovará
1. renovamos	renovábamos	renovaremos
2. renováis	renovabais	renovaréis
3. renuevan	renovaban	renovarán

PRETERITE	PERFECT	PLUPERFECT
1. renové	he renovado	había renovado
2. renovaste	has renovado	habías renovado
3. renovó	ha renovado	había renovado
1. renovamos	hemos renovado	habíamos renovado
2. renovasteis	habéis renovado	habíais renovado
3. renovaron	han renovado	habían renovado

PAST ANTERIOR	FUTURE PERFECT
hube renovado *etc*	habré renovado *etc*

CONDITIONAL

IMPERATIVE

PRESENT	PAST	
1. renovaría	habría renovado	
2. renovarías	habrías renovado	(tú) renueva
3. renovaría	habría renovado	(Vd) renueve
1. renovaríamos	habríamos renovado	(nosotros) renovemos
2. renovaríais	habríais renovado	(vosotros) renovad
3. renovarían	habrían renovado	(Vds) renueven

SUBJUNCTIVE

PRESENT	IMPERFECT	PLUPERFECT
1. renueve	renov-ara/ase	hubiera renovado
2. renueves	renov-aras/ases	hubieras renovado
3. renueve	renov-ara/ase	hubiera renovado
1. renovemos	renov-áramos/ásemos	hubiéramos renovado
2. renovéis	renov-arais/aseis	hubierais renovado
3. renueven	renov-aran/asen	hubieran renovado

PERFECT   haya renovado *etc*

INFINITIVE

PARTICIPLE

PRESENT	PRESENT
renovar	renovando

PAST	PAST
haber renovado	renovado

PRESENT	IMPERFECT	FUTURE
1. riño	reñía	reñiré
2. riñes	reñías	reñirás
3. riñe	reñía	reñirá
1. reñimos	reñíamos	reñiremos
2. reñís	reñíais	reñiréis
3. riñen	reñían	reñirán

PRETERITE	PERFECT	PLUPERFECT
1. reñí	he reñido	había reñido
2. reñiste	has reñido	habías reñido
3. riñó	ha reñido	había reñido
1. reñimos	hemos reñido	habíamos reñido
2. reñisteis	habéis reñido	habíais reñido
3. riñeron	han reñido	habían reñido

PAST ANTERIOR	FUTURE PERFECT
hube reñido *etc*	habré reñido *etc*

CONDITIONAL

IMPERATIVE

PRESENT	PAST
1. reñiría	habría reñido
2. reñirías	habrías reñido
3. reñiría	habría reñido
1. reñiríamos	habríamos reñido
2. reñiríais	habríais reñido
3. reñirían	habrían reñido

(tú) riñe
(Vd) riña
(nosotros) riñamos
(vosotros) reñid
(Vds) riñan

SUBJUNCTIVE

PRESENT	IMPERFECT	PLUPERFECT
1. riña	riñ-era/ese	hubiera reñido
2. riñas	riñ-eras/eses	hubieras reñido
3. riña	riñ-era/ese	hubiera reñido
1. riñamos	riñ-éramos/ésemos	hubiéramos reñido
2. riñáis	riñ-erais/eseis	hubierais reñido
3. riñan	riñ-eran/esen	hubieran reñido

PERFECT	haya reñido *etc*

INFINITIVE

PARTICIPLE

PRESENT	PRESENT
reñir	riñendo

PAST	PAST
haber reñido	reñido

PRESENT	IMPERFECT	FUTURE
1. repito	repetía	repetiré
2. repites	repetías	repetirás
3. repite	repetía	repetirá
1. repetimos	repetíamos	repetiremos
2. repetís	repetíais	repetiréis
3. repiten	repetían	repetirán

PRETERITE	PERFECT	PLUPERFECT
1. repetí	he repetido	había repetido
2. repetiste	has repetido	habías repetido
3. repitió	ha repetido	había repetido
1. repetimos	hemos repetido	habíamos repetido
2. repetisteis	habéis repetido	habíais repetido
3. repitieron	han repetido	habían repetido

PAST ANTERIOR	FUTURE PERFECT
hube repetido *etc*	habré repetido *etc*

CONDITIONAL

IMPERATIVE

PRESENT	PAST	
1. repetiría	habría repetido	
2. repetirías	habrías repetido	(tú) repite
3. repetiría	habría repetido	(Vd) repita
1. repetiríamos	habríamos repetido	(nosotros) repitamos
2. repetiríais	habríais repetido	(vosotros) repetid
3. repetirían	habrían repetido	(Vds) repitan

SUBJUNCTIVE

PRESENT	IMPERFECT	PLUPERFECT
1. repita	repit-iera/iese	hubiera repetido
2. repitas	repit-ieras/ieses	hubieras repetido
3. repita	repit-iera/iese	hubiera repetido
1. repitamos	repit-iéramos/iésemos	hubiéramos repetido
2. repitáis	repit-ierais/ieseis	hubierais repetido
3. repitan	repit-ieran/iesen	hubieran repetido

PERFECT	haya repetido *etc*

INFINITIVE

PARTICIPLE

PRESENT	PRESENT
repetir	repitiendo

PAST	PAST
haber repetido	repetido

PRESENT	IMPERFECT	FUTURE
1. reúno	reunía	reuniré
2. reúnes	reunías	reunirás
3. reúne	reunía	reunirá
1. reunimos	reuníamos	reuniremos
2. reunís	reuníais	reuniréis
3. reúnen	reunían	reunirán

PRETERITE	PERFECT	PLUPERFECT
1. reuní	he reunido	había reunido
2. reuniste	has reunido	habías reunido
3. reunió	ha reunido	había reunido
1. reunimos	hemos reunido	habíamos reunido
2. reunisteis	habéis reunido	habíais reunido
3. reunieron	han reunido	habían reunido

PAST ANTERIOR	FUTURE PERFECT
hube reunido *etc*	habré reunido *etc*

CONDITIONAL

PRESENT	PAST
1. reuniría	habría reunido
2. reunirías	habrías reunido
3. reuniría	habría reunido
1. reuniríamos	habríamos reunido
2. reuniríais	habríais reunido
3. reunirían	habrían reunido

IMPERATIVE

(tú) reúne
(Vd) reúna
(nosotros) reunamos
(vosotros) reunid
(Vds) reúnan

SUBJUNCTIVE

PRESENT	IMPERFECT	PLUPERFECT
1. reúna	reun-iera/iese	hubiera reunido
2. reúnas	reun-ieras/ieses	hubieras reunido
3. reúna	reun-iera/iese	hubiera reunido
1. reunamos	reun-iéramos/iésemos	hubiéramos reunido
2. reunáis	reun-ierais/ieseis	hubierais reunido
3. reúnan	reun-ieran/iesen	hubieran reunido

PERFECT	haya reunido *etc*

INFINITIVE

PRESENT	PARTICIPLE

PRESENT	PRESENT
reunir	reuniendo

PAST	PAST
haber reunido	reunido

PRESENT	IMPERFECT	FUTURE
1. roo/roigo/royo	roía	roeré
2. roes	roías	roerás
3. roe	roía	roerá
1. roemos	roíamos	roeremos
2. roéis	roíais	roeréis
3. roen	roían	roerán

PRETERITE	PERFECT	PLUPERFECT
1. roí	he roído	había roído
2. roíste	has roído	habías roído
3. royó	ha roído	había roído
1. roímos	hemos roído	habíamos roído
2. roísteis	habéis roído	habíais roído
3. royeron	han roído	habían roído

PAST ANTERIOR	FUTURE PERFECT
hube roído *etc*	habré roído *etc*

CONDITIONAL

IMPERATIVE

PRESENT	PAST	
1. roería	habría roído	
2. roerías	habrías roído	(tú) roe
3. roería	habría roído	(Vd) roa
1. roeríamos	habríamos roído	(nosotros) roamos
2. roeríais	habríais roído	(vosotros) roed
3. roerían	habrían roído	(Vds) roan

SUBJUNCTIVE

PRESENT	IMPERFECT	PLUPERFECT
1. roa/roiga/roya	ro-yera/yese	hubiera roído
2. roas	ro-yeras/yeses	hubieras roído
3. roa	ro-yera/yese	hubiera roído
1. roamos	ro-yéramos/yésemos	hubiéramos roído
2. roáis	ro-yerais/yeseis	hubierais roído
3. roan	ro-yeran/yesen	hubieran roído

PERFECT   haya roído *etc*

INFINITIVE

PARTICIPLE

PRESENT	PRESENT
roer	royendo

PAST	PAST
haber roído	roído

PRESENT	IMPERFECT	FUTURE
1. ruego	rogaba	rogaré
2. ruegas	rogabas	rogarás
3. ruega	rogaba	rogará
1. rogamos	rogábamos	rogaremos
2. rogáis	rogabais	rogaréis
3. ruegan	rogaban	rogarán

PRETERITE	PERFECT	PLUPERFECT
1. rogué	he rogado	había rogado
2. rogaste	has rogado	habías rogado
3. rogó	ha rogado	había rogado
1. rogamos	hemos rogado	habíamos rogado
2. rogasteis	habéis rogado	habíais rogado
3. rogaron	han rogado	habían rogado

PAST ANTERIOR		FUTURE PERFECT
hube rogado *etc*		habré rogado *etc*

CONDITIONAL		*IMPERATIVE*

PRESENT	PAST	
1. rogaría	habría rogado	
2. rogarías	habrías rogado	(tú) ruega
3. rogaría	habría rogado	(Vd) ruegue
1. rogaríamos	habríamos rogado	(nosotros) roguemos
2. rogaríais	habríais rogado	(vosotros) rogad
3. rogarían	habrían rogado	(Vds) rueguen

SUBJUNCTIVE

PRESENT	IMPERFECT	PLUPERFECT
1. ruegue	rog-ara/ase	hubiera rogado
2. ruegues	rog-aras/ases	hubieras rogado
3. ruegue	rog-ara/ase	hubiera rogado
1. roguemos	rog-áramos/ásemos	hubiéramos rogado
2. roguéis	rog-arais/aseis	hubierais rogado
3. rueguen	rog-aran/asen	hubieran rogado

PERFECT   haya rogado *etc*

INFINITIVE	*PARTICIPLE*
PRESENT	PRESENT
rogar	rogando
PAST	PAST
haber rogado	rogado

PRESENT	IMPERFECT	FUTURE
1. rompo	rompía	romperé
2. rompes	rompías	romperás
3. rompe	rompía	romperá
1. rompemos	rompíamos	romperemos
2. rompéis	rompíais	romperéis
3. rompen	rompían	romperán

PRETERITE	PERFECT	PLUPERFECT
1. rompí	he roto	había roto
2. rompiste	has roto	habías roto
3. rompió	ha roto	había roto
1. rompimos	hemos roto	habíamos roto
2. rompisteis	habéis roto	habíais roto
3. rompieron	han roto	habían roto

PAST ANTERIOR	FUTURE PERFECT
hube roto *etc*	habré roto *etc*

CONDITIONAL

IMPERATIVE

PRESENT	PAST	
1. rompería	habría roto	
2. romperías	habrías roto	
3. rompería	habría roto	(tú) rompe
1. romperíamos	habríamos roto	(Vd) rompa
2. romperíais	habríais roto	(nosotros) rompamos
3. romperían	habrían roto	(vosotros) romped
		(Vds) rompan

SUBJUNCTIVE

PRESENT	IMPERFECT	PLUPERFECT
1. rompa	romp-iera/iese	hubiera roto
2. rompas	romp-ieras/ieses	hubieras roto
3. rompa	romp-iera/iese	hubiera roto
1. rompamos	romp-iéramos/iésemos	hubiéramos roto
2. rompáis	romp-ierais/ieseis	hubierais roto
3. rompan	romp-ieran/iesen	hubieran roto

PERFECT   haya roto *etc*

INFINITIVE

PARTICIPLE

PRESENT	PRESENT
romper	rompiendo

PAST	PAST
haber roto	roto

SABER
173 *to know*

PRESENT	IMPERFECT	FUTURE
1. sé	sabía	sabré
2. sabes	sabías	sabrás
3. sabe	sabía	sabrá
1. sabemos	sabíamos	sabremos
2. sabéis	sabíais	sabréis
3. saben	sabían	sabrán

PRETERITE	PERFECT	PLUPERFECT
1. supe	he sabido	había sabido
2. supiste	has sabido	habías sabido
3. supo	ha sabido	había sabido
1. supimos	hemos sabido	habíamos sabido
2. supisteis	habéis sabido	habíais sabido
3. supieron	han sabido	habían sabido

PAST ANTERIOR	FUTURE PERFECT
hube sabido *etc*	habré sabido *etc*

CONDITIONAL

PRESENT	PAST
1. sabría	habría sabido
2. sabrías	habrías sabido
3. sabría	habría sabido
1. sabríamos	habríamos sabido
2. sabríais	habríais sabido
3. sabrían	habrían sabido

IMPERATIVE

(tú) sabe
(Vd) sepa
(nosotros) sepamos
(vosotros) sabed
(Vds) sepan

SUBJUNCTIVE

PRESENT	IMPERFECT	PLUPERFECT
1. sepa	sup-iera/iese	hubiera sabido
2. sepas	sup-ieras/ieses	hubieras sabido
3. sepa	sup-iera/iese	hubiera sabido
1. sepamos	sup-iéramos/iésemos	hubiéramos sabido
2. sepáis	sup-ierais/ieseis	hubierais sabido
3. sepan	sup-ieran/iesen	hubieran sabido

PERFECT   haya sabido *etc*

INFINITIVE

PRESENT
saber

PAST
haber sabido

PARTICIPLE

PRESENT
sabiendo

PAST
sabido

PRESENT	IMPERFECT	FUTURE
1. saco	sacaba	sacaré
2. sacas	sacabas	sacarás
3. saca	sacaba	sacará
1. sacamos	sacábamos	sacaremos
2. sacáis	sacabais	sacaréis
3. sacan	sacaban	sacarán

PRETERITE	PERFECT	PLUPERFECT
1. saqué	he sacado	había sacado
2. sacaste	has sacado	habías sacado
3. sacó	ha sacado	había sacado
1. sacamos	hemos sacado	habíamos sacado
2. sacasteis	habéis sacado	habíais sacado
3. sacaron	han sacado	habían sacado

PAST ANTERIOR	FUTURE PERFECT
hube sacado *etc*	habré sacado *etc*

CONDITIONAL

IMPERATIVE

PRESENT	PAST	
1. sacaría	habría sacado	
2. sacarías	habrías sacado	(tú) saca
3. sacaría	habría sacado	(Vd) saque
1. sacaríamos	habríamos sacado	(nosotros) saquemos
2. sacaríais	habríais sacado	(vosotros) sacad
3. sacarían	habrían sacado	(Vds) saquen

SUBJUNCTIVE

PRESENT	IMPERFECT	PLUPERFECT
1. saque	sac-ara/ase	hubiera sacado
2. saques	sac-ara/ases	hubieras sacado
3. saque	sac-ara/ase	hubiera sacado
1. saquemos	sac-áramos/ásemos	hubiéramos sacado
2. saquéis	sac-arais/aseis	hubierais sacado
3. saquen	sac-aran/asen	hubieran sacado

PERFECT	haya sacado *etc*

INFINITIVE

PARTICIPLE

PRESENT	PRESENT
sacar	sacando

PAST	PAST
haber sacado	sacado

SALIR

175 *to go out; to leave*

PRESENT	IMPERFECT	FUTURE
1. salgo	salía	saldré
2. sales	salías	saldrás
3. sale	salía	saldrá
1. salimos	salíamos	saldremos
2. salís	salíais	saldréis
3. salen	salían	saldrán

PRETERITE	PERFECT	PLUPERFECT
1. salí	he salido	había salido
2. saliste	has salido	habías salido
3. salió	ha salido	había salido
1. salimos	hemos salido	habíamos salido
2. salisteis	habéis salido	habíais salido
3. salieron	han salido	habían salido

PAST ANTERIOR	FUTURE PERFECT
hube salido *etc*	habré salido *etc*

CONDITIONAL

IMPERATIVE

PRESENT	PAST	
1. saldría	habría salido	
2. saldrías	habrías salido	(tú) sal
3. saldría	habría salido	(Vd) salga
1. saldríamos	habríamos salido	(nosotros) salgamos
2. saldríais	habríais salido	(vosotros) salid
3. saldrían	habrían salido	(Vds) salgan

SUBJUNCTIVE

PRESENT	IMPERFECT	PLUPERFECT
1. salga	sal-iera/iese	hubiera salido
2. salgas	sal-ieras/ieses	hubieras salido
3. salga	sal-iera/iese	hubiera salido
1. salgamos	sal-iéramos/iésemos	hubiéramos salido
2. salgáis	sal-ierais/ieseis	hubierais salido
3. salgan	sal-ieran/iesen	hubieran salido

PERFECT   haya salido *etc*

INFINITIVE

PARTICIPLE

PRESENT	PRESENT
salir	saliendo

PAST	PAST
haber salido	salido

PRESENT	IMPERFECT	FUTURE
1. satisfago	satisfacía	satisfaré
2. satisfaces	satisfacías	satisfarás
3. satisface	satisfacía	satisfará
1. satisfacemos	satisfacíamos	satisfaremos
2. satisfacéis	satisfacíais	satisfaréis
3. satisfacen	satisfacían	satisfarán

PRETERITE	PERFECT	PLUPERFECT
1. satisfice	he satisfecho	había satisfecho
2. satisficiste	has satisfecho	habías satisfecho
3. satisfizo	ha satisfecho	había satisfecho
1. satisficimos	hemos satisfecho	habíamos satisfecho
2. satisficisteis	habéis satisfecho	habíais satisfecho
3. satisficieron	han satisfecho	habían satisfecho

PAST ANTERIOR	FUTURE PERFECT
hube satisfecho *etc*	habré satisfecho *etc*

CONDITIONAL

IMPERATIVE

PRESENT	PAST	
1. satisfaría	habría satisfecho	
2. satisfarías	habrías satisfecho	(tú) satisface/satisfaz
3. satisfaría	habría satisfecho	(Vd) satisfaga
1. satisfaríamos	habríamos satisfecho	(nosotros) satisfagamos
2. satisfaríais	habríais satisfecho	(vosotros) satisfaced
3. satisfarían	habrían satisfecho	(Vds) satisfagan

SUBJUNCTIVE

PRESENT	IMPERFECT	PLUPERFECT
1. satisfaga	satisfic-iera/iese	hubiera satisfecho
2. satisfagas	satisfic-ieras/ieses	hubieras satisfecho
3. satisfaga	satisfic-iera/iese	hubiera satisfecho
1. satisfagamos	satisfic-iéramos/iésemos	hubiéramos satisfecho
2. satisfagáis	satisfic-ierais/ieseis	hubierais satisfecho
3. satisfagan	satisfic-ieran/iesen	hubieran satisfecho

PERFECT haya satisfecho *etc*

INFINITIVE

PARTICIPLE

PRESENT	PRESENT
satisfacer	satisfaciendo

PAST	PAST
haber satisfecho	satisfecho

PRESENT	IMPERFECT	FUTURE
1. seco	secaba	secaré
2. secas	secabas	secarás
3. seca	secaba	secará
1. secamos	secábamos	secaremos
2. secáis	secabais	secaréis
3. secan	secaban	secarán

PRETERITE	PERFECT	PLUPERFECT
1. sequé	he secado	había secado
2. secaste	has secado	habías secado
3. secó	ha secado	había secado
1. secamos	hemos secado	habíamos secado
2. secasteis	habéis secado	habíais secado
3. secaron	han secado	habían secado

PAST ANTERIOR	FUTURE PERFECT
hube secado _etc_	habré secado _etc_

CONDITIONAL

IMPERATIVE

PRESENT	PAST	
1. secaría	habría secado	
2. secarías	habrías secado	(tú) seca
3. secaría	habría secado	(Vd) seque
1. secaríamos	habríamos secado	(nosotros) sequemos
2. secaríais	habríais secado	(vosotros) secad
3. secarían	habrían secado	(Vds) sequen

SUBJUNCTIVE

PRESENT	IMPERFECT	PLUPERFECT
1. seque	sec-ara/ase	hubiera secado
2. seques	sec-aras/ases	hubieras secado
3. seque	sec-ara/ase	hubiera secado
1. sequemos	sec-áramos/ásemos	hubiéramos secado
2. sequéis	sec-arais/aseis	hubierais secado
3. sequen	sec-aran/asen	hubieran secado

PERFECT   haya secado _etc_

INFINITIVE

PARTICIPLE

PRESENT	PRESENT
secar	secando

PAST	PAST
haber secado	secado

PRESENT	IMPERFECT	FUTURE
1. sigo	seguía	seguiré
2. sigues	seguías	seguirás
3. sigue	seguía	seguirá
1. seguimos	seguíamos	seguiremos
2. seguís	seguíais	seguiréis
3. siguen	seguían	seguirán

PRETERITE	PERFECT	PLUPERFECT
1. seguí	he seguido	había seguido
2. seguiste	has seguido	habías seguido
3. siguió	ha seguido	había seguido
1. seguimos	hemos seguido	habíamos seguido
2. seguisteis	habéis seguido	habíais seguido
3. siguieron	han seguido	habían seguido

PAST ANTERIOR		FUTURE PERFECT
hube seguido *etc*		habré seguido *etc*

CONDITIONAL

IMPERATIVE

PRESENT	PAST	
1. seguiría	habría seguido	
2. seguirías	habrías seguido	(tú) sigue
3. seguiría	habría seguido	(Vd) siga
1. seguiríamos	habríamos seguido	(nosotros) sigamos
2. seguiríais	habríais seguido	(vosotros) seguid
3. seguirían	habrían seguido	(Vds) sigan

SUBJUNCTIVE

PRESENT	IMPERFECT	PLUPERFECT
1. siga	sigu-iera/iese	hubiera seguido
2. sigas	sigu-ieras/ieses	hubieras seguido
3. siga	sigu-iera/iese	hubiera seguido
1. sigamos	sigu-iéramos/iésemos	hubiéramos seguido
2. sigáis	sigu-ierais/ieseis	hubierais seguido
3. sigan	sigu-ieran/iesen	hubieran seguido
PERFECT	haya seguido *etc*	

INFINITIVE

PARTICIPLE

PRESENT	PRESENT
seguir	siguiendo

PAST	PAST
haber seguido	seguido

SENTARSE
179 *to sit down*

PRESENT	IMPERFECT	FUTURE
1. me siento	me sentaba	me sentaré
2. te sientas	te sentabas	te sentarás
3. se sienta	se sentaba	se sentará
1. nos sentamos	nos sentábamos	nos sentaremos
2. os sentáis	os sentabais	os sentaréis
3. se sientan	se sentaban	se sentarán

PRETERITE	PERFECT	PLUPERFECT
1. me senté	me he sentado	me había sentado
2. te sentaste	te has sentado	te habías sentado
3. se sentó	se ha sentado	se había sentado
1. nos sentamos	nos hemos sentado	nos habíamos sentado
2. os sentasteis	os habéis sentado	os habíais sentado
3. se sentaron	se han sentado	se habían sentado

PAST ANTERIOR
me hube sentado *etc*

FUTURE PERFECT
me habré sentado *etc*

CONDITIONAL

IMPERATIVE

PRESENT	PAST
1. me sentaría	me habría sentado
2. te sentarías	te habrías sentado
3. se sentaría	se habría sentado
1. nos sentaríamos	nos habríamos sentado
2. os sentaríais	os habríais sentado
3. se sentarían	se habrían sentado

(tú) siéntate
(Vd) siéntese
(nosotros) sentémonos
(vosotros) sentaos
(Vds) siéntense

SUBJUNCTIVE

PRESENT	IMPERFECT	PLUPERFECT
1. me siente	me sent-ara/ase	me hubiera sentado
2. te sientes	te sent-aras/ases	te hubieras sentado
3. se siente	se sent-ara/ase	se hubiera sentado
1. nos sentemos	nos sent-áramos/ásemos	nos hubiéramos sentado
2. os sentéis	os sent-arais/aseis	os hubierais sentado
3. se sienten	se sent-aran/asen	se hubieran sentado

PERFECT   me haya sentado *etc*

INFINITIVE

PARTICIPLE

PRESENT	PRESENT
sentarse	sentándose

PAST	PAST
haberse sentado	sentado

PRESENT	IMPERFECT	FUTURE
1. siento	sentía	sentiré
2. sientes	sentías	sentirás
3. siente	sentía	sentirá
1. sentimos	sentíamos	sentiremos
2. sentís	sentíais	sentiréis
3. sienten	sentían	sentirán

PRETERITE	PERFECT	PLUPERFECT
1. sentí	he sentido	había sentido
2. sentiste	has sentido	habías sentido
3. sintió	ha sentido	había sentido
1. sentimos	hemos sentido	habíamos sentido
2. sentisteis	habéis sentido	habíais sentido
3. sintieron	han sentido	habían sentido

PAST ANTERIOR	FUTURE PERFECT
hube sentido *etc*	habré sentido *etc*

CONDITIONAL

IMPERATIVE

PRESENT	PAST	
1. sentiría	habría sentido	
2. sentirías	habrías sentido	(tú) siente
3. sentiría	habría sentido	(Vd) sienta
1. sentiríamos	habríamos sentido	(nosotros) sintamos
2. sentiríais	habríais sentido	(vosotros) sentid
3. sentirían	habrían sentido	(Vds) sientan

SUBJUNCTIVE

PRESENT	IMPERFECT	PLUPERFECT
1. sienta	sint-iera/iese	hubiera sentido
2. sientas	sint-ieras/ieses	hubieras sentido
3. sienta	sint-iera/iese	hubiera sentido
1. sintamos	sint-iéramos/iésemos	hubiéramos sentido
2. sintáis	sint-ierais/ieseis	hubierais sentido
3. sientan	sint-ieran/iesen	hubieran sentido

PERFECT	haya sentido *etc*

INFINITIVE

PARTICIPLE

PRESENT	PRESENT
sentir	sintiendo

PAST	PAST
haber sentido	sentido

PRESENT	IMPERFECT	FUTURE
1. soy	era	seré
2. eres	eras	serás
3. es	era	será
1. somos	éramos	seremos
2. sois	erais	seréis
3. son	eran	serán

PRETERITE	PERFECT	PLUPERFECT
1. fui	he sido	había sido
2. fuiste	has sido	habías sido
3. fue	ha sido	había sido
1. fuimos	hemos sido	habíamos sido
2. fuisteis	habéis sido	habíais sido
3. fueron	han sido	habían sido

PAST ANTERIOR		FUTURE PERFECT
hube sido *etc*		habré sido *etc*

CONDITIONAL

PRESENT	PAST
1. sería	habría sido
2. serías	habrías sido
3. sería	habría sido
1. seríamos	habríamos sido
2. seríais	habríais sido
3. serían	habrían sido

IMPERATIVE

(tú) sé
(Vd) sea
(nosotros) seamos
(vosotros) sed
(Vds) sean

SUBJUNCTIVE

PRESENT	IMPERFECT	PLUPERFECT
1. sea	fu-era/ese	hubiera sido
2. seas	fu-eras/eses	hubieras sido
3. sea	fu-era/ese	hubiera sido
1. seamos	fu-éramos/ésemos	hubiéramos sido
2. seáis	fu-erais/eseis	hubierais sido
3. sean	fu-eran/esen	hubieran sido

PERFECT	haya sido *etc*

INFINITIVE

PRESENT
ser

PAST
haber sido

PARTICIPLE

PRESENT
siendo

PAST
sido

PRESENT	IMPERFECT	FUTURE
1. sirvo	servía	serviré
2. sirves	servías	servirás
3. sirve	servía	servirá
1. servimos	servíamos	serviremos
2. servís	servíais	serviréis
3. sirven	servían	servirán

PRETERITE	PERFECT	PLUPERFECT
1. serví	he servido	había servido
2. serviste	has servido	habías servido
3. sirvió	ha servido	había servido
1. servimos	hemos servido	habíamos servido
2. servisteis	habéis servido	habíais servido
3. sirvieron	han servido	habían servido

PAST ANTERIOR		FUTURE PERFECT
hube servido *etc*		habré servido *etc*

CONDITIONAL

IMPERATIVE

PRESENT	PAST	
1. serviría	habría servido	
2. servirías	habrías servido	
3. serviría	habría servido	(tú) sirve
1. serviríamos	habríamos servido	(Vd) sirva
2. serviríais	habríais servido	(nosotros) sirvamos
3. servirían	habrían servido	(vosotros) servid
		(Vds) sirvan

SUBJUNCTIVE

PRESENT	IMPERFECT	PLUPERFECT
1. sirva	sirv-iera/iese	hubiera servido
2. sirvas	sirv-ieras/ieses	hubieras servido
3. sirva	sirv-iera/iese	hubiera servido
1. sirvamos	sirv-iéramos/iésemos	hubiéramos servido
2. sirváis	sirv-ierais/ieseis	hubierais servido
3. sirvan	sirv-ieran/iesen	hubieran servido
PERFECT	haya servido *etc*	

INFINITIVE	PARTICIPLE
PRESENT	PRESENT
servir	sirviendo
PAST	PAST
haber servido	servido

SITUAR
183 *to situate*

PRESENT	IMPERFECT	FUTURE
1. sitúo	situaba	situaré
2. sitúas	situabas	situarás
3. sitúa	situaba	situará
1. situamos	situábamos	situaremos
2. situáis	situabais	situaréis
3. sitúan	situaban	situarán

PRETERITE	PERFECT	PLUPERFECT
1. situé	he situado	había situado
2. situaste	has situado	habías situado
3. situó	ha situado	había situado
1. situamos	hemos situado	habíamos situado
2. situasteis	habéis situado	habíais situado
3. situaron	han situado	habían situado

PAST ANTERIOR		FUTURE PERFECT
hube situado *etc*		habré situado *etc*

CONDITIONAL		IMPERATIVE

PRESENT	PAST	
1. situaría	habría situado	
2. situarías	habrías situado	(tú) sitúa
3. situaría	habría situado	(Vd) sitúe
1. situaríamos	habríamos situado	(nosotros) situemos
2. situaríais	habríais situado	(vosotros) situad
3. situarían	habrían situado	(Vds) sitúen

SUBJUNCTIVE

PRESENT	IMPERFECT	PLUPERFECT
1. sitúe	situ-ara/ase	hubiera situado
2. sitúes	situ-aras/ases	hubieras situado
3. sitúe	situ-ara/ase	hubiera situado
1. situemos	situ-áramos/ásemos	hubiéramos situado
2. situéis	situ-arais/aseis	hubierais situado
3. sitúen	situ-aran/asen	hubieran situado

PERFECT	haya situado *etc*	

INFINITIVE	PARTICIPLE	

PRESENT	PRESENT
situar	situando

PAST	PAST
haber situado	situado

PRESENT	IMPERFECT	FUTURE
1. suelo	solía	
2. sueles	solías	
3. suele	solía	
1. solemos	solíamos	
2. soléis	solíais	
3. suelen	solían	

PRETERITE	PERFECT	PLUPERFECT
PAST ANTERIOR		FUTURE PERFECT

CONDITIONAL		*IMPERATIVE*
PRESENT	PAST	

SUBJUNCTIVE		
PRESENT	IMPERFECT	PLUPERFECT
1. suela		
2. suelas		
3. suela		
1. solamos		
2. soláis		
3. suelan		
PERFECT		

INFINITIVE	*PARTICIPLE*	*NOTE*
PRESENT	PRESENT	The other tenses rarely occur.
soler		
PAST	PAST	

203

SOÑAR
185 to dream

PRESENT	IMPERFECT	FUTURE
1. sueño	soñaba	soñaré
2. sueñas	soñabas	soñarás
3. sueña	soñaba	soñará
1. soñamos	soñábamos	soñaremos
2. soñáis	soñabais	soñaréis
3. sueñan	soñaban	soñarán

PRETERITE	PERFECT	PLUPERFECT
1. soñé	he soñado	había soñado
2. soñaste	has soñado	habías soñado
3. soñó	ha soñado	había soñado
1. soñamos	hemos soñado	habíamos soñado
2. soñasteis	habéis soñado	habíais soñado
3. soñaron	han soñado	habían soñado

PAST ANTERIOR	FUTURE PERFECT
hube soñado *etc*	habré soñado *etc*

CONDITIONAL		IMPERATIVE

PRESENT	PAST	
1. soñaría	habría soñado	
2. soñarías	habrías soñado	(tú) sueña
3. soñaría	habría soñado	(Vd) sueñe
1. soñaríamos	habríamos soñado	(nosotros) soñemos
2. soñaríais	habríais soñado	(vosotros) soñad
3. soñarían	habrían soñado	(Vds) sueñen

SUBJUNCTIVE

PRESENT	IMPERFECT	PLUPERFECT
1. sueñe	soñ-ara/ase	hubiera soñado
2. sueñes	soñ-aras/ases	hubieras soñado
3. sueñe	soñ-ara/ase	hubiera soñado
1. soñemos	soñ-áramos/ásemos	hubiéramos soñado
2. soñéis	soñ-arais/aseis	hubierais soñado
3. sueñen	soñ-aran/asen	hubieran soñado
PERFECT	haya soñado *etc*	

INFINITIVE	PARTICIPLE
PRESENT	PRESENT
soñar	soñando
PAST	PAST
haber soñado	soñado

PRESENT	**IMPERFECT**	**FUTURE**
1. subo	subía	subiré
2. subes	subías	subirás
3. sube	subía	subirá
1. subimos	subíamos	subiremos
2. subís	subíais	subiréis
3. suben	subían	subirán

PRETERITE	**PERFECT**	**PLUPERFECT**
1. subí	he subido	había subido
2. subiste	has subido	habías subido
3. subió	ha subido	había subido
1. subimos	hemos subido	habíamos subido
2. subisteis	habéis subido	habíais subido
3. subieron	han subido	habían subido

PAST ANTERIOR	**FUTURE PERFECT**
hube subido *etc*	habré subido *etc*

CONDITIONAL

IMPERATIVE

PRESENT	**PAST**	
1. subiría	habría subido	
2. subirías	habrías subido	(tú) sube
3. subiría	habría subido	(Vd) suba
1. subiríamos	habríamos subido	(nosotros) subamos
2. subiríais	habríais subido	(vosotros) subid
3. subirían	habrían subido	(Vds) suban

SUBJUNCTIVE

PRESENT	**IMPERFECT**	**PLUPERFECT**
1. suba	sub-iera/iese	hubiera subido
2. subas	sub-ieras/ieses	hubieras subido
3. suba	sub-iera/iese	hubiera subido
1. subamos	sub-iéramos/iésemos	hubiéramos subido
2. subáis	sub-ierais/ieseis	hubierais subido
3. suban	sub-ieran/iesen	hubieran subido

PERFECT   haya subido *etc*

INFINITIVE

PARTICIPLE

PRESENT	**PRESENT**
subir	subiendo

PAST	**PAST**
haber subido	subido

SUGERIR
187 *to suggest*

PRESENT	IMPERFECT	FUTURE
1. sugiero	sugería	sugeriré
2. sugieres	sugerías	sugerirás
3. sugiere	sugería	sugerirá
1. sugerimos	sugeríamos	sugeriremos
2. sugerís	sugeríais	sugeriréis
3. sugieren	sugerían	sugerirán

PRETERITE	PERFECT	PLUPERFECT
1. sugerí	he sugerido	había sugerido
2. sugeriste	has sugerido	habías sugerido
3. sugirió	ha sugerido	había sugerido
1. sugerimos	hemos sugerido	habíamos sugerido
2. sugeristeis	habéis sugerido	habíais sugerido
3. sugirieron	han sugerido	habían sugerido

PAST ANTERIOR	FUTURE PERFECT
hube sugerido *etc*	habré sugerido *etc*

CONDITIONAL

PRESENT	PAST
1. sugeriría	habría sugerido
2. sugerirías	habrías sugerido
3. sugeriría	habría sugerido
1. sugeriríamos	habríamos sugerido
2. sugeriríais	habríais sugerido
3. sugerirían	habrían sugerido

IMPERATIVE

(tú) sugiere
(Vd) sugiera
(nosotros) sugiramos
(vosotros) sugerid
(Vds) sugieran

SUBJUNCTIVE

PRESENT	IMPERFECT	PLUPERFECT
1. sugiera	sugir-iera/iese	hubiera sugerido
2. sugieras	sugir-ieras/ieses	hubieras sugerido
3. sugiera	sugir-iera/iese	hubiera sugerido
1. sugiramos	sugir-iéramos/iésemos	hubiéramos sugerido
2. sugiráis	sugir-ierais/ieseis	hubierais sugerido
3. sugieran	sugir-ieran/iesen	hubieran sugerido

PERFECT   haya sugerido *etc*

INFINITIVE

PRESENT	PARTICIPLE PRESENT
sugerir	sugiriendo

PAST	PAST
haber sugerido	sugerido

PRESENT	**IMPERFECT**	**FUTURE**
1. taño	tañía	tañeré
2. tañes	tañías	tañerás
3. tañe	tañía	tañerá
1. tañemos	tañíamos	tañeremos
2. tañéis	tañíais	tañeréis
3. tañen	tañían	tañerán

PRETERITE	**PERFECT**	**PLUPERFECT**
1. tañí	he tañido	había tañido
2. tañiste	has tañido	habías tañido
3. tañó	ha tañido	había tañido
1. tañimos	hemos tañido	habíamos tañido
2. tañisteis	habéis tañido	habíais tañido
3. tañeron	han tañido	habían tañido

PAST ANTERIOR	**FUTURE PERFECT**
hube tañido *etc*	habré tañido *etc*

CONDITIONAL

IMPERATIVE

PRESENT	**PAST**	
1. tañería	habría tañido	
2. tañerías	habrías tañido	(tú) tañe
3. tañería	habría tañido	(Vd) taña
1. tañeríamos	habríamos tañido	(nosotros) tañamos
2. tañeríais	habríais tañido	(vosotros) tañed
3. tañerían	habrían tañido	(Vds) tañan

SUBJUNCTIVE

PRESENT	**IMPERFECT**	**PLUPERFECT**
1. taña	tañ-iera/iese	hubiera tañido
2. tañas	tañ-ieras/ieses	hubieras tañido
3. taña	tañ-iera/iese	hubiera tañido
1. tañamos	tañ-iéramos/iésemos	hubiéramos tañido
2. tañáis	tañ-ierais/ieseis	hubierais tañido
3. tañan	tañ-ieran/iesen	hubieran tañido
PERFECT	haya tañido *etc*	

INFINITIVE	**PARTICIPLE**
PRESENT	**PRESENT**
tañer	tañendo
PAST	**PAST**
haber tañido	tañido

PRESENT	IMPERFECT	FUTURE
1. tengo	tenía	tendré
2. tienes	tenías	tendrás
3. tiene	tenía	tendrá
1. tenemos	teníamos	tendremos
2. tenéis	teníais	tendréis
3. tienen	tenían	tendrán

PRETERITE	PERFECT	PLUPERFECT
1. tuve	he tenido	había tenido
2. tuviste	has tenido	habías tenido
3. tuvo	ha tenido	había tenido
1. tuvimos	hemos tenido	habíamos tenido
2. tuvisteis	habéis tenido	habíais tenido
3. tuvieron	han tenido	habían tenido

PAST ANTERIOR	FUTURE PERFECT
hube tenido *etc*	habré tenido *etc*

CONDITIONAL

IMPERATIVE

PRESENT	PAST	
1. tendría	habría tenido	
2. tendrías	habrías tenido	(tú) ten
3. tendría	habría tenido	(Vd) tenga
1. tendríamos	habríamos tenido	(nosotros) tengamos
2. tendríais	habríais tenido	(vosotros) tened
3. tendrían	habrían tenido	(Vds) tengan

SUBJUNCTIVE

PRESENT	IMPERFECT	PLUPERFECT
1. tenga	tuv-iera/iese	hubiera tenido
2. tengas	tuv-ieras/ieses	hubieras tenido
3. tenga	tuv-iera/iese	hubiera tenido
1. tengamos	tuv-iéramos/iésemos	hubiéramos tenido
2. tengáis	tuv-ierais/ieseis	hubierais tenido
3. tengan	tuv-ieran/iesen	hubieran tenido
PERFECT	haya tenido *etc*	

INFINITIVE

PARTICIPLE

PRESENT	PRESENT
tener	teniendo
PAST	PAST
haber tenido	tenido

PRESENT	IMPERFECT	FUTURE
1. toco	tocaba	tocaré
2. tocas	tocabas	tocarás
3. toca	tocaba	tocará
1. tocamos	tocábamos	tocaremos
2. tocáis	tocabais	tocaréis
3. tocan	tocaban	tocarán

PRETERITE	PERFECT	PLUPERFECT
1. toqué	he tocado	había tocado
2. tocaste	has tocado	habías tocado
3. tocó	ha tocado	había tocado
1. tocamos	hemos tocado	habíamos tocado
2. tocasteis	habéis tocado	habíais tocado
3. tocaron	han tocado	habían tocado

PAST ANTERIOR	FUTURE PERFECT
hube tocado *etc*	habré tocado *etc*

CONDITIONAL

IMPERATIVE

PRESENT	PAST	
1. tocaría	habría tocado	
2. tocarías	habrías tocado	(tú) toca
3. tocaría	habría tocado	(Vd) toque
1. tocaríamos	habríamos tocado	(nosotros) toquemos
2. tocaríais	habríais tocado	(vosotros) tocad
3. tocarían	habrían tocado	(Vds) toquen

SUBJUNCTIVE

PRESENT	IMPERFECT	PLUPERFECT
1. toque	toc-ara/ase	hubiera tocado
2. toques	toc-aras/ases	hubieras tocado
3. toque	toc-ara/ase	hubiera tocado
1. toquemos	toc-áramos/ásemos	hubiéramos tocado
2. toquéis	toc-arais/aseis	hubierais tocado
3. toquen	toc-aran/asen	hubieran tocado
PERFECT	haya tocado *etc*	

INFINITIVE

PARTICIPLE

PRESENT	PRESENT
tocar	tocando

PAST	PAST
haber tocado	tocado

PRESENT	IMPERFECT	FUTURE
1. tomo	tomaba	tomaré
2. tomas	tomabas	tomarás
3. toma	tomaba	tomará
1. tomamos	tomábamos	tomaremos
2. tomáis	tomabais	tomaréis
3. toman	tomaban	tomarán

PRETERITE	PERFECT	PLUPERFECT
1. tomé	he tomado	había tomado
2. tomaste	has tomado	habías tomado
3. tomó	ha tomado	había tomado
1. tomamos	hemos tomado	habíamos tomado
2. tomasteis	habéis tomado	habíais tomado
3. tomaron	han tomado	habían tomado

PAST ANTERIOR	FUTURE PERFECT
hube tomado *etc*	habré tomado *etc*

CONDITIONAL

IMPERATIVE

PRESENT	PAST	
1. tomaría	habría tomado	
2. tomarías	habrías tomado	(tú) toma
3. tomaría	habría tomado	(Vd) tome
1. tomaríamos	habríamos tomado	(nosotros) tomemos
2. tomaríais	habríais tomado	(vosotros) tomad
3. tomarían	habrían tomado	(Vds) tomen

SUBJUNCTIVE

PRESENT	IMPERFECT	PLUPERFECT
1. tome	tom-ara/ase	hubiera tomado
2. tomes	tom-ara/ases	hubieras tomado
3. tome	tom-ara/ase	hubiera tomado
1. tomemos	tom-áramos/ásemos	hubiéramos tomado
2. toméis	tom-arais/aseis	hubierais tomado
3. tomen	tom-aran/asen	hubieran tomado

PERFECT	haya tomado *etc*

INFINITIVE

PARTICIPLE

PRESENT	PRESENT
tomar	tomando

PAST	PAST
haber tomado	tomado

PRESENT	IMPERFECT	FUTURE
1. tuerzo	torcía	torceré
2. tuerces	torcías	torcerás
3. tuerce	torcía	torcerá
1. torcemos	torcíamos	torceremos
2. torcéis	torcíais	torceréis
3. tuercen	torcían	torcerán

PRETERITE	PERFECT	PLUPERFECT
1. torcí	he torcido	había torcido
2. torciste	has torcido	habías torcido
3. torció	ha torcido	había torcido
1. torcimos	hemos torcido	habíamos torcido
2. torcisteis	habéis torcido	habíais torcido
3. torcieron	han torcido	habían torcido

PAST ANTERIOR
hube torcido *etc*

FUTURE PERFECT
habré torcido *etc*

CONDITIONAL

IMPERATIVE

PRESENT	PAST	
1. torcería	habría torcido	
2. torcerías	habrías torcido	(tú) tuerce
3. torcería	habría torcido	(Vd) tuerza
1. torceríamos	habríamos torcido	(nosotros) torzamos
2. torceríais	habríais torcido	(vosotros) torced
3. torcerían	habrían torcido	(Vds) tuerzan

SUBJUNCTIVE

PRESENT	IMPERFECT	PLUPERFECT
1. tuerza	torc-iera/iese	hubiera torcido
2. tuerzas	torc-ieras/ieses	hubieras torcido
3. tuerza	torc-iera/iese	hubiera torcido
1. torzamos	torc-iéramos/iésemos	hubiéramos torcido
2. torzáis	torc-ierais/ieseis	hubierais torcido
3. tuerzan	torc-ieran/iesen	hubieran torcido

PERFECT   haya torcido *etc*

INFINITIVE

PARTICIPLE

PRESENT	PRESENT
torcer	torciendo

PAST	PAST
haber torcido	torcido

TOSER
193 *to cough*

PRESENT	IMPERFECT	FUTURE
1. toso	tosía	toseré
2. toses	tosías	toserás
3. tose	tosía	toserá
1. tosemos	tosíamos	toseremos
2. toséis	tosíais	toseréis
3. tosen	tosían	toserán

PRETERITE	PERFECT	PLUPERFECT
1. tosí	he tosido	había tosido
2. tosiste	has tosido	habías tosido
3. tosió	ha tosido	había tosido
1. tosimos	hemos tosido	habíamos tosido
2. tosisteis	habéis tosido	habíais tosido
3. tosieron	han tosido	habían tosido

PAST ANTERIOR	FUTURE PERFECT
hube tosido *etc*	habré tosido *etc*

CONDITIONAL | IMPERATIVE

PRESENT	PAST	
1. tosería	habría tosido	
2. toserías	habrías tosido	(tú) tose
3. tosería	habría tosido	(Vd) tosa
1. toseríamos	habríamos tosido	(nosotros) tosamos
2. toseríais	habríais tosido	(vosotros) tosed
3. toserían	habrían tosido	(Vds) tosan

SUBJUNCTIVE

PRESENT	IMPERFECT	PLUPERFECT
1. tosa	tos-iera/iese	hubiera tosido
2. tosas	tos-ieras/ieses	hubieras tosido
3. tosa	tos-iera/iese	hubiera tosido
1. tosamos	tos-iéramos/iésemos	hubiéramos tosido
2. tosáis	tos-ierais/ieseis	hubierais tosido
3. tosan	tos-ieran/iesen	hubieran tosido

PERFECT	haya tosido *etc*

INFINITIVE | PARTICIPLE

PRESENT	PRESENT
toser	tosiendo

PAST	PAST
haber tosido	tosido

PRESENT	**IMPERFECT**	**FUTURE**
1. trabajo	trabajaba	trabajaré
2. trabajas	trabajabas	trabajarás
3. trabaja	trabajaba	trabajará
1. trabajamos	trabajábamos	trabajaremos
2. trabajáis	trabajabais	trabajaréis
3. trabajan	trabajaban	trabajarán

PRETERITE	**PERFECT**	**PLUPERFECT**
1. trabajé	he trabajado	había trabajado
2. trabajaste	has trabajado	habías trabajado
3. trabajó	ha trabajado	había trabajado
1. trabajamos	hemos trabajado	habíamos trabajado
2. trabajasteis	habéis trabajado	habíais trabajado
3. trabajaron	han trabajado	habían trabajado

PAST ANTERIOR	**FUTURE PERFECT**
hube trabajado *etc*	habré trabajado *etc*

CONDITIONAL

IMPERATIVE

PRESENT	**PAST**	
1. trabajaría	habría trabajado	
2. trabajarías	habrías trabajado	(tú) trabaja
3. trabajaría	habría trabajado	(Vd) trabaje
1. trabajaríamos	habríamos trabajado	(nosotros) trabajemos
2. trabajaríais	habríais trabajado	(vosotros) trabajad
3. trabajarían	habrían trabajado	(Vds) trabajen

SUBJUNCTIVE

PRESENT	**IMPERFECT**	**PLUPERFECT**
1. trabaje	trabaj-ara/ase	hubiera trabajado
2. trabajes	trabaj-aras/ases	hubieras trabajado
3. trabaje	trabaj-ara/ase	hubiera trabajado
1. trabajemos	trabaj-áramos/ásemos	hubiéramos trabajado
2. trabajéis	trabaj-arais/aseis	hubierais trabajado
3. trabajen	trabaj-aran/asen	hubieran trabajado

PERFECT   haya trabajado *etc*

INFINITIVE

PARTICIPLE

PRESENT	**PRESENT**
trabajar	trabajando
PAST	**PAST**
haber trabajado	trabajado

PRESENT	IMPERFECT	FUTURE
1. traduzco	traducía	traduciré
2. traduces	traducías	traducirás
3. traduce	traducía	traducirá
1. traducimos	traducíamos	traduciremos
2. traducís	traducíais	traduciréis
3. traducen	traducían	traducirán

PRETERITE	PERFECT	PLUPERFECT
1. traduje	he traducido	había traducido
2. tradujiste	has traducido	habías traducido
3. tradujo	ha traducido	había traducido
1. tradujimos	hemos traducido	habíamos traducido
2. tradujisteis	habéis traducido	habíais traducido
3. tradujeron	han traducido	habían traducido

PAST ANTERIOR	FUTURE PERFECT
hube traducido *etc*	habré traducido *etc*

CONDITIONAL

IMPERATIVE

PRESENT	PAST	
1. traduciría	habría traducido	
2. traducirías	habrías traducido	
3. traduciría	habría traducido	(tú) traduce
1. traduciríamos	habríamos traducido	(Vd) traduzca
2. traduciríais	habríais traducido	(nosotros) traduzcamos
3. traducirían	habrían traducido	(vosotros) traducid
		(Vds) traduzcan

SUBJUNCTIVE

PRESENT	IMPERFECT	PLUPERFECT
1. traduzca	traduj-era/ese	hubiera traducido
2. traduzcas	traduj-eras/eses	hubieras traducido
3. traduzca	traduj-era/ese	hubiera traducido
1. traduzcamos	traduj-éramos/ésemos	hubiéramos traducido
2. traduzcáis	traduj-erais/eseis	hubierais traducido
3. traduzcan	traduj-eran/esen	hubieran traducido
PERFECT	haya traducido *etc*	

INFINITIVE

PARTICIPLE

PRESENT	PRESENT
traducir	traduciendo

PAST	PAST
haber traducido	traducido

PRESENT	IMPERFECT	FUTURE
1. traigo	traía	traeré
2. traes	traías	traerás
3. trae	traía	traerá
1. traemos	traíamos	traeremos
2. traéis	traíais	traeréis
3. traen	traían	traerán

PRETERITE	PERFECT	PLUPERFECT
1. traje	he traído	había traído
2. trajiste	has traído	habías traído
3. trajo	ha traído	había traído
1. trajimos	hemos traído	habíamos traído
2. trajisteis	habéis traído	habíais traído
3. trajeron	han traído	habían traído

PAST ANTERIOR	FUTURE PERFECT
hube traído *etc*	habré traído *etc*

CONDITIONAL

IMPERATIVE

PRESENT	PAST	
1. traería	habría traído	
2. traerías	habrías traído	
3. traería	habría traído	(tú) trae
1. traeríamos	habríamos traído	(Vd) traiga
2. traeríais	habríais traído	(nosotros) traigamos
3. traerían	habrían traído	(vosotros) traed
		(Vds) traigan

SUBJUNCTIVE

PRESENT	IMPERFECT	PLUPERFECT
1. traiga	traj-era/ese	hubiera traído
2. traigas	traj-eras/eses	hubieras traído
3. traiga	traj-era/ese	hubiera traído
1. traigamos	traj-éramos/ésemos	hubiéramos traído
2. traigáis	traj-erais/eseis	hubierais traído
3. traigan	traj-eran/esen	hubieran traído

PERFECT	haya traído *etc*

INFINITIVE

PARTICIPLE

PRESENT	PRESENT
traer	trayendo

PAST	PAST
haber traído	traído

TRONAR
197 *to thunder*

PRESENT	**IMPERFECT**	**FUTURE**
3. truena	tronaba	tronará
PRETERITE	**PERFECT**	**PLUPERFECT**
3. tronó	ha tronado	había tronado
PAST ANTERIOR		**FUTURE PERFECT**
hubo tronado		habrá tronado

CONDITIONAL

PRESENT
3. tronaría

PAST
habría tronado

IMPERATIVE

SUBJUNCTIVE

PRESENT	**IMPERFECT**	**PLUPERFECT**
3. truene	tron-ara/ase	hubiera tronado
PERFECT haya tronado		

INFINITIVE

PRESENT
tronar

PAST
haber tronado

PARTICIPLE

PRESENT
tronando

PAST
tronado

PRESENT	IMPERFECT	FUTURE
1. tropiezo	tropezaba	tropezaré
2. tropiezas	tropezabas	tropezarás
3. tropieza	tropezaba	tropezará
1. tropezamos	tropezábamos	tropezaremos
2. tropezáis	tropezabais	tropezaréis
3. tropiezan	tropezaban	tropezarán

PRETERITE	PERFECT	PLUPERFECT
1. tropecé	he tropezado	había tropezado
2. tropezaste	has tropezado	habías tropezado
3. tropezó	ha tropezado	había tropezado
1. tropezamos	hemos tropezado	habíamos tropezado
2. tropezasteis	habéis tropezado	habíais tropezado
3. tropezaron	han tropezado	habían tropezado

PAST ANTERIOR	FUTURE PERFECT
hube tropezado *etc*	habré tropezado *etc*

CONDITIONAL

IMPERATIVE

PRESENT	PAST	
1. tropezaría	habría tropezado	
2. tropezarías	habrías tropezado	(tú) tropieza
3. tropezaría	habría tropezado	(Vd) tropiece
1. tropezaríamos	habríamos tropezado	(nosotros) tropecemos
2. tropezaríais	habríais tropezado	(vosotros) tropezad
3. tropezarían	habrían tropezado	(Vds) tropiecen

SUBJUNCTIVE

PRESENT	IMPERFECT	PLUPERFECT
1. tropiece	tropez-ara/ase	hubiera tropezado
2. tropieces	tropez-aras/ases	hubieras tropezado
3. tropiece	tropez-ara/ase	hubiera tropezado
1. tropecemos	tropez-áramos/ásemos	hubiéramos tropezado
2. tropecéis	tropez-arais/aseis	hubierais tropezado
3. tropiecen	tropez-aran/asen	hubieran tropezado

PERFECT haya tropezado *etc*

INFINITIVE

PARTICIPLE

PRESENT	PRESENT
tropezar	tropezando

PAST	PAST
haber tropezado	tropezado

PRESENT	**IMPERFECT**	**FUTURE**
1. vacío	vaciaba	vaciaré
2. vacías	vaciabas	vaciarás
3. vacía	vaciaba	vaciará
1. vaciamos	vaciábamos	vaciaremos
2. vaciáis	vaciabais	vaciaréis
3. vacían	vaciaban	vaciarán

PRETERITE	**PERFECT**	**PLUPERFECT**
1. vacié	he vaciado	había vaciado
2. vaciaste	has vaciado	habías vaciado
3. vació	ha vaciado	había vaciado
1. vaciamos	hemos vaciado	habíamos vaciado
2. vaciasteis	habéis vaciado	habíais vaciado
3. vaciaron	han vaciado	habían vaciado

PAST ANTERIOR		**FUTURE PERFECT**
hube vaciado *etc*		habré vaciado *etc*

CONDITIONAL

IMPERATIVE

PRESENT	**PAST**	
1. vaciaría	habría vaciado	
2. vaciarías	habrías vaciado	(tú) vacía
3. vaciaría	habría vaciado	(Vd) vacíe
1. vaciaríamos	habríamos vaciado	(nosotros) vaciemos
2. vaciaríais	habríais vaciado	(vosotros) vaciad
3. vaciarían	habrían vaciado	(Vds) vacíen

SUBJUNCTIVE

PRESENT	**IMPERFECT**	**PLUPERFECT**
1. vacíe	vaci-ara/ase	hubiera vaciado
2. vacíes	vaci-aras/ases	hubieras vaciado
3. vacíe	vaci-ara/ase	hubiera vaciado
1. vaciemos	vaci-áramos/ásemos	hubiéramos vaciado
2. vaciéis	vaci-arais/aseis	hubierais vaciado
3. vacíen	vaci-aran/asen	hubieran vaciado

PERFECT	haya vaciado *etc*

INFINITIVE

PARTICIPLE

PRESENT	**PRESENT**
vaciar	vaciando

PAST	**PAST**
haber vaciado	vaciado

PRESENT	IMPERFECT	FUTURE
1. valgo	valía	valdré
2. vales	valías	valdrás
3. vale	valía	valdrá
1. valemos	valíamos	valdremos
2. valéis	valíais	valdréis
3. valen	valían	valdrán

PRETERITE	PERFECT	PLUPERFECT
1. valí	he valido	había valido
2. valiste	has valido	habías valido
3. valió	ha valido	había valido
1. valimos	hemos valido	habíamos valido
2. valisteis	habéis valido	habíais valido
3. valieron	han valido	habían valido

PAST ANTERIOR		FUTURE PERFECT
hube valido *etc*		habré valido *etc*

CONDITIONAL

IMPERATIVE

PRESENT	PAST	
1. valdría	habría valido	
2. valdrías	habrías valido	
3. valdría	habría valido	(tú) vale
1. valdríamos	habríamos valido	(Vd) valga
2. valdríais	habríais valido	(nosotros) valgamos
3. valdrían	habrían valido	(vosotros) valed
		(Vds) valgan

SUBJUNCTIVE

PRESENT	IMPERFECT	PLUPERFECT
1. valga	val-iera/iese	hubiera valido
2. valgas	val-ieras/ieses	hubieras valido
3. valga	val-iera/iese	hubiera valido
1. valgamos	val-iéramos/iésemos	hubiéramos valido
2. valgáis	val-ierais/ieseis	hubierais valido
3. valgan	val-ieran/iesen	hubieran valido

PERFECT   haya valido *etc*

INFINITIVE

PARTICIPLE

PRESENT	PRESENT
valer	valiendo
PAST	PAST
haber valido	valido

VENCER
201 *to win; to defeat*

PRESENT	IMPERFECT	FUTURE
1. venzo	vencía	venceré
2. vences	vencías	vencerás
3. vence	vencía	vencerá
1. vencemos	vencíamos	venceremos
2. vencéis	vencíais	venceréis
3. vencen	vencían	vencerán

PRETERITE	PERFECT	PLUPERFECT
1. vencí	he vencido	había vencido
2. venciste	has vencido	habías vencido
3. venció	ha vencido	había vencido
1. vencimos	hemos vencido	habíamos vencido
2. vencisteis	habéis vencido	habíais vencido
3. vencieron	han vencido	habían vencido

PAST ANTERIOR		FUTURE PERFECT
hube vencido *etc*		habré vencido *etc*

CONDITIONAL

IMPERATIVE

PRESENT	PAST	
1. vencería	habría vencido	
2. vencerías	habrías vencido	(tú) vence
3. vencería	habría vencido	(Vd) venza
1. venceríamos	habríamos vencido	(nosotros) venzamos
2. venceríais	habríais vencido	(vosotros) venced
3. vencerían	habrían vencido	(Vds) venzan

SUBJUNCTIVE

PRESENT	IMPERFECT	PLUPERFECT
1. venza	venc-iera/iese	hubiera vencido
2. venzas	venc-ieras/ieses	hubieras vencido
3. venza	venc-iera/iese	hubiera vencido
1. venzamos	venc-iéramos/iésemos	hubiéramos vencido
2. venzáis	venc-ierais/ieseis	hubierais vencido
3. venzan	venc-ieran/iesen	hubieran vencido

PERFECT	haya vencido *etc*

INFINITIVE

PARTICIPLE

PRESENT	PRESENT
vencer	venciendo

PAST	PAST
haber vencido	vencido

PRESENT	IMPERFECT	FUTURE
1. vendo	vendía	venderé
2. vendes	vendías	venderás
3. vende	vendía	venderá
1. vendemos	vendíamos	venderemos
2. vendéis	vendíais	venderéis
3. venden	vendían	venderán

PRETERITE	PERFECT	PLUPERFECT
1. vendí	he vendido	había vendido
2. vendiste	has vendido	habías vendido
3. vendió	ha vendido	había vendido
1. vendimos	hemos vendido	habíamos vendido
2. vendisteis	habéis vendido	habíais vendido
3. vendieron	han vendido	habían vendido

PAST ANTERIOR		FUTURE PERFECT
hube vendido *etc*		habré vendido *etc*

CONDITIONAL

IMPERATIVE

PRESENT	PAST	IMPERATIVE
1. vendería	habría vendido	
2. venderías	habrías vendido	(tú) vende
3. vendería	habría vendido	(Vd) venda
1. venderíamos	habríamos vendido	(nosotros) vendamos
2. venderíais	habríais vendido	(vosotros) vended
3. venderían	habrían vendido	(Vds) vendan

SUBJUNCTIVE

PRESENT	IMPERFECT	PLUPERFECT
1. venda	vend-iera/iese	hubiera vendido
2. vendas	vend-ieras/ieses	hubieras vendido
3. venda	vend-iera/iese	hubiera vendido
1. vendamos	vend-iéramos/iésemos	hubiéramos vendido
2. vendáis	vend-ierais/ieseis	hubierais vendido
3. vendan	vend-ieran/iesen	hubieran vendido
PERFECT	haya vendido *etc*	

INFINITIVE

PARTICIPLE

PRESENT	PRESENT
vender	vendiendo

PAST	PAST
haber vendido	vendido

VENIR
203 *to come*

PRESENT	IMPERFECT	FUTURE
1. vengo	venía	vendré
2. vienes	venías	vendrás
3. viene	venía	vendrá
1. venimos	veníamos	vendremos
2. venís	veníais	vendréis
3. vienen	venían	vendrán

PRETERITE	PERFECT	PLUPERFECT
1. vine	he venido	había venido
2. viniste	has venido	habías venido
3. vino	ha venido	había venido
1. vinimos	hemos venido	habíamos venido
2. vinisteis	habéis venido	habíais venido
3. vinieron	han venido	habían venido

PAST ANTERIOR		FUTURE PERFECT
hube venido *etc*		habré venido *etc*

CONDITIONAL

IMPERATIVE

PRESENT	PAST	
1. vendría	habría venido	
2. vendrías	habrías venido	(tú) ven
3. vendría	habría venido	(Vd) venga
1. vendríamos	habríamos venido	(nosotros) vengamos
2. vendríais	habríais venido	(vosotros) venid
3. vendrían	habrían venido	(Vds) vengan

SUBJUNCTIVE

PRESENT	IMPERFECT	PLUPERFECT
1. venga	vin-iera/iese	hubiera venido
2. vengas	vin-ieras/ieses	hubieras venido
3. venga	vin-iera/iese	hubiera venido
1. vengamos	vin-iéramos/iésemos	hubiéramos venido
2. vengáis	vin-ierais/ieseis	hubierais venido
3. vengan	vin-ieran/iesen	hubieran venido

PERFECT	haya venido *etc*

INFINITIVE

PARTICIPLE

PRESENT	PRESENT
venir	viniendo

PAST	PAST
haber venido	venido

PRESENT	IMPERFECT	FUTURE
1. veo	veía	veré
2. ves	veías	verás
3. ve	veía	verá
1. vemos	veíamos	veremos
2. veis	veíais	veréis
3. ven	veían	verán

PRETERITE	PERFECT	PLUPERFECT
1. vi	he visto	había visto
2. viste	has visto	habías visto
3. vio	ha visto	había visto
1. vimos	hemos visto	habíamos visto
2. visteis	habéis visto	habíais visto
3. vieron	han visto	habían visto

PAST ANTERIOR	FUTURE PERFECT
hube visto _etc_	habré visto _etc_

CONDITIONAL

IMPERATIVE

PRESENT	PAST	
1. vería	habría visto	
2. verías	habrías visto	(tú) ve
3. vería	habría visto	(Vd) vea
1. veríamos	habríamos visto	(nosotros) veamos
2. veríais	habríais visto	(vosotros) ved
3. verían	habrían visto	(Vds) vean

SUBJUNCTIVE

PRESENT	IMPERFECT	PLUPERFECT
1. vea	v-iera/iese	hubiera visto
2. veas	v-ieras/ieses	hubieras visto
3. vea	v-iera/iese	hubiera visto
1. veamos	v-iéramos/iésemos	hubiéramos visto
2. veáis	v-ierais/ieseis	hubierais visto
3. vean	v-ieran/iesen	hubieran visto
PERFECT	haya visto _etc_	

INFINITIVE

PARTICIPLE

PRESENT	PRESENT
ver	viendo

PAST	PAST
haber visto	visto

VESTIRSE

to get dressed, to dress

PRESENT	**IMPERFECT**	**FUTURE**
1. me visto	me vestía	me vestiré
2. te vistes	te vestías	te vestirás
3. se viste	se vestía	se vestirá
1. nos vestimos	nos vestíamos	nos vestiremos
2. os vestís	os vestíais	os vestiréis
3. se visten	se vestían	se vestirán

PRETERITE	**PERFECT**	**PLUPERFECT**
1. me vestí	me he vestido	me había vestido
2. te vestiste	te has vestido	te habías vestido
3. se vistió	se ha vestido	se había vestido
1. nos vestimos	nos hemos vestido	nos habíamos vestido
2. os vestisteis	os habéis vestido	os habíais vestido
3. se vistieron	se han vestido	se habían vestido

PAST ANTERIOR	**FUTURE PERFECT**
me hube vestido *etc*	me habré vestido *etc*

CONDITIONAL

PRESENT	**PAST**
1. me vestiría	me habría vestido
2. te vestirías	te habrías vestido
3. se vestiría	se habría vestido
1. nos vestiríamos	nos habríamos vestido
2. os vestiríais	os habríais vestido
3. se vestirían	se habrían vestido

IMPERATIVE

(tú) vístete
(Vd) vístase
(nosotros) vistámonos
(vosotros) vestíos
(Vds) vístanse

SUBJUNCTIVE

PRESENT	**IMPERFECT**	**PLUPERFECT**
1. me vista	me vist-iera/iese	me hubiera vestido
2. te vistas	te vist-ieras/ieses	te hubieras vestido
3. se vista	se vist-iera/iese	se hubiera vestido
1. nos vistamos	nos vist-iéramos/iésemos	nos hubiéramos vestido
2. os vistáis	os vist-ierais/ieseis	os hubierais vestido
3. se vistan	se vist-ieran/iesen	se hubieran vestido

PERFECT me haya vestido *etc*

INFINITIVE

PRESENT
vestirse

PAST
haberse vestido

PARTICIPLE

PRESENT
vistiéndose

PAST
vestido

PRESENT
1. viajo
2. viajas
3. viaja
1. viajamos
2. viajáis
3. viajan

IMPERFECT
viajaba
viajabas
viajaba
viajábamos
viajabais
viajaban

FUTURE
viajaré
viajarás
viajará
viajaremos
viajaréis
viajarán

PRETERITE
1. viajé
2. viajaste
3. viajó
1. viajamos
2. viajasteis
3. viajaron

PERFECT
he viajado
has viajado
ha viajado
hemos viajado
habéis viajado
han viajado

PLUPERFECT
había viajado
habías viajado
había viajado
habíamos viajado
habíais viajado
habían viajado

PAST ANTERIOR
hube viajado *etc*

FUTURE PERFECT
habré viajado *etc*

CONDITIONAL

PRESENT
1. viajaría
2. viajarías
3. viajaría
1. viajaríamos
2. viajaríais
3. viajarían

PAST
habría viajado
habrías viajado
habría viajado
habríamos viajado
habríais viajado
habrían viajado

IMPERATIVE

(tú) viaja
(Vd) viaje
(nosotros) viajemos
(vosotros) viajad
(Vds) viajen

SUBJUNCTIVE

PRESENT
1. viaje
2. viajes
3. viaje
1. viajemos
2. viajéis
3. viajen

IMPERFECT
viaj-ara/ase
viaj-aras/ases
viaj-ara/ase
viaj-áramos/ásemos
viaj-arais/aseis
viaj-aran/asen

PLUPERFECT
hubiera viajado
hubieras viajado
hubiera viajado
hubiéramos viajado
hubierais viajado
hubieran viajado

PERFECT haya viajado *etc*

INFINITIVE

PRESENT
viajar

PAST
haber viajado

PARTICIPLE

PRESENT
viajando

PAST
viajado

PRESENT	IMPERFECT	FUTURE
1. vivo	vivía	viviré
2. vives	vivías	vivirás
3. vive	vivía	vivirá
1. vivimos	vivíamos	viviremos
2. vivís	vivíais	viviréis
3. viven	vivían	vivirán

PRETERITE	PERFECT	PLUPERFECT
1. viví	he vivido	había vivido
2. viviste	has vivido	habías vivido
3. vivió	ha vivido	había vivido
1. vivimos	hemos vivido	habíamos vivido
2. vivisteis	habéis vivido	habíais vivido
3. vivieron	han vivido	habían vivido

PAST ANTERIOR		FUTURE PERFECT
hube vivido *etc*		habré vivido *etc*

CONDITIONAL

IMPERATIVE

PRESENT	PAST	
1. viviría	habría vivido	
2. vivirías	habrías vivido	(tú) vive
3. viviría	habría vivido	(Vd) viva
1. viviríamos	habríamos vivido	(nosotros) vivamos
2. viviríais	habríais vivido	(vosotros) vivid
3. vivirían	habrían vivido	(Vds) vivan

SUBJUNCTIVE

PRESENT	IMPERFECT	PLUPERFECT
1. viva	viv-iera/iese	hubiera vivido
2. vivas	viv-ieras/ieses	hubieras vivido
3. viva	viv-iera/iese	hubiera vivido
1. vivamos	viv-iéramos/iésemos	hubiéramos vivido
2. viváis	viv-ierais/ieseis	hubierais vivido
3. vivan	viv-ieran/iesen	hubieran vivido
PERFECT	haya vivido *etc*	

INFINITIVE

PARTICIPLE

PRESENT	PRESENT
vivir	viviendo

PAST	PAST
haber vivido	vivido

PRESENT	**IMPERFECT**	**FUTURE**
1. vuelo	volaba	volaré
2. vuelas	volabas	volarás
3. vuela	volaba	volará
1. volamos	volábamos	volaremos
2. voláis	volabais	volaréis
3. vuelan	volaban	volarán

PRETERITE	**PERFECT**	**PLUPERFECT**
1. volé	he volado	había volado
2. volaste	has volado	habías volado
3. voló	ha volado	había volado
1. volamos	hemos volado	habíamos volado
2. volasteis	habéis volado	habíais volado
3. volaron	han volado	habían volado

PAST ANTERIOR		**FUTURE PERFECT**
hube volado *etc*		habré volado *etc*

CONDITIONAL		**IMPERATIVE**

PRESENT	**PAST**	
1. volaría	habría volado	
2. volarías	habrías volado	(tú) vuela
3. volaría	habría volado	(Vd) vuele
1. volaríamos	habríamos volado	(nosotros) volemos
2. volaríais	habríais volado	(vosotros) volad
3. volarían	habrían volado	(Vds) vuelen

SUBJUNCTIVE

PRESENT	**IMPERFECT**	**PLUPERFECT**
1. vuele	vol-ara/ase	hubiera volado
2. vueles	vol-aras/ases	hubieras volado
3. vuele	vol-ara/ase	hubiera volado
1. volemos	vol-áramos/ásemos	hubiéramos volado
2. voléis	vol-arais/aseis	hubierais volado
3. vuelen	vol-aran/asen	hubieran volado

PERFECT   haya volado *etc*

INFINITIVE	**PARTICIPLE**
PRESENT	**PRESENT**
volar	volando
PAST	**PAST**
haber volado	volado

PRESENT	IMPERFECT	FUTURE
1. vuelco	volcaba	volcaré
2. vuelcas	volcabas	volcarás
3. vuelca	volcaba	volcará
1. volcamos	volcábamos	volcaremos
2. volcáis	volcabais	volcaréis
3. vuelcan	volcaban	volcarán

PRETERITE	PERFECT	PLUPERFECT
1. volqué	he volcado	había volcado
2. volcaste	has volcado	habías volcado
3. volcó	ha volcado	había volcado
1. volcamos	hemos volcado	habíamos volcado
2. volcasteis	habéis volcado	habíais volcado
3. volcaron	han volcado	habían volcado

PAST ANTERIOR	FUTURE PERFECT
hube volcado *etc*	habré volcado *etc*

CONDITIONAL

IMPERATIVE

PRESENT	PAST	
1. volcaría	habría volcado	
2. volcarías	habrías volcado	(tú) vuelca
3. volcaría	habría volcado	(Vd) vuelque
1. volcaríamos	habríamos volcado	(nosotros) volquemos
2. volcaríais	habríais volcado	(vosotros) volcad
3. volcarían	habrían volcado	(Vds) vuelquen

SUBJUNCTIVE

PRESENT	IMPERFECT	PLUPERFECT
1. vuelque	volc-ara/ase	hubiera volcado
2. vuelques	volc-aras/ases	hubieras volcado
3. vuelque	volc-ara/ase	hubiera volcado
1. volquemos	volc-áramos/ásemos	hubiéramos volcado
2. volquéis	volc-arais/aseis	hubierais volcado
3. vuelquen	volc-aran/asen	hubieran volcado

PERFECT   haya volcado *etc*

INFINITIVE

PARTICIPLE

PRESENT	PRESENT
volcar	volcando

PAST	PAST
haber volcado	volcado

PRESENT	IMPERFECT	FUTURE
1. vuelvo	volvía	volveré
2. vuelves	volvías	volverás
3. vuelve	volvía	volverá
1. volvemos	volvíamos	volveremos
2. volvéis	volvíais	volveréis
3. vuelven	volvían	volverán

PRETERITE	PERFECT	PLUPERFECT
1. volví	he vuelto	había vuelto
2. volviste	has vuelto	habías vuelto
3. volvió	ha vuelto	había vuelto
1. volvimos	hemos vuelto	habíamos vuelto
2. volvisteis	habéis vuelto	habíais vuelto
3. volvieron	han vuelto	habían vuelto

PAST ANTERIOR		FUTURE PERFECT
hube vuelto *etc*		habré vuelto *etc*

CONDITIONAL

IMPERATIVE

PRESENT	PAST	
1. volvería	habría vuelto	
2. volverías	habrías vuelto	(tú) vuelve
3. volvería	habría vuelto	(Vd) vuelva
1. volveríamos	habríamos vuelto	(nosotros) volvamos
2. volveríais	habríais vuelto	(vosotros) volved
3. volverían	habrían vuelto	(Vds) vuelvan

SUBJUNCTIVE

PRESENT	IMPERFECT	PLUPERFECT
1. vuelva	volv-iera/iese	hubiera vuelto
2. vuelvas	volv-ieras/ieses	hubieras vuelto
3. vuelva	volv-iera/iese	hubiera vuelto
1. volvamos	volv-iéramos/iésemos	hubiéramos vuelto
2. volváis	volv-ierais/ieseis	hubierais vuelto
3. vuelvan	volv-ieran/iesen	hubieran vuelto

PERFECT	haya vuelto *etc*

INFINITIVE

PARTICIPLE

PRESENT	PRESENT
volver	volviendo

PAST	PAST
haber vuelto	vuelto

PRESENT	IMPERFECT	FUTURE
1. yazgo/yago/yazco	yacía	yaceré
2. yaces	yacías	yacerás
3. yace	yacía	yacerá
1. yacemos	yacíamos	yaceremos
2. yacéis	yacíais	yaceréis
3. yacen	yacían	yacerán

PRETERITE	PERFECT	PLUPERFECT
1. yací	he yacido	había yacido
2. yaciste	has yacido	habías yacido
3. yació	ha yacido	había yacido
1. yacimos	hemos yacido	habíamos yacido
2. yacisteis	habéis yacido	habíais yacido
3. yacieron	han yacido	habían yacido

PAST ANTERIOR		FUTURE PERFECT
hube yacido *etc*		habré yacido *etc*

CONDITIONAL

IMPERATIVE

PRESENT	PAST	
1. yacería	habría yacido	
2. yacerías	habrías yacido	
3. yacería	habría yacido	(tú) yace
1. yaceríamos	habríamos yacido	(Vd) yazga
2. yaceríais	habríais yacido	(nosotros) yazgamos
3. yacerían	habrían yacido	(vosotros) yaced
		(Vds) yazgan

SUBJUNCTIVE

PRESENT	IMPERFECT	PLUPERFECT
1. yazga	yac-iera/iese	hubiera yacido
2. yazgas	yac-ieras/ieses	hubieras yacido
3. yazga	yac-iera/iese	hubiera yacido
1. yazgamos	yac-iéramos/iésemos	hubiéramos yacido
2. yazgáis	yac-ierais/ieseis	hubierais yacido
3. yazgan	yac-ieran/iesen	hubieran yacido

PERFECT	haya yacido *etc*	

INFINITIVE	PARTICIPLE	NOTE
PRESENT	**PRESENT**	Present subjunctive:
yacer	yaciendo	The following forms are also found:
PAST	**PAST**	
haber yacido	yacido	**yazca/yaga**

230

PRESENT	IMPERFECT	FUTURE
1. zurzo	zurcía	zurciré
2. zurces	zurcías	zurcirás
3. zurce	zurcía	zurcirá
1. zurcimos	zurcíamos	zurciremos
2. zurcís	zurcíais	zurciréis
3. zurcen	zurcían	zurcirán

PRETERITE	PERFECT	PLUPERFECT
1. zurcí	he zurcido	había zurcido
2. zurciste	has zurcido	habías zurcido
3. zurció	ha zurcido	había zurcido
1. zurcimos	hemos zurcido	habíamos zurcido
2. zurcisteis	habéis zurcido	habíais zurcido
3. zurcieron	han zurcido	habían zurcido

PAST ANTERIOR
hube zurcido *etc*

FUTURE PERFECT
habré zurcido *etc*

CONDITIONAL

IMPERATIVE

PRESENT	PAST	
1. zurciría	habría zurcido	
2. zurcirías	habrías zurcido	(tú) zurce
3. zurciría	habría zurcido	(Vd) zurza
1. zurciríamos	habríamos zurcido	(nosotros) zurzamos
2. zurciríais	habríais zurcido	(vosotros) zurcid
3. zurcirían	habrían zurcido	(Vds) zurzan

SUBJUNCTIVE

PRESENT	IMPERFECT	PLUPERFECT
1. zurza	zurc-iera/iese	hubiera zurcido
2. zurzas	zurc-ieras/ieses	hubieras zurcido
3. zurza	zurc-iera/iese	hubiera zurcido
1. zurzamos	zurc-iéramos/iésemos	hubiéramos zurcido
2. zurzáis	zurc-ierais/ieseis	hubierais zurcido
3. zurzan	zurc-ieran/iesen	hubieran zurcido

PERFECT   haya zurcido *etc*

INFINITIVE

PARTICIPLE

PRESENT	PRESENT
zurcir	zurciendo

PAST	PAST
haber zurcido	zurcido

INDEX OF SPANISH VERBS

The verbs given in full in the tables on the preceding pages are used as models for all other Spanish verbs given in this index. The number in the index is that of the corresponding verb table, rather than the page number.

The index also contains irregular verb forms. These are each referred to the respective infinitive form of the same verb.

All verbs in this index have been referred to model verbs with corresponding features wherever possible. Most reflexive verbs have been referred to reflexive model verbs. However, if this model is not reflexive, the reflexive pronouns have to be added.

A verb shown in blue is itself given as a model.

Note that in the Spanish alphabet, 'ñ' comes after 'n' in alphabetical order.

A

abalanzar 12
abandonar 1
abanicar 23
abaratar 112
abarcar 23
abarrotar 112
abastecer 60
abatir 207
abdicar 23
abierto *see* **abrir**
ablandar 112
abochornar 112
abofetear 147
abolir 2

abollar 112
abominar 112
abonar 112
abordar 112
aborrecer 3
abortar 112
abotonar 112
abrasar 112
abrazar 62
abreviar 17
abrigar 38
abrir 4
abrochar 112
abrumar 112
absolver 210

absorber 45
abstenerse 189
abstraer 196
abultar 112
abundar 112
aburrir 207
abusar 112
acabar 5
acalorarse 32
acampar 112
acaparar 112
acariciar 17
acarrear 147
acatar 112
acatarrarse 32

acaudalar 112
acaudillar 112
acceder 45
accionar 112
aceitar 112
acelerar 112
acentuar 6
aceptar 112
acercarse 7
acertar 149
achacar 174
achicar 174
achicharrar 112
acicalar 112
aclamar 112
aclarar 112
aclimatar 112
acobardar 112
acoger 42
acolchar 112
acometer 45
acomodar 112
acompañar 112
acomplejar 31
acondicionar 112
aconsejar 31
acontecer 60
acoplar 112
acordarse 8
acorralar 112
acortar 112
acosar 112
acostarse 8
acostumbrar 112
acrecentar 149
acreditar 112
acribillar 112
activar 112
actualizar 62

actuar 6
acuciar 17
acudir 207
acuerdo *see* **acordarse**
acumular 112
acunar 112
acuñar 112
acurrucar 112
acusar 112
adaptar 112
adecuar 112
adelantar 112
adelgazar 62
adeudar 112
adherir 116
adiestrar 112
adivinar 112
adjudicar 174
adjuntar 112
administrar 112
admirar 112
admitir 207
adoptar 112
adorar 112
adormecer 60
adornar 112
adosar 112
adquiero *see* **adquirir**
adquirir 9
adscribir 99
aducir 195
adueñarse 32
adular 112
adulterar 112
advertir 180
afear 147
afectar 112
afeitar 112
aferrar 112

afianzar 62
aficionar 112
afilar 112
afiliar 17
afinar 112
afirmar 112
afligir 76
aflojar 31
afrentar 112
afrontar 112
agachar 112
agarrar 112
agarrotar 112
agasajar 31
agitar 112
aglomerarse 32
agobiar 17
agolparse 32
agonizar 62
agorar 10
agotar 112
agradar 112
agradecer 11
agrandar 112
agravar 112
agraviar 17
agredir 207
agregar 38
agriar 95
agrietarse 32
agrupar 112
aguantar 112
aguardar 112
aguijonear 147
agujerear 147
ahogar 38
ahorcar 174
ahorrar 112
ahuecar 174

ahumar 112
ahuyentar 112
airear 147
aislar 95
ajar 112
ajustar 112
ajusticiar 112
alabar 112
alardear 147
alargar 38
albergar 38
alborotar 112
alcanzar 12
aleccionar 112
alegar 38
alegrar 112
alejar 112
alentar 149
aletargar 38
alfombrar 112
aliarse 95
aligerar 112
alimentar 112
alinear 147
aliñar 112
alisar 112
alistar 112
aliviar 112
allanar 112
almacenar 112
almidonar 112
almorzar 13
alojar 112
alquilar 112
alterar 112
alternar 112
alucinar 112
aludir 207
alumbrar 112

alunizar 62
alzar 62
amaestrar 112
amainar 112
amalgamar 112
amamantar 112
amanecer 14
amansar 112
amar 112
amargar 38
amarrar 112
amartillar 112
ambicionar 112
amedrentar 112
amenazar 62
amilanar 112
aminorar 112
amodorrar 112
amoldar 112
amonestar 112
amontonar 112
amordazar 62
amortajar 112
amortiguar 30
amortizar 62
amotinar 112
amparar 112
ampliar 95
amputar 112
amueblar 112
amurallar 112
analizar 62
anclar 112

andar 15
anduve see **andar**
anexionar 112
angustiar 112
anhelar 112
anidar 112

animar 112
aniquilar 112
anochecer 16
anotar 112
ansiar 95
anteponer 153
anticipar 112
antojarse 32
anudar 112
anular 112
anunciar 17
añadir 207
apaciguar 30
apadrinar 112
apagar 38
apalear 147
aparcar 174
aparecer 18
aparejar 31
aparentar 112
apartar 112
apasionar 112
apearse 147
apedrear 147
apelar 112
apellidarse 32
apenar 112
apestar 112
apetecer 19
apiadarse 32
apiñar 112
apisonar 112
aplacar 174
aplanar 112
aplastar 112
aplaudir 207
aplazar 62
aplicar 174
apodar 112

apoderarse 32
aportar 112
apostar 59
apoyar 112
apreciar 17
apremiar 17
aprender 45
apresar 112
apresurar 112
apretar 20
aprieto *see* **apretar**
aprisionar 112
aprobar 21
apropiarse 32
aprovechar 112
aproximar 112
apruebo *see* **aprobar**
apuntalar 112
apuntar 112
apuñalar 112
aquejar 31
arañar 112
arar 112
arbitrar 112
archivar 112
arder 45
arengar 38
argüir 22
argumentar 112
armar 112
armonizar 62
arquear 147
arraigar 38
arrancar 23
arranqué *see* **arrancar**
arrasar 112
arrastrar 112
arrear 147
arrebatar 112

arreglar 24
arremangar 38
arremeter 45
arrendar 149
arrepentirse 180
arrestar 112
arriar 95
arriesgar 38
arrimar 112
arrinconar 112
arrodillarse 32
arrojar 31
arropar 112
arrugar 38
arruinar 112
arrullar 114
articular 112
asaltar 112
asar 112
ascender 25
asciendo *see* **ascender**
asear 147
asediar 17
asegurar 112
asemejarse 32
asentar 149
asentir 180
asesinar 112
asfixiar 112
asgo *see* **asir**
asignar 112
asimilar 112
asir 26
asistir 207
asociar 17
asolar 112
asomar 112
asombrar 112
aspirar 112

asquear 147
asumir 207
asustar 112
atacar 174
atañer 188
atar 112
atardecer 60
atarear 147
atascar 174
ataviar 95
atemorizar 62
atender 93
atenerse 189
atentar 112
atenuar 6
aterrar 112
aterrizar 27
aterrorizar 62
atesorar 112
atestar 112
atestiguar 30
atiborrar 112
atizar 62
atontar 112
atormentar 112
atornillar 114
atracar 174
atraer 196
atragantarse 32
atrancar 174
atrapar 112
atrasar 112
atravesar 28
atreverse 45
atribuir 74
atrofiar 17
atropellar 114
aturdir 207
augurar 112

aullar 6
aumentar 112
aunar 6
ausentarse 32
automatizar 62
autorizar 62
auxiliar 17
avalar 112
avanzar 62
avasallar 114
avenirse 203
aventajar 31
avergonzarse 29
avergüenzo *see*
    avergonzarse
averiar 95
averiguar 30
avinagrarse 32
avisar 112
avituallar 114
avivar 112
ayudar 112
ayunar 112
azotar 112
azuzar 62

B
babear 147
bailar 112
bajar 31
balancear 147
balar 112
balbucear 147
bambolearse 32
bañarse 32
barajar 31
barnizar 62
barrer 45
barruntar 112

basar 112
bastar 112
batallar 114
batir 207
bautizar 62
beber 33
bendecir 34
bendigo *see* **bendecir**
bendije *see* **bendecir**
beneficiar 17
berrear 147
besar 112
bifurcar 174
birlar 112
bizquear 147
blandir 207
blanquear 147
blasfemar 112
blindar 112
bloquear 147
boicotear 147
bombardear 147
bordar 112
bordear 147
borrar 112
bosquejar 31
bostezar 62
botar 112
boxear 147
bracear 147
bramar 112
brillar 114
brincar 174
brindar 112
bromear 147
broncearse 32
brotar 112
bucear 147
burlar 112

buscar 35
busqué *see* **buscar**

C
cabalgar 38
cabecear 147
caber 36
cacarear 147
cacé *see* **cazar**
cachear 147
caducar 174
caer 37
caigo *see* **caer**
calar 112
calcar 174
calcinar 112
calcular 112
caldear 147
calentar 149
calibrar 112
calificar 174
callarse 32
callejear 147
calmar 112
calumniar 17
calzar 62
cambiar 17
camelar 112
caminar 112
camuflar 112
canalizar 62
cancelar 112
cansar 112
cantar 112
capar 112
capitalizar 62
capitanear 147
capitular 112
captar 112

capturar 112
caracterizar 62
carbonizar 62
carcomer 45
carecer 60
cargar 38
cargué *see* **cargar**
casarse 32
cascar 174
castigar 38
castrar 112
catar 112
causar 112
cautivar 112
cavar 112
cavilar 112
cayó *see* **caer**
cazar 39
cebar 112
cecear 147
ceder 45
cegar 138
cejar 31
celebrar 112
cementar 112
cenar 112
censurar 112
centellear 147
centralizar 62
centrar 112
centrifugar 38
ceñir 167
cepillar 114
cercar 174
cerciorarse 32
cerner 93
cerrar 40
certificar 174
cesar 112

chamuscar 174
chantajear 147
chapotear 147
chapurrear 147
chapuzar 62
charlar 112
chequear 147
chiflar 112
chillar 114
chirriar 95
chispear 147
chisporrotear 147
chocar 174
chochear 147
chorrear 147
chupar 112
cicatrizar 62
cierro *see* **cerrar**
cifrar 112
cimentar 149
cinchar 112
circular 112
circuncidar 112
circundar 112
circunscribir 99
citar 112
civilizar 62
clamar 112
clarear 147
clarificar 174
clasificar 174
claudicar 174
clavar 112
coartar 112
cobijar 17
cobrar 112
cocear 147
cocer 41
cocinar 112

codearse 147
codiciar 17
codificar 174
coexistir 207
coger 42
cohabitar 112
cohibir 156
coincidir 207
cojear 147
cojo *see* **coger**
colaborar 112
colar 59
colear 147
coleccionar 112
colegir 83
colgar 43
colmar 112
colocar 174
colonizar 62
colorear 147
columpiar 17
comadrear 147
combatir 207
combinar 112
comedir 148
comentar 112
comenzar 44
comer 45
comercializar 62
comerciar 17
cometer 45
comisionar 112
compadecer 60
comparar 112
comparecer 60
compartir 207
compensar 112
competer 46
competir 148

INDEX OF SPANISH VERBS

complacer 135
completar 112
complicar 174
componer 153
comportarse 32
comprar 47
comprender 45
comprimir 207
comprobar 155
comprometer 45
computar 112
comulgar 38
comunicar 174
concebir 48
conceder 45
concentrar 112
concernir 49
concertar 149
concibo see concebir
concierne see concernir
conciliar 17
concluir 74
concordar 8
concretar 112
concurrir 207
condecorar 112
condenar 112
condensar 112
condescender 71
conducir 50
conduje see conducir
conduzco see conducir
conectar 112
confeccionar 112
conferir 180
confesar 149
confiar 95
configurar 112
confinar 112

confirmar 112
confiscar 174
conformarse 32
confortar 112
confrontar 112
confundir 207
congelar 112
congeniar 17
congratular 112
conjugar 38
conmemorar 112
conmover 134
conocer 51
conozco see conocer
conquistar 112
consagrar 112
conseguir 178
consentir 180
conservar 112
considerar 112
consistir 207
consolar 52
consolidar 112
conspirar 112
constar 112
constiparse 32
constituir 74
construir 53
construyo
   see construir
consuelo see consolar
consultar 112
consumar 112
consumir 207
contagiar 17
contaminar 112
contar 54
contemplar 112
contender 93

contener 189
contentar 112
contestar 55
continuar 56
contradecir 67
contraer 196
contrapesar 112
contrariar 95
contrarrestar 112
contrastar 112
contratar 112
contravenir 203
contribuir 74
controlar 112
convalecer 60
convencer 201
convenir 203
converger 42
conversar 112
convertir 180
convidar 112
convocar 174
cooperar 112
coordinar 112
copiar 17
coquetear 147
coronar 112
corregir 57
correr 58
corresponder 45
corrijo see corregir
corroborar 112
corroer 170
corromper 45
cortar 112
cortejar 31
cosechar 112
coser 45
costar 59

cotejar 31
cotizar 62
crear 147
crecer 60
creer 61
creyó see **creer**
crezco see **crecer**
criar 95
cribar 112
crispar 112
cristalizar 62
criticar 174
crucé see **cruzar**
crucificar 174
crujir 207
cruzar 62
cuadrar 112
cuajar 31
cubierto see **cubrir**
cubrir 63
cuchichear 147
cuelgo see **colgar**
cuento see **contar**
cuesta see **costar**
cuezo see **cocer**
cuidar 112
culebrear 147
culpar 112
cultivar 112
cumplimentar 112
cumplir 207
cupe see **caber**
cupieron see **caber**
cupimos see **caber**
cupiste see **caber**
curar 112
curiosear 147
cursar 112
custodiar 17

D
damnificar 174
danzar 62
dañar 112
dar 64
datar 112
deambular 112
debatir 207
deber 65
debilitar 112
debutar 112
decaer 37
decapitar 112
decepcionar 112
decidir 66
decir 67
declamar 112
declarar 112
declinar 112
decolorar 112
decorar 112
decretar 112
dedicar 174
deducir 195
defender 93
definir 207
deformar 112
defraudar 112
degenerar 112
degollar 68
degradar 112
dejar 69
delatar 112
delegar 38
deleitar 112
deletrear 147
deliberar 112
delinquir 70
delirar 112

demandar 112
democratizar 62
demoler 134
demorar 112
demostrar 59
denegar 138
denigrar 112
denominar 112
denotar 112
denunciar 17
depender 45
deplorar 112
deponer 153
deportar 112
depositar 112
depravar 112
depreciar 17
deprimir 207
depurar 112
derivar 112
derramar 112
derretir 148
derribar 112
derrocar 174
derrochar 112
derrotar 112
derrumbar 112
desabotonar 112
desabrochar 112
desaconsejar 31
desacreditar 112
desafiar 95
desafinar 112
desagradar 112
desagraviar 17
desahogar 38
desahuciar 17
desairar 112
desajustar 112

desalentar 149
desalojar 31
desamparar 112
desandar 15
desanimar 112
desaparecer 18
desaprobar 21
desaprovechar 112
desarmar 112
desarraigar 38
desarrollar 114
desarticular 112
desasir 26
desatar 112
desatender 93
desatornillar 114
desautorizar 62
desayunar 112
desbandar 112
desbaratar 112
desbordar 112
descabalgar 38
descabezar 62
descalzar 62
descansar 112
descargar 38
descarriar 95
descartar 112
descender 71
descendiendo
    see **descender**
descifrar 112
descolgar 43
descolorirse 207
descomponer 153
desconcertar 149
desconectar 112
desconfiar 95
desconocer 51

desconsolar 52
descontar 54
descorchar 112
descorrer 58
descoser 207
descoyuntar 112
describir 99
descubierto
    see **descubrir**
descubrir 72
descuidar 112
desdecir 67
desdeñar 112
desdoblar 112
desear 147
desechar 112
desembarazar 62
desembarcar 84
desembocar 174
desempeñar 112
desencadenar 112
desencajar 31
desengañar 112
desenredar 112
desentenderse 93
desenterrar 149
desentrañar 112
desentumecer 60
desenvolver 210
desertar 149
desesperar 101
desfallecer 60
desfigurar 112
desfilar 112
desgajar 31
desgañitarse 32
desgarrar 112
desgastar 112
desgravar 112

desguazar 62
deshacer 113
deshelar 115
desheredar 112
deshilar 112
deshilvanar 112
deshinchar 112
deshonrar 112
designar 112
desilusionar 112
desinfectar 112
desinflar 112
desistir 207
desligar 38
deslizar 62
deslumbrar 112
desmandarse 32
desmantelar 112
desmayarse 32
desmejorar 112
desmentir 130
desmenuzar 62
desmontar 112
desmoralizar 62
desmoronarse 32
desnudar 112
desobedecer 140
desocupar 112
desolar 112
desorientar 112
despabilar 112
despachar 112
desparramar 112
despedazar 62
despedir 148
despegar 38
despeinar 112
despejar 31
despenalizar 62

despertarse 73
despierto *see*
  despertarse
despistar 112
desplegar 138
despoblar 155
despojar 31
desposeer 125
despreciar 17
desprender 45
despreocuparse 32
destacar 174
destapar 112
desteñir 167
desterrar 149
destilar 112
destinar 112
destituir 74
destornillar 114
destrozar 62
destruir 74
destruye *see* **destruir**
desunir 207
desvanecer 60
desvariar 95
desvelar 112
desviar 95
desvivirse 207
detallar 114
detener 189
deteriorar 112
determinar 112
detestar 112
detonar 112
devolver 210
devorar 112
di *see* **decir, dar**
dibujar 31
dice *see* **decir**

dicho *see* **decir**
dictar 112
dieron *see* **dar**
diferenciar 17
dificultar 112
difundir 186
diga *see* **decir**
digerir 75
dignarse 32
digo *see* **decir**
dije *see* **decir**
dilatar 112
diluir 74
dimitir 207
diré *see* **decir**
dirigir 76
dirijo *see* **dirigir**
discernir 77
discierno *see* **discernir**
disciplinar 112
discrepar 112
disculpar 112
discurrir 207
discutir 207
disecar 174
diseminar 112
diseñar 112
disfrazar 62
disfrutar 112
disgustar 110
disimular 112
disipar 112
disminuir 74
disolver 210
disparar 112
dispensar 112
dispersar 112
disponer 153
disputar 112

distanciar 17
diste *see* **dar**
distingo *see* **distinguir**
distinguir 78
distraer 196
distribuir 74
disuadir 207
divagar 38
diversificar 174
divertirse 79
dividir 207
divierto *see* **divertirse**
divorciarse 32
divulgar 38
doblar 112
doblegar 38
doler 80
domar 112
domesticar 174
dominar 112
dormir 81
dotar 112
doy *see* **dar**
drogar 38
ducharse 32
dudar 112
duele *see* **doler**
duermo *see* **dormir**
duplicar 174
durar 112

E
echar 112
editar 112
educar 82
efectuar 6
ejecutar 112
ejercer 201
elaborar 112

electrizar 62
electrocutar 112
elegir 83
elevar 112
elijo *see* **elegir**
eliminar 112
elogiar 17
eludir 207
emanar 112
emancipar 112
embadurnar 112
embalar 112
embarazar 62
embarcar 84
embargar 38
embarqué
   see **embarcar**
embellecer 60
embestir 205
embobar 112
embolsar 112
emborrachar 112
embotar 112
embotellar 114
embragar 38
embravecer 60
embriagar 38
embrollar 114
embrutecer 60
embutir 207
emerger 175
emigrar 112
emitir 207
emocionar 112
empalmar 112
empañar 112
empapar 112
empapelar 112
empaquetar 112

empastar 112
empatar 112
empeñar 112
empeorar 112
empequeñecer 60
empezar 85
empiezo *see* **empezar**
empinar 112
emplazar 62
emplear 147
empotrar 112
emprender 45
empujar 86
empuñar 112
emular 112
enamorarse 32
enardecer 60
encabezar 62
encadenar 112
encajar 31
encaminar 112
encantar 112
encaramar 112
encarcelar 112
encarecer 60
encargar 38
encauzar 62
encender 87
encerrar 40
enchufar 112o
enciendo *see* **encender**
encoger 42
encolar 112
encolerizar 62
encomendar 149
encontrar 88
encorvar 112
encrespar 112
encubrir 63

encuentro *see*
   encontrar
enderezar 62
endeudarse 32
endosar 112
endulzar 62
endurecer 60
enemistar 112
enfadarse 32
enfermar 112
enflaquecer 60
enfocar 174
enfrentar 112
enfriar 89
enfurecerse 90
enfurezco
   see **enfurecerse**
enganchar 112
engañar 112
engatusar 112
engendrar 112
engordar 112
engrasar 112
engreírse 165
engrosar 112
enhebrar 112
enjabonar 112
enjaular 112
enjuagar 38
enlazar 62
enloquecer 60
enlutar 112
enmarañar 112
enmascarar 112
enmendar 149
enmohecer 60
enmudecer 91
enmudezco
   see **enmudecer**

ennegrecer 60
ennoblecer 60
enojar 31
enorgullecerse 90
enraizar 92
enredar 112
enriquecer 60
enrojecer 60
enrollar 114
enroscar 174
ensalzar 62
ensanchar 112
ensangrentar 112
ensañarse 32
ensayar 112
enseñar 112
ensillar 114
ensimismar 112
ensordecer 60
ensortijar 31
ensuciar 17
entablar 112
entallar 114
entender 93
enterarse 32
enternecer 60
enterrar 149
entibiar 17
entiendo *see* **entender**
entonar 112
entornar 112
entorpecer 60
entrar 94
entreabrir 4
entregar 38
entrelazar 62
entremezclar 112
entrenar 112
entreoír 143

entretener 189
entrever 204
entrevistar 112
entristecer 60
entrometer 45
entumecer 60
enturbiar 17
entusiasmar 112
enumerar 112
enunciar 17
envanecerse 90
envasar 112
envejecer 60
envenenar 112
enviar 95
envidiar 112
envilecer 60
enviudar 112
envolver 210
equilibrar 112
equipar 112
equivaler 200
equivocarse 96
era *see* **ser**
erguir 97
erigir 76
erizar 62
erradicar 174
errar 98
eructar 137
es *see* **ser**
escabullirse 109
escalar 112
escampar 112
escandalizar 62
escapar 112
escarbar 112
escarmentar 149
escasear 147

escatimar 112
esclarecer 60
esclavizar 62
escocer 41
escoger 42
escoltar 112
esconder 45
escribir 99
escrito *see* **escribir**
escrutar 112
escuchar 112
escudar 112
escudriñar 112
esculpir 207
escupir 207
escurrir 207
esforzarse 100
esfuerzo *see* **esforzarse**
esfumarse 32
esmaltar 112
esmerarse 32
espabilar 112
espaciar 17
espantar 112
esparcir 212
especificar 174
especular 112
esperar 101
espesar 112
espiar 95
espirar 112
espolear 147
espolvorear 147
esponjar 31
esposar 112
esquematizar 62
esquilar 112
esquivar 112
establecer 60

estacionar 112
estafar 112
estallar 114
estampar 112
estancar 174
estandarizar 62
estar 102
esterilizar 62
estilarse 32
estimar 112
estimular 112
estipular 112
estirar 112
estofar 112
estorbar 112
estornudar 112
estoy *see* **estar**
estrangular 112
estrechar 112
estrellar 114
estremecer 60
estrenar 112
estreñir 167
estribar 112
estropear 147
estructurar 112
estrujar 31
estudiar 17
evacuar 103
evadir 207
evaluar 6
evaporar 112
evitar 112
evocar 174
evolucionar 112
exacerbar 112
exagerar 112
exaltar 112
examinar 112

exasperar 112
exceder 45
exceptuar 6
excitar 112
exclamar 112
excluir 74
excomulgar 38
excusar 112
exhalar 112
exhibir 207
exhortar 112
exigir 104
exijo *see* **exigir**
existir 207
exonerar 112
expansionar 112
expatriar 17
expedir 148
experimentar 112
expiar 95
expirar 112
explayarse 32
explicar 105
expliqué *see* **explicar**
explorar 112
explosionar 112
explotar 112
exponer 153
exportar 112
expresar 112
exprimir 207
expropiar 17
expulsar 112
expurgar 38
extender 93
extenuar 6
exterminar 112
extinguir 78
extirpar 112

extraer 196
extrañar 112
extraviar 95
extremar 112
eyacular 112

F
fabricar 174
facilitar 112
facturar 112
fallar 114
fallecer 60
falsificar 174
faltar 112
familiarizar 62
fascinar 112
fastidiar 17
fatigar 38
favorecer 60
fecundar 112
felicitar 112
fermentar 112
fertilizar 62
festejar 31
fiarse 95
fichar 112
figurar 112
fijar 31
filmar 112
filtrar 112
finalizar 62
financiar 17
fingir 76
firmar 112
fisgar 38
flirtear 147
florecer 60
flotar 112
fluctuar 6

fluir 74
fomentar 112
forjar 31
formalizar 62
formar 112
forrar 112
fortalecer 60
forzar 13
fotocopiar 17
fotografiar 95
fracasar 112
fraccionar 112
fraguar 30
franquear 147
fregar 106
freír 107
frenar 112
friego *see* **fregar**
frío *see* **freír**
frotar 112
fruncir 212
frustrar 112
fue *see* **ser, ir**
fuera *see* **ser, ir**
fuéramos *see* **ser, ir**
fueron *see* **ser, ir**
fugarse 38
fui *see* **ser, ir**
fulminar 112
fumar 112
funcionar 112
fundar 112
fundir 186
fusilar 112

G
galopar 112
ganar 112
garantizar 62

gastar 112
gatear 147
gemir 108
generalizar 62
generar 112
germinar 112
gestionar 112
gimo *see* **gemir**
gimotear 147
girar 112
glorificar 174
glosar 112
gobernar 40
golpear 147
gorjear 147
gotear 147
gozar 62
grabar 112
graduar 6
granizar 62
granjear 147
gravar 112
gravitar 112
graznar 112
gritar 112
gruñir 109
guardar 112
guarnecer 60
guasear 147
guerrear 147
guiar 95
guiñar 112
guisar 112
gustar 110

H
ha *see* **haber**
haber 111
habilitar 112

habitar 112
habituarse 6
hablar 112
habré *see* **haber**
habremos *see* **haber**
habría *see* **haber**
hacer 113
hacinar 112
hago *see* **hacer**
halagar 38
hallarse 114
han *see* **haber**
haré *see* **hacer**
hartar 112
has *see* **haber**
hastiar 95
hay *see* **haber**
haya *see* **haber**
haz *see* **hacer**
he *see* **haber**
hechizar 62
hecho *see* **hacer**
heder 93
helar 115
hemos *see* **haber**
heredar 112
herir 116
hermanar 112
herrar 149
hervir 116
hice *see* **hacer**
hiela *see* **helar**
hiere *see* **herir**
hilar 112
hilvanar 112
hincar 174
hinchar 112
hipar 112
hipnotizar 62

hizo *see* **hacer**
hojear 147
hollar 59
homogeneizar 62
honrar 112
horadar 112
horripilar 112
horrorizar 62
hospedar 112
hospitalizar 62
hostigar 38
hube *see* **haber**
hubieron *see* **haber**
huelo *see* **oler**
huir 117
humanizar 62
humear 147
humedecer 60
humillar 114
hundir 186
hurgar 38
hurtar 112
husmear 147
huyo *see* **huir**

I
idealizar 62
idear 147
identificar 174
ignorar 112
igualar 112
iluminar 112
ilustrar 112
imaginar 112
imitar 112
impartir 207
impedir 148
impeler 45
imperar 112

implicar 174
implorar 112
imponer 153
importar 112
importunar 112
imposibilitar 112
imprecar 174
impregnar 112
impresionar 112
imprimir 207
improvisar 112
impugnar 112
impulsar 112
imputar 112
inaugurar 112
incapacitar 112
incautar 112
incendiar 17
incidir 66
incinerar 112
incitar 112
inclinar 112
incluir 74
incomodar 112
incorporar 112
increpar 112
incrustar 112
incubar 112
inculcar 174
inculpar 112
incurrir 186
indagar 38
indemnizar 62
indicar 118
indignar 112
inducir 195
indultar 112
industrializar 62
infectar 112

inferir 180
infestar 112
inflamar 112
inflar 112
infligir 76
influenciar 17
influir 74
informar 112
infringir 76
infundir 186
ingeniar 17
ingerir 180
ingresar 112
inhibir 207
iniciar 17
injertar 112
injuriar 17
inmiscuirse 74
inmolar 112
inmortalizar 62
inmutar 112
innovar 112
inquietar 112
inquirir 9
inscribir 99
insertar 112
insinuar 6
insistir 207
insonorizar 62
inspeccionar 112
inspirar 112
instalar 112
instar 112
instigar 38
instituir 74
instruir 74
insubordinarse 32
insultar 112
integrar 112

intentar 119
intercalar 112
interceder 45
interesar 112
interferir 116
internar 112
interpelar 112
interponer 153
interpretar 112
interrogar 38
interrumpir 186
intervenir 203
intimar 112
intrigar 38
introducir 120
introduzco
   see **introducir**
inundar 112
inutilizar 62
invadir 207
inventar 112
invertir 180
investigar 38
invitar 112
invocar 174
inyectar 112
ir 121
irrigar 38
irritar 112
irrumpir 186
izar 62

J
jabonar 112
jactarse 32
jadear 147
jubilarse 32
juego see **jugar**
juegue see **jugar**

jugar 122
juntar 112
jurar 112
justificar 174
juzgar 123

L
labrar 112
lacrar 112
ladear 147
ladrar 112
lamentar 112
lamer 45
laminar 112
languidecer 60
lanzar 62
lapidar 112
largar 38
lastimar 112
latir 207
lavar 124
leer 125
legalizar 62
legar 38
legislar 112
legitimar 112
lesionar 112
levantar 112
leyó see **leer**
liar 95
libar 112
liberar 112
libertar 112
librar 112
licenciar 17
licuar 112
lidiar 17
ligar 38
limar 112

limitar 112
limpiar 17
linchar 112
liquidar 112
lisiar 17
lisonjear 147
litigar 38
llamar 126
llamear 147
llegar 127
llenar 112
llevar 112
llorar 112
lloriquear 147
llover 128
lloviznar 112
llueve see **llover**
localizar 62
lograr 112
lubricar 174
luchar 112
lucir 129
lustrar 112
luzco see **lucir**

M
macerar 112
machacar 174
madrugar 38
madurar 112
magnetizar 62
magullar 114
maldecir 67
malgastar 112
malograr 112
maltratar 112
malversar 112
malvivir 207
mamar 112

manar 112
manchar 112
mandar 112
manejar 31
mangonear 147
maniatar 112
manifestar 149
maniobrar 112
manipular 112
manosear 147
mantener 189
maquillar 114
maquinar 112
maravillar 114
marcar 174
marcharse 32
marchitar 112
marear 147
marginar 112
martillear 147
martirizar 62
mascar 174
mascullar 114
masticar 174
matar 112
matizar 62
matricular 112
mecanizar 62
mecer 201
mediar 17
medicar 174
medir 148
meditar 112
mejorar 112
mencionar 1
mendigar 38
menear 147
menguar 112
menoscabar 112

menospreciar 17
mentar 112
mentir 130
merecer 131
merendar 112
mermar 112
meter 45
mezclar 112
miento *see* **mentir**
militar 112
mimar 112
minar 112
mirar 112
modelar 112
moderar 112
modernizar 62
modificar 174
mofar 112
mojar 31
moler 134
molestar 112
mondar 112
montar 112
moralizar 62
morder 132
morir 133
mortificar 174
mostrar 59
motivar 112
motorizar 62
mover 134
movilizar 62
mudar 112
muerdo *see* **morder**
muero *see* **morir**
muevo *see* **mover**
mugir 76
mullir 109
multar 112

multiplicar 174
murmurar 112
musitar 112
mutilar 112

N
nacer 135
nacionalizar 62
nadar 136
narcotizar 62
narrar 112
naturalizar 62
naufragar 38
navegar 38
nazco *see* **nacer**
necesitar 137
negar 138
negociar 17
neutralizar 62
nevar 139
neviscar 174
niego *see* **negar**
nieva *see* **nevar**
niquelar 112
nivelar 112
nombrar 112
normalizar 62
notar 112
notificar 174
nublarse 32
numerar 112
nutrir 186

O
obcecarse 96
obedecer 140
obedezco *see* **obedecer**
objetar 112
obligar 141

obrar 112
obsequiar 17
observar 112
obsesionar 112
obstaculizar 62
obstinarse 32
obstruir 74
obtener 189
ocasionar 112
ocultar 112
ocupar 112
ocurrir 186
odiar 17
ofender 202
ofrecer 142
ofrezco *see* **ofrecer**
ofuscarse 96
oiga *see* **oír**
oido *see* **oír**
oír 143
ojear 147
oler 144
olfatear 147
olvidar 112
omitir 207
ondear 147
ondular 112
operar 112
opinar 112
oponer 153
opositar 112
oprimir 207
optar 112
opugnar 112
orar 112
ordenar 112
ordeñar 112
organizar 62
orientar 112

originar 112
orillar 114
orinar 112
ornar 112
osar 112
oscilar 112
oscurecer 60
ostentar 112
otear 147
otorgar 38
ovacionar 112
ovillar 114
ovular 112
oxidar 112
oxigenar 112
oye *see* **oír**

P

pacer 60
pacificar 174
pactar 112
padecer 60
pagar 145
paladear 147
paliar 17
palidecer 60
palpar 112
palpitar 112
paralizar 62
parar 112
parecer 146
parir 207
parlamentar 112
parodiar 17
parpadear 147
participar 112
partir 207
pasar 112
pasear 147

pasmar 112
pastar 112
patalear 147
patear 147
patentizar 62
patinar 112
patrocinar 112
pecar 174
pedalear 147
pedir 148
pegar 38
peinar 112
pelar 112
pelear 147
pellizcar 174
penar 112
pender 202
penetrar 112
pensar 149
percatarse 32
percibir 160
perder 150
perdonar 112
perdurar 112
perecer 60
perfeccionar 112
perfilar 112
perforar 112
perjudicar 174
perjurar 112
permanecer 14
permitir 207
permutar 112
perpetrar 112
perpetuar 6
perseguir 178
perseverar 112
persignarse 32
persistir 207

personarse 32
personificar 174
persuadir 207
pertenecer 151
perturbar 112
pervertir 180
pesar 112
pescar 174
pestañear 177
petrificar 174
piar 95
picar 174
pidió *see* **pedir**
pido *see* **pedir**
pienso *see* **pensar**
pierdo *see* **perder**
pillar 114
pinchar 112
pintar 112
pisar 112
pisotear 147
pitar 112
plagar 38
planchar 112
planear 147
planificar 174
plantar 112
plantear 147
plañir 109
plasmar 112
platicar 174
plegar 138
poblar 166
podar 112
poder 152
podrido *see* **pudrir**
polarizar 62
pon *see* **poner**
ponderar 112

pondré *see* **poner**
poner 153
pongo *see* **poner**
popularizar 62
porfiar 95
portarse 32
posar 112
poseer 125
posibilitar 112
posponer 153
postrar 112
postular 112
practicar 174
precaver 45
preceder 45
preciarse 32
precintar 112
precipitar 112
precisar 112
preconizar 62
predecir 67
predicar 174
predisponer 153
predominar 112
prefabricar 174
preferir 154
prefiero *see* **preferir**
pregonar 112
preguntar 112
premeditar 112
premiar 17
prendarse 32
prender 45
prensar 112
preocupar 112
preparar 112
presagiar 17
prescindir 207
prescribir 99

presenciar 17
presentar 112
presentir 180
preservar 112
presidir 207
presionar 112
prestar 112
presumir 207
presuponer 153
pretender 45
prevalecer 60
prevenir 203
prever 204
principiar 17
privar 112
probar 155
proceder 45
procesar 112
proclamar 112
procrear 147
procurar 112
producir 195
profanar 112
proferir 180
profesar 112
profetizar 62
profundizar 62
programar 112
progresar 112
prohibir 156
prohijar 92
proliferar 112
prolongar 38
prometer 45
promover 134
promulgar 38
pronosticar 174
pronunciar 17
propagar 38

proponer 153
proporcionar 112
propulsar 112
prorrogar 38
prorrumpir 207
proscribir 99
proseguir 178
prosperar 112
prostituir 74
proteger 157
protestar 112
proveer 125
provenir 203
provocar 174
proyectar 112
pruebo *see* **probar**
publicar 174
pudrir 158
puedo *see* **poder**
pugnar 112
pulimentar 112
pulir 186
pulsar 112
pulular 112
pulverizar 62
puntear 147
puntualizar 62
punzar 62
purgar 38
purificar 174
puse *see* **poner**

Q
quebrantar 112
quebrar 149
quedar 112
quejarse 31
quemar 112
quepo *see* **caber**

querellar 114
querer 159
quiero *see* **querer**
quisiera *see* **querer**
quiso *see* **querer**
quitar 112

R
rabiar 17
racionalizar 62
racionar 112
radiar 17
radicar 174
radiografiar 95
raer 37
rajar 31
rallar 114
ramificar 174
rapar 112
raptar 112
rasar 112
rascar 174
rasgar 38
raspar 112
rasurar 112
ratificar 174
rayar 112
razonar 112
reabastecer 60
reaccionar 112
reactivar 112
reafirmar 112
reagrupar 112
realizar 62
reanimar 112
reanudar 112
rebajar 31
rebasar 112
rebatir 207

rebelar 112
reblandecer 60
rebosar 112
rebotar 112
rebozar 62
rebuscar 34
rebuznar 112
recaer 37
recalcar 174
recalentar 112
recapacitar 112
recatar 112
recelar 112
rechazar 62
rechinar 112
recibir 160
reciclar 112
recitar 112
reclamar 112
reclinar 112
recluir 74
reclutar 112
recobrar 112
recoger 42
recomendar 149
recompensar 112
reconciliar 17
reconocer 51
reconstruir 74
recopilar 112
recordar 161
recorrer 58
recortar 112
recostar 112
recrear 147
recriminar 112
rectificar 174
recubrir 63
recuerdo *see* **recordar**

recular 112
recuperar 112
recurrir 207
redactar 112
redimir 207
redoblar 112
redondear 147
reducir 162
reembolsar 112
reemplazar 62
referir 180
refinar 112
reflejar 31
reflexionar 112
reformar 112
reforzar 62
refractar 112
refrenar 112
refrendar 112
refrescar 174
refrigerar 112
refugiarse 32
refulgir 76
refunfuñar 112
refutar 112
regalar 112
regañar 112
regar 138
regatear 147
regenerar 112
regentar 112
regir 83
registrar 112
reglamentar 112
reglar 112
regocijar 31
regresar 112
regular 112
rehabilitar 112

rehacer 113
rehogar 38
rehuir 163
rehusar 164
rehúyo *see* **rehuir**
reinar 112
reincidir 66
reincorporar 112
reintegrar 112
reír 165
reiterar 112
reivindicar 174
rejonear 147
rejuvenecer 60
relacionar 112
relajar 31
relamer 45
relampaguear 147
relatar 112
relegar 38
relevar 112
relinchar 112
rellenar 112
relucir 129
relumbrar 112
remachar 112
remar 112
rematar 112
remediar 17
remendar 149
remitir 207
remojar 31
remolcar 174
remolinarse 32
remontar 112
remorder 132
remover 134
remunerar 112
renacer 135

rendir 148
renegar 138
renovar 166
renuevo *see* **renovar**
renunciar 17
reñir 167
reorganizar 62
reparar 112
repartir 207
repasar 112
repatriar 17
repeler 45
repercutir 186
repetir 168
repicar 174
replegar 138
replicar 174
repoblar 166
reponer 153
reposar 112
reprender 45
representar 112
reprimir 207
reprobar 155
reprochar 112
reproducir 195
repudiar 17
repugnar 112
repujar 31
requerir 180
requisar 112
resaltar 112
resarcir 212
resbalar 112
rescatar 112
rescindir 207
resecar 174
resentir 180
reseñar 112

reservar 112
resfriarse 95
resguardar 112
residir 207
resignarse 32
resistir 207
resolver 210
resonar 185
resoplar 112
respaldar 112
respetar 112
respirar 112
resplandecer 60
responder 45
resquebrajar 31
restablecer 60
restallar 114
restar 112
restaurar 112
restituir 74
restregar 138
restringir 76
resucitar 112
resultar 112
resumir 186
retar 112
retardar 112
retener 189
retirar 112
retocar 190
retorcer 192
retornar 112
retozar 62
retractarse 32
retraer 196
retransmitir 207
retrasar 112
retratar 112
retribuir 74

retroceder 45
retumbar 112
reunificar 174
reunir 169
revalidar 112
revalorizar 62
revelar 112
reventar 149
reverberar 112
reverdecer 60
reverenciar 17
revertir 180
revestir 205
revisar 112
revivir 207
revocar 174
revolcar 209
revolotear 149
revolucionar 112
revolver 210
rezagar 38
rezar 62
rezongar 38
ribetear 147
ridiculizar 62
rifar 112
rimar 112
riño *see* **reñir**
río *see* **reír**
rivalizar 62
rizar 62
robar 112
robustecer 60
rociar 95
rodar 59
rodear 147
roer 170
rogar 171
romper 172

roncar 174
rondar 112
ronronear 147
roto *see* **romper**
rotular 112
roturar 112
rozar 62
ruborizarse 62
rubricar 174
ruego *see* **rogar**
rugir 76
rumiar 17
rumorearse 32

S

saber 173
saborear 147
sabotear 147
sacar 174
saciar 17
sacrificar 174
sacudir 186
sal *see* **salir**
salar 112
saldar 112
salgo *see* **salir**
salir 175
salpicar 174
saltar 112
saltear 147
saludar 112
salvaguardar 112
salvar 112
sanar 112
sancionar 112
sanear 147
sangrar 112
santificar 174
santiguar 30

saqué *see* **sacar**
saquear 147
satisfacer 176
satisfago *see* **satisfacer**
saturar 112
sazonar 112
se *see* **saber, ser**
sé *see* **saber, ser**
secar 177
secuestrar 112
secundar 112
sedimentar 112
seducir 195
segar 138
segregar 38
seguir 178
seleccionar 112
sellar 114
sembrar 149
semejar 31
sentarse 179
sentenciar 17
sentir 180
señalar 112
sepa *see* **saber**
separar 112
sepultar 112
sequé *see* **secar**
ser 181
serenar 112
serpentear 147
serrar 149
servir 182
sido *see* **ser**
siento *see* **sentir, sentarse**
significar 174
sigo *see* **seguir**
sigue *see* **seguir**

silbar 112
silenciar 17
simpatizar 62
simplificar 174
simular 112
sincronizar 62
sintetizar 62
sirvo *see* **servir**
sisear 147
sitiar 17
situar 183
sobornar 112
sobrar 112
sobrecargar 38
sobrellevar 112
sobrepasar 112
sobreponer 153
sobresalir 175
sobresaltar 112
sobrevivir 207
socorrer 58
sofocar 174
sois *see* **ser**
soldar 112
soler 184
solicitar 112
sollozar 62
soltar 59
solucionar 112
solventar 112
someter 45
somos *see* **ser**
son *see* **ser**
sonar 185
sondear 147
sonreír 165
soñar 185
sopesar 112
soplar 112

soportar 112
sorber 33
sorprender 45
sortear 147
sosegar 38
sospechar 112
sostener 189
soterrar 112
soy *see* **ser**
suavizar 62
subastar 112
subdividir 207
subestimar 112
subir 186
subrayar 112
subsanar 112
subscribir 99
subsistir 207
subvencionar 112
subyugar 38
suceder 45
sucumbir 186
sudar 112
suelo *see* **soler**
sueño *see* **soñar**
sufrir 207
sugerir 187
sugestionar 112
sugiero *see* **sugerir**
suicidarse 32
sujetar 112
sumar 112
sumergir 76
suministrar 112
sumir 186
supe *see* **saber**
supeditar 112
superar 112
supervisar 112

suplicar 174
suplir 186
suponer 153
suprimir 207
surcar 174
surgir 76
surtir 186
suscitar 112
suscribir 99
suspender 202
suspirar 112
sustentar 112
sustituir 74
sustraer 196
susurrar 112

T

tabular 112
tachar 112
taladrar 112
talar 112
tallar 114
tambalearse 32
tamizar 62
tantear 147
tañer 188
tapar 112
tapiar 17
tapizar 62
tararear 147
tardar 112
tartamudear 147
tasar 112
tatuar 6
teclear 147
tejer 45
telefonear 147
televisar 112
temblar 149

temer 45
templar 112
ten see **tener**
tender 93
tener 189
tengo see **tener**
tensar 112
tentar 149
teñir 167
teorizar 62
terciar 17
tergiversar 112
terminar 112
tersar 112
testar 112
testificar 174
testimoniar 17
tildar 112
timar 112
tintinear 147
tirar 112
tiritar 112
tirotear 147
titilar 112
titubear 147
titular 112
tiznar 112
tocar 190
tolerar 112
tomar 191
tonificar 174
topar 112
toqué see **tocar**
torcer 192
torear 147
tornar 112
torpedear 147
torturar 112
toser 193

tostar 59
trabajar 194
trabar 112
traducir 195
traer 196
traficar 174
tragar 38
traicionar 112
traigo see **traer**
traje see **traer**
trajinar 112
tramar 112
tramitar 112
tranquilizar 62
transbordar 112
transcurrir 207
transferir 116
transfigurar 112
transformar 112
transigir 76
transitar 112
transmitir 207
transparentarse 32
transpirar 112
transponer 153
transportar 112
trascender 25
trasegar 138
trasgredir 207
trasladar 112
traslucir 129
trasnochar 112
traspasar 112
trasplantar 112
trastornar 112
tratar 112
trazar 62
trenzar 62
trepar 112

trepidar 112
tributar 112
trillar 114
trincar 174
trinchar 112
tripular 112
triturar 112
triunfar 112
trivializar 62
trocar 209
tronar 197
tronchar 112
tropezar 198
tropiezo *see* **tropezar**
trotar 112
truena *see* **tronar**
truncar 174
tuerzo *see* **torcer**
tumbar 112
turbar 112
turnarse 32
tutear 147
tutelar 112

U
ubicar 174
ufanarse 32
ulcerar 112
ultimar 112
ultrajar 31
ulular 112
uncir 212
undular 112
ungir 76
unificar 174
uniformar 112
unir 207
untar 112
urbanizar 62

urdir 186
urgir 76
usar 112
usurpar 112
utilizar 62

V
va *see* **ir**
vaciar 199
vacilar 112
vacunar 112
vadear 147
vagar 38
vais *see* **ir**
valer 200
valgo *see* **valer**
vallar 114
valorar 112
valuar 6
vamos *see* **ir**
van *see* **ir**
vanagloriarse 32
vaporizar 62
variar 95
vas *see* **ir**
vaya *see* **ir**
ve *see* **ir, ver**
vedar 112
velar 112
ven *see* **venir**
vencer 201
vendar 112
vender 202
venerar 112
vengar 38
vengo *see* **venir**
venir 203
ventilar 112
ver 204

veranear 147
verdear 147
verificar 174
versar 112
verter 93
vestirse 205
vetar 112
vi *see* **ver**
viajar 206
vibrar 112
viciar 17
vigilar 112
vincular 112
vindicar 174
vine *see* **venir**
violar 112
violentar 112
virar 112
visitar 112
vislumbrar 112
visto *see*
    vestirse, ver
vitorear 147
vivificar 174
vivir 207
vocalizar 62
vocear 147
vociferar 112
volar 208
volcar 209
voltear 147
volver 210
vomitar 112
votar 112
voy *see* **ir**
vuelco *see* **volcar**
vuelo *see* **volar**
vuelvo *see* **volver**
vulnerar 112

Y

yacer 211
yazco *see* **yacer**
yazgo *see* **yacer**
yergo *see* **erguir**
yerro *see* **errar**
yuxtaponer 153

Z

zafar 112
zaherir 116
zambullir 109
zampar 112
zanjar 31
zapatear 147

zarandear 147
zarpar 112
zigzaguear 147
zozobrar 112
zumbar 112
zurcir 212
zurrar 112

ENGLISH-SPANISH INDEX

The following index contains over 1700 common English verbs and their main translations. Note that the correct translation for the English verb depends entirely on the context in which the verb is used and the user should consult a dictionary if in any doubt.

The verbs given in full in the tables in the main part of this book are used as models for the Spanish verbs given in this index. The number in this index is that of the corresponding verb table.

A verb shown in blue is itself given as a model.

A

abandon	abandonar 1
abdicate	abdicar 23
abolish	abolir 2
abound	abundar 112
absolve	absolver 210
absorb	absorber 45
abstain	abstenerse 189
abuse	abusar 112
accelerate	acelerar 112
accent	acentuar 6
accept	aceptar 112
acclaim	aclamar 112
acclimatize	aclimatar 112
accommodate	alojar 112
accompany	acompañar 112
accomplish	conseguir 178
accredit	acreditar 112
accumulate	acumular 112
accuse	acusar 112
achieve	lograr 112
acknowledge	reconocer 51, admitir 207

acquire	adquirir 9
act	actuar 6
activate	activar 112
adapt	adaptar 112
add	añadir 207, sumar 112
adhere	adherir 116
adjust	ajustar 112
administer	administrar 112
admire	admirar 112
admit	admitir 207, reconocer 51
adopt	adoptar 112
adore	adorar 112
advance	adelantar 112, avanzar 62
advise	aconsejar 31
advocate	preconizar 62
affect	afectar 112
affiliate	afiliar 17
afflict	afligir 76
affront	afrentar 112
age	envejecer 60
aggravate	agravar 112
agree	acceder 45, concordar 8
agree to	pactar 112
aim	apuntar 112
air	ventilar 112
align	alinear 147
alleviate	paliar 17
allow	permitir 207
alter	alterar 112
alternate	alternar 112
amalgamate	amalgamar 112
amaze	asombrar 112
amputate	amputar 112
amuse	recrear 147
analyse	analizar 62
anchor	anclar 112
anger	enojar 31
annex	anexionar 112
annihilate	aniquilar 112

announce	anunciar 17
annoy	fastidiar 17
answer	contestar 55, responder 45
answer back	replicar 174
appear	aparecer 18
applaud	aplaudir 207
apply	aplicar 174
apply for	solicitar 112
appoint	nombrar 112
appreciate	apreciar 17
approach	acercarse 7
appropriate	apropiarse 32
approve	aprobar 21
argue	argüir 22, discutir 207
arise	surgir 76
arm	armar 112
arouse	suscitar 112
arrange	arreglar 24
arrest	arrestar 112, prender 45
arrive	llegar 127, acudir 207
articulate	articular 112
ascend	ascender 25
ask	preguntar 112
ask for	pedir 148
assassinate	asesinar 112
assault	agredir 207
assemble	armar 112
assign	destinar 112
assimilate	asimilar 112
associate	asociar 17
assume	asumir 207
assure	asegurar 112
attach	acoplar 112
attack	atacar 174
attempt	procurar 112
attend to	atender 93
attract	atraer 196
attribute	atribuir 74
auction	subastar 112

authorize	**autorizar** 62
automate	**automatizar** 62
avenge	**vengar** 38
avoid	**evitar** 112, **rehuir** 163
await	**aguardar** 112
award	**conceder** 45

B

back	**secundar** 112
back up	**respaldar** 112
balance	**equilibrar** 112
ban	**proscribir** 99
bandage	**vendar** 112
bang	**golpear** 147
baptize	**bautizar** 62
bark	**ladrar** 112
barter	**trocar** 209
base	**basar** 112
batter	**rebozar** 62
be	**estar** 102, **ser** 181
bear	**llevar** 112, **soportar** 112
beat	**apalear** 147, **ganar** 112, **latir** 207
become	**hacerse** 113, **ponerse** 153
beg	**rogar** 171, **mendigar** 38
begin	**empezar** 85, **comenzar** 44
behave	**portarse** 32
behead	**degollar** 68, **decapitar** 112
belch	**eructar** 137
believe	**creer** 61
belittle	**empequeñecer** 60
bellow	**berrear** 147
belong	**pertenecer** 151
bend	**doblar** 112, **encorvar** 112
benefit	**beneficiar** 17
bequeath	**legar** 38
besiege	**sitiar** 17
bet	**apostar** 59
betray	**traicionar** 112
bewitch	**hechizar** 62

bite	morder 132, picar 174
blacken	ennegrecer 60
blackmail	chantajear 147
blame	culpar 112
bleach	decolorar 112
bleat	balar 112
bleed	sangrar 112
bless	bendecir 34
blind	cegar 138
blink	parpadear 147, pestañear 177
block	atascar 174, bloquear 147
blow	soplar 112
blow up	inflar 112
blush	ruborizarse 62
board	abordar 112
boast	jactarse 32
boil	cocer 41, hervir 116
bolt	atrancar 174
bomb	bombardear 147
book	reservar 112
bore	aburrir 207
born, be	nacer 135
bother	estorbar 112, molestar 112
bottle	embotellar 114
bounce	botar 112, rebotar 112
box	boxear 147
boycott	boicotear 147
brag	alardear 147, jactarse 32
brake	frenar 112
brand	tildar 112
brandish	blandir 207
bray	rebuznar 112
break	romper 172, averiar 95
break down	descomponer 153
break up	desarticular 112, fraccionar 112
breathe	respirar 112
breathe in	inspirar 112
breathe out	espirar 112
breed	criar 95

bribe	sobornar 112
bring	traer 196
bring about	producir 195
bring down	derribar 112
bring forward	adelantar 112
bring together	reunir 169
broadcast	transmitir 207
bruise	magullar 114
brush	cepillar 114
brush against	rozar 62
build	construir 53
burgle	robar 112
burn	arder 45, quemar 112
burst	estallar 114, reventar 149
bury	enterrar 149
button	abrochar 112
buy	comprar 47
buzz	zumbar 112

C

cage	enjaular 112
calculate	calcular 112
call	llamar 126
call for	pedir 148
call off	suspender 202
calm (down)	calmar 112, tranquilizar 62
camp	acampar 112
cancel	anular 112, cancelar 112
capitalize	capitalizar 62
capture	capturar 112
caress	acariciar 17
carpet	alfombrar 112
carry	llevar 112
carry on	continuar 56
carry out	ejecutar 112, realizar 62
carve	esculpir 207, trinchar 112
catch	alcanzar 12, coger 42, atrapar 112
cause	causar 112, ocasionar 112
celebrate	celebrar 112

cease	cesar 112
certify	certificar 174
chain	encadenar 112
chair	presidir 207
challenge	retar 112
change	cambiar 17
channel	canalizar 62
char	carbonizar 62
characterize	caracterizar 62
charge	cobrar 112
charm	cautivar 112
chase	perseguir 178
chat	charlar 112
cheat	engaar 112
check	comprobar 155
cheer	vitorear 147
cheer up	animar 112
chew	masticar 174
chirp	gorjear 147, piar 95
choke	atragantarse 32
choose	elegir 83, escoger 42
circulate	circular 112
civilize	civilizar 62
claim	alegar 38, reclamar 112
clarify	aclarar 112
classify	clasificar 174
clean	limpiar 17
clean up	sanear 147
clear	despejar 31
climb	escalar 112, trepar 112
close	cerrar 40
clot	cuajar 31
cloud over	nublarse 32
coat	revestir 205
coax	engatusar 112
coexist	coexistir 207
cohabit	cohabitar 112
coincide	coincidir 207
collaborate	colaborar 112

collect	coleccionar 112
colonize	colonizar 62
colour	colorear 147
comb	peinar 112
combat	combatir 207
combine	combinar 112
come	venir 203
come back	volver 210
come down	bajar 31
come from	provenir 203
come in	entrar 94
come out	salir 175
come up	subir 186
comfort	confortar 112
command	mandar 112
commemorate	conmemorar 112
commit	perpetrar 112
communicate	comunicar 174
compare	comparar 112
compel	obligar 141
compensate	compensar 112
compete	competir 148
compete for	disputar 112
compile	recopilar 112
complain	quejarse 31
complete	completar 112
complicate	complicar 174
comply with	acatar 112
compose	componer 153
compress	comprimir 207
compromise	comprometer 45, transigir 76
conceal	disimular 112, encubrir 63
conceive	concebir 48
concentrate	concentrar 112
concern	concernir 49
conclude	concluir 74
condemn	condenar 112
condense	condensar 112
conduct	guiar 95, dirigir 76

confess	confesar 149
confide	confiar 95
confine	internar 112
confirm	confirmar 112
confiscate	confiscar 174
confront	confrontar 112, enfrentar 112
confuse	confundir 207
congratulate	felicitar 112
connect	conectar 112, relacionar 112
conquer	conquistar 112
consider	considerar 112
consist	consistir 207
console	consolar 52
constitute	constituir 74
construct	construir 53
consult	consultar 112
consume	consumir 207
contain	contener 189
continue	continuar 56
contract	contraer 196
contradict	contradecir 67
contrast	contrastar 112
contravene	contravenir 203
contribute	contribuir 74
control	controlar 112, regular 112
converge	converger 42
convert	convertir 180
convict	condenar 112
convince	convencer 201
cook	cocinar 112
cool (down)	enfriar 89
co-operate	cooperar 112
co-ordinate	coordinar 112
copy	copiar 17
corner	acorralar 112
correct	corregir 57
correspond	corresponder 45
corroborate	corroborar 112
corrode	corroer 170

corrupt	**corromper** 45
cost	**costar** 59
cough	**toser** 193
count	**contar** 54
counteract	**contrarrestar** 112
court	**cortejar** 31
cover	**cubrir** 63, **abarcar** 23
cover up	**cubrir** 63
covet	**codiciar** 17
crack	**agrietarse** 32, **rajar** 31
cram	**abarrotar** 112
crash	**chocar** 174
crawl	**gatear** 147
creak	**crujir** 207
create	**crear** 147
cremate	**incinerar** 112
criticize	**criticar** 174
cross	**atravesar** 28, **cruzar** 62
cross out	**tachar** 112
crown	**coronar** 112
crucify	**crucificar** 174
crumble	**desmenuzar** 62, **desmoronarse** 32
crunch	**crujir** 207
crush	**machacar** 174
cry	**llorar** 112
crystallize	**cristalizar** 62
curdle	**cuajar** 31
cure	**curar** 112
curl	**rizar** 62
curse	**maldecir** 67
cut	**cortar** 112
cut down	**talar** 112
cut out	**recortar** 112

D

damage	**dañar** 112
dance	**bailar** 112
dare	**atreverse** 45
darken	**oscurecer** 60

darn	zurcir 212
dash	correr 58
date	datar 112
dawn	amanecer 14
dazzle	deslumbrar 112
deafen	ensordecer 60
debate	debatir 207
deceive	engañar 112
decide	decidir 66
decipher	descifrar 112
declare	declarar 112
decline	declinar 112
decorate	adornar 112, decorar 112
decrease	mermar 112
decree	decretar 112
dedicate	dedicar 174
deduce	deducir 195
deduct	descontar 54
deepen	profundizar 62
defeat	vencer 201, derrotar 112
defend	defender 93
define	definir 207
deflate	desinflar 112
deform	deformar 112
defraud	defraudar 112
degenerate	degenerar 112
degrade	degradar 112
deign	dignarse 32
delay	retrasar 112
delegate	delegar 38
delete	suprimir 207
delight	deleitar 112
deliver	entregar 38, repartir 207
demand	exigir 104
demolish	demoler 134
demonstrate	demostrar 59
demoralize	desmoralizar 62
dent	abollar 112
deny	negar 138

depend	depender	45
depict	retratar	112
deploy	desplegar	138
deport	deportar	112
deposit	depositar	112
depress	deprimir	207
deprive	privar	112
descend	descender	71
describe	describir	99
desecrate	profanar	112
desert	desertar	149
deserve	merecer	131
design	disear	112
designate	designar	112
desire	desear	147
desist	desistir	207
despise	despreciar	17
destroy	destruir	74
detain	detener	189
deteriorate	decaer	37
detest	detestar	112
detonate	detonar	112
devastate	arrasar	112
develop	desarrollar	114
devise	idear	147
devour	devorar	112
dictate	dictar	112
die	morir	133
dig	cavar	112
digest	digerir	75
digress	divagar	38
dilute	diluir	74
diminish	atenuar	6
direct	dirigir,	76
disagree	discrepar	112
disappear	desaparecer	18
disappoint	decepcionar 112, desilusionar	112
disapprove of	desaprobar	21
discern	discernir	77

disclose	**revelar** 112
discolour	**desteñir** 167
disconcert	**desconcertar** 149
disconnect	**desconectar** 112
discourage	**desanimar** 112
discover	**descubrir** 72
discredit	**desacreditar** 112
discuss	**discutir** 207
disdain	**desdeñar** 112
disembark	**desembarcar** 84
disguise	**disfrazar** 62
disgust	**repugnar** 112
dishonour	**deshonrar** 112
disinfect	**desinfectar** 112
disinherit	**desheredar** 112
dislocate	**desencajar** 31
dismantle	**desmontar** 112
dismiss	**destituir** 74
disobey	**desobedecer** 140
disorientate	**desorientar** 112
disown	**renegar** 138
dispel	**disipar** 112
disperse	**dispersar** 112
display	**mostrar** 59
displease	**desagradar** 112
disrupt	**trastornar** 112
dissolve	**disolver** 210
dissuade	**disuadir** 207
distil	**destilar** 112
distinguish	**distinguir** 78
distort	**deformar** 112, **tergiversar** 112
distract	**distraer** 196
distress	**angustiar** 112
distribute	**distribuir** 74
distrust	**recelar** 112
disturb	**molestar** 112, **turbar** 112
dive	**bucear** 147
divert	**desviar** 95
divide	**dividir** 207

do	**hacer** 113
do without	**prescindir** 207
dodge	**esquivar** 112
dominate	**dominar** 112
dot	**puntear** 147
double	**doblar** 112
doubt	**dudar** 112
draft	**redactar** 112
drag	**arrastrar** 112
drain	**escurrir** 207
draw	**dibujar** 31, **empatar** 112
draw back	**descorrer** 58
dream	**soñar** 185
dress	**vestirse** 205
dribble	**babear** 147
drill	**taladrar** 112
drink	**beber** 33
drip	**gotear** 147
drive	**conducir** 50
drive in	**hincar** 174
drizzle	**lloviznar** 112
drop	**tirar** 112
drown	**ahogar** 38
drug	**drogar** 38
dry	**secar** 177
dump	**verter** 93
duplicate	**duplicar** 174
dye	**teñir** 167

E

earn	**ganar** 112
eat	**comer** 45
echo	**resonar** 185
edit	**editar** 112
educate	**educar** 82
ejaculate	**eyacular** 112
electrocute	**electrocutar** 112
elect	**elegir** 83
eliminate	**eliminar** 112

embark	embarcar 84
embarrass	**abochornar 112**
embellish	**embellecer 60**
embroider	**bordar 112**
emerge	**emerger 175**
emigrate	**emigrar 112**
emit	**emitir 207**
emphasize	**destacar 174, subrayar 112**
employ	**emplear 147**
empty	**vaciar 199**
emulate	**emular 112**
enclose	**adjuntar 112**
encourage	**animar 112**
end	**terminar 112, acabar 5**
endorse	**refrendar 112**
endure	**perdurar 112, sobrellevar 112**
enjoy	**disfrutar 112**
enlarge	**agrandar 112, ampliar 95**
enliven	**avivar 112**
ennoble	**ennoblecer 60**
enrich	**enriquecer 60**
enrol	**matricular 112**
enslave	**esclavizar 62**
entangle	**enredar 112**
enter	**entrar 94**
entertain	**entretener 189**
entitle	**habilitar 112**
entrust	**encomendar 149**
enumerate	**enumerar 112**
envy	**envidiar 112**
equip	**equipar 112**
eradicate	**erradicar 174**
erase	**borrar 112**
erect	**erigir 76**
err	**errar 98**
escape	**escapar 112**
escort	**escoltar 112**
establish	**establecer 60**
esteem	**estimar 112**

evacuate	evacuar 103
evaluate	evaluar 6
evaporate	evaporar 112
evict	desalojar 31
evolve	evolucionar 112
exaggerate	exagerar 112
examine	examinar 112
exasperate	exasperar 112
exceed	exceder 45
except	exceptuar 6
exchange	cambiar 17, intercambiar 17
excite	excitar 112
exclaim	exclamar 112
exclude	excluir 74
excuse	disculpar 112
execute	ejecutar 112
exempt	dispensar 112
exercise	ejercitar 112
exhale	exhalar 112
exhaust	agotar 112
exhibit	exhibir 207, exponer 153
exhort	exhortar 112
exile	desterrar 149
exist	existir 207
exonerate	exonerar 112
expand	dilatar 112
expect	esperar 101
expel	expulsar 112
experience	experimentar 112
expire	caducar 174, expirar 112
explain	explicar 105
explode	estallar 114, explotar 112
exploit	explotar 112
explore	explorar 112
export	exportar 112
expose	exponer 153
express	expresar 112
expropriate	expropiar 17
extend	extender 93, prolongar 38

exterminate	**exterminar** 112
extinguish	**extinguir** 78
extract	**extraer** 196

F

fail	**fallar** 114, **suspender** 202
faint	**desfallecer** 60, **desmayarse** 32
fall	**caer** 37
fall out	**enfadarse** 32
falsify	**falsificar** 174
falter	**vacilar** 112
fascinate	**fascinar** 112
fast	**ayunar** 112
fasten	**prender** 45
fatten	**cebar** 112
favour	**favorecer** 60
fear	**temer** 45
feed	**alimentar** 112
feel	**sentir** 180
feign	**fingir** 76
fell	**talar** 112
fence	**vallar** 114
ferment	**fermentar** 112
fertilize	**fertilizar** 62
fight	**luchar** 112
figure	**figurar** 112
file	**archivar** 112, **limar** 112
fill	**llenar** 112, **empastar** 112
film	**filmar** 112, **rodar** 59
filter	**filtrar** 112
finance	**financiar** 17
find	**encontrar** 88
find out	**enterarse** 32, **averiguar** 30
fine	**multar** 112
finish	**acabar** 5, **terminar** 112
finish off	**rematar** 112
fish	**pescar** 174
fit	**caber** 36, **encajar** 31

fix	**determinar** 112, **fijar** 31
flash	**relampaguear** 147
flatten	**allanar** 112, **aplastar** 112
flatter	**adular** 112
flaunt	**ostentar** 112
flicker	**vacilar** 112
flirt	**flirtear** 147
float	**flotar** 112
flood	**inundar** 112
flourish	**florecer** 60
flow	**fluir** 74
flower	**florecer** 60
fluctuate	**fluctuar** 6
flutter	**ondear** 147
fly	**volar** 208
focus	**enfocar** 174
fold	**doblar** 112
follow	**seguir** 178
forbid	**prohibir** 156
force	**obligar** 141
ford	**vadear** 147
foresee	**prever** 204
foretell	**predecir** 67
forge	**falsificar** 174, **forjar** 31
forget	**olvidar** 112
forgive	**perdonar** 112
form	**formar** 112
formalize	**formalizar** 62
found	**fundar** 112
function	**funcionar** 112
free	**liberar** 112, **librar** 112
freeze	**helar** 115, **congelar** 112
frighten	**asustar** 112, **espantar** 112
frolic	**retozar** 62
frustrate	**frustrar** 112
fry	**freír** 107
fulfil	**cumplir** 207
furnish	**amueblar** 112

G

gain	**granjear** 147
gallop	**galopar** 112
garnish	**guarnecer** 60
gather	**recoger** 42
gather together	**aglomerarse** 32
generalize	**generalizar** 62
generate	**generar** 112
germinate	**germinar** 112
get	**conseguir** 178
get down	**bajar** 31
get off	**apearse** 147
get on	**subir** 186, **montar** 112
give	**dar** 64
give away	**obsequiar** 17
give in	**claudicar** 174
give off	**soltar** 59
give up	**desistir** 207, **renunciar** 17
glimpse	**vislumbrar** 112
glorify	**glorificar** 174
glue	**pegar** 38
gnaw	**roer** 170
go	**ir** 121, **andar** 15
go out	**salir** 175
go through	**traspasar** 112
go up	**subir** 186
govern	**gobernar** 112
graft	**injertar** 112
grasp	**agarrar** 112
grate	**rallar** 114
gravitate	**gravitar** 112
graze	**pastar** 112
grease	**engrasar** 112
greet	**saludar** 112
grieve	**doler** 80
grind	**moler** 134
groan	**gemir** 108
group	**agrupar** 112
grow	**crecer** 60, **cultivar** 112

grumble	**refunfuñar** 112
grunt	**gruñir** 109
guarantee	**garantizar** 62
guard	**vigilar** 112
guess	**adivinar** 112
guide	**guiar** 95

H

haggle	**regatear** 147
hail	**granizar** 62
hallucinate	**alucinar** 112
hammer	**martillear** 147
hand	**tender** 93
hand out	**repartir** 207
hand over	**entregar** 38
handcuff	**esposar** 112
hang	**colgar** 43
hang out	**tender** 93
happen	**pasar** 112, **ocurrir** 186
harangue	**arengar** 38
harass	**acosar** 112
harden	**endurecer** 60
harm	**daar** 112, **perjudicar** 174
harmonize	**armonizar** 62
harvest	**cosechar** 112
hate	**odiar** 17
have	**tener** 189, **haber** 111
have to	**deber** 65
head	**encabezar** 62
heal	**sanar** 112
hear	**oír** 143
heat	**calentar** 149
help	**ayudar** 112
hesitate	**vacilar** 112
hide	**esconder** 45, **ocultar** 112
hijack	**secuestrar** 112
hinder	**dificultar** 112, **impedir** 148
hire	**alquilar** 112, **contratar** 112
hiss	**silbar** 112

hit	**golpear** 147, **pegar** 38
hoard	**acaparar** 112
hoist	**izar** 62
hold	**contener** 189, **sujetar** 112
hold up	**sostener** 189
hollow out	**ahuecar** 174
honour	**honrar** 112
hook	**enganchar** 112
hoot	**ulular** 112
hope	**esperar** 101
horrify	**horrorizar** 62
house	**albergar** 38
howl	**aullar** 6
hug	**abrazar** 62
hum	**tararear** 147
humiliate	**humillar** 114
hunt	**cazar** 39
hurry	**precipitar** 112
hurt	**doler** 80, **herir** 116
hush up	**silenciar** 17
hypnotize	**hipnotizar** 62

I

idealize	**idealizar** 62
identify	**identificar** 174
illustrate	**ilustrar** 112
imagine	**imaginar** 112
imitate	**imitar** 112
immerse	**sumergir** 76
immobilize	**trabar** 112
immortalize	**inmortalizar** 62
impel	**impulsar** 112
implicate	**implicar** 174
implore	**implorar** 112
imply	**implicar** 174
impose	**imponer** 153
impregnate	**impregnar** 112
impress	**impresionar** 112
imprison	**encarcelar** 112

improve	**mejorar** 112
improvise	**improvisar** 112
impute	**imputar** 112
inaugurate	**inaugurar** 112
incapacitate	**incapacitar** 112
incinerate	**incinerar** 112
incite	**incitar** 112
include	**incluir** 74
inconvenience	**incomodar** 112
incorporate	**incorporar** 112
increase	**aumentar** 112
incubate	**incubar** 112
indicate	**indicar** 118
induce	**inducir** 195
industrialize	**industrializar** 62
infect	**infectar** 112
infer	**inferir** 180
infest	**infestar** 112
inflame	**inflamar** 112
inflate	**hinchar** 112
inflict	**infligir** 76
influence	**influir** 74
inform	**informar** 112
infringe	**infringir** 112
infuriate	**indignar** 112
infuse	**infundir** 186
inhabit	**poblar** 166
inhale	**aspirar** 112
inherit	**heredar** 112
inhibit	**cohibir** 156
inject	**inyectar** 112
injure	**lesionar** 112
innovate	**innovar** 112
insert	**insertar** 112
insinuate	**insinuar** 6
insist	**insistir** 207
inspect	**inspeccionar** 112
inspire	**inspirar** 112
install	**instalar** 112

instigate	**instigar** 38
instil	**inculcar** 174
institute	**instituir** 74
instruct	**instruir** 74
insult	**injuriar** 17, **insultar** 112
insure	**asegurar** 112
intercede	**interceder** 45
interest	**interesar** 112
interfere	**inmiscuirse** 74
interfere with	**interferir** 116
interpret	**interpretar** 112
interrupt	**interrumpir** 186
intervene	**intervenir** 203
intervene	**terciar** 17
interview	**entrevistar** 112
intimidate	**achicar** 174
intrigue	**intrigar** 38
introduce	**introducir** 120
invade	**invadir** 207
invent	**inventar** 112
invest	**invertir** 180
investigate	**investigar** 38
invigorate	**tonificar** 174
invite	**invitar** 112
invoice	**facturar** 112
invoke	**invocar** 174
involve	**suponer** 153
iron	**planchar** 112
irrigate	**irrigar** 38
irritate	**irritar** 112
isolate	**aislar** 95
issue	**expedir** 148
itch	**picar** 174

J

jingle	**tintinear** 147
join	**juntar** 112
joke	**bromear** 147
judge	**juzgar** 123

jump	**saltar** 112
justify	**justificar** 174
jut out	**resaltar** 112
juxtapose	**yuxtaponer** 153

K

keep	**guardar** 112
key in	**teclear** 147
kick	**patear** 147
kidnap	**secuestrar** 112
kill	**matar** 112
kiss	**besar** 112
kneel	**arrodillarse** 32
knit	**tejer** 45
knock	**golpear** 147
knock down	**atropellar** 114, **tumbar** 112
knock over	**tirar** 112
knot	**anudar** 112
know	**saber** 173, **conocer** 51

L

label	**rotular** 112
lack	**carecer** 60
land	**aterrizar** 27
languish	**languidecer** 60
last	**durar** 112
laugh	**reír** 165
launch	**lanzar** 62
lay	**poner** 153, **colocar** 174
lay out	**tender** 93
leaf through	**hojear** 147
lead	**conducir** 50
lean	**apoyar** 112
learn	**aprender** 45
leave	**dejar** 69, **marcharse** 32
leave out	**omitir** 207
legalize	**legalizar** 62
legislate	**legislar** 112
legitimize	**legitimar** 112

lend	**prestar** 112
lengthen	**alargar** 38
let	**dejar** 69
let go of	**soltar** 59
level	**aplanar** 112, **igualar** 112
level out	**nivelar** 112
liberate	**liberar** 112
lick	**lamer** 45
lie	**mentir** 130, **yacer** 211
lie down	**acostarse** 8
lift	**levantar** 112
light	**encender** 87
light up	**iluminar** 112
lighten	**aligerar** 112
like	**gustar** 110
limit	**limitar** 112
limp	**cojear** 147
line	**forrar** 112
link	**enlazar** 62
liquidize	**licuar** 112
lisp	**cecear** 147
listen	**escuchar** 112
litigate	**litigar** 38
live	**vivir** 207
live in	**habitar** 112
load	**cargar** 38
loathe	**aborrecer** 3
locate	**ubicar** 174
lodge	**acomodar** 112
long for	**anhelar** 112, **ansiar** 95
look	**mirar** 112
look after	**cuidar** 112
look at	**mirar** 112
look for	**buscar** 35
loosen	**aflojar** 31
loot	**saquear** 147
lose	**perder** 150
love	**querer** 159

lower	**agachar** 112
lubricate	**lubricar** 174

M

magnetize	**magnetizar** 62
maim	**lisiar** 17
maintain	**mantener** 189
make	**hacer** 113
make up	**componer** 153, **inventar** 112, **maquillar** 114
make up for	**compensar** 112
man	**tripular** 112
manage	**manejar** 31
manipulate	**manipular** 112
manoeuvre	**maniobrar** 112
manufacture	**fabricar** 174
mark	**marcar** 174
market	**comercializar** 62
marry	**casarse** 32
mask	**enmascarar** 112
matter	**importar** 112
mature	**madurar** 112
mean	**significar** 174
measure	**medir** 148
mechanize	**mecanizar** 62
meddle	**mangonear** 147
mediate	**mediar** 17
meditate	**meditar** 112
meet	**encontrar** 88
melt	**derretir** 148
mend	**arreglar** 24
mention	**mencionar** 1
milk	**ordeñar** 112
mince	**picar** 174
mine	**minar** 112
mint	**acuñar** 112
mislay	**extraviar** 95
mislead	**despistar** 112
miss	**perder** 150

mistreat	**maltratar** 112
mistrust	**desconfiar** 95
mix	**mezclar** 112
mobilize	**movilizar** 62
model	**modelar** 112
moderate	**moderar** 112
modernize	**modernizar** 62
modify	**modificar** 174
moisten	**humedecer** 60
moor	**amarrar** 112
motivate	**motivar** 112
motorize	**motorizar** 62
move	**mover** 134, **conmover** 134
move away	**apartar** 112
move back	**retroceder** 45
muffle	**amortiguar** 30
multiply	**multiplicar** 174
mumble	**mascullar** 114
murder	**asesinar** 112
murmur	**murmurar** 112
mutilate	**mutilar** 112
mutter	**murmurar** 112
muzzle	**amordazar** 62

N

nail	**clavar** 112
name	**nombrar** 112
narrate	**narrar** 112
narrow	**estrechar** 112
nationalize	**nacionalizar** 62
naturalize	**naturalizar** 62
navigate	**navegar** 38
need	**necesitar** 137
neglect	**descuidar** 112
negotiate	**negociar** 17
neigh	**relinchar** 112
nest	**anidar** 112
neutralize	**neutralizar** 62
nibble	**picar** 174

normalize	**normalizar** 62
note	**notar** 112
notice	**notar** 112
notify	**notificar** 174
nourish	**nutrir** 186
number	**numerar** 112

O

obey	**obedecer** 140
observe	**observar** 112
obsess	**obsesionar** 112
obstruct	**obstaculizar** 62, **obstruir** 74
obtain	**obtener** 189
occupy	**ocupar** 112
occur	**ocurrir** 186
offend	**ofender** 202
offer	**ofrecer** 142
omit	**omitir** 207
open	**abrir** 4
operate	**operar** 112
oppress	**oprimir** 207
order	**ordenar** 112, **encargar** 38
organize	**organizar** 62
outline	**perfilar** 112
outrage	**ultrajar** 31
overcome	**superar** 112
overflow	**desbordar** 112, **rebosar** 112
overload	**sobrecargar** 38
overtake	**rebasar** 112
overthrow	**derrocar** 174
overturn	**volcar** 209
overwhelm	**abrumar** 112
owe	**deber** 65
own	**poseer** 125

P

pacify	**pacificar** 174
pack	**empaquetar** 112, **envasar** 112
pad	**acolchar** 112

paint	pintar 112
pamper	mimar 112
pant	jadear 147
paralyse	paralizar 62
pardon	perdonar 112
park	aparcar 174
parody	parodiar 17
participate	participar 112
pass	aprobar 21, pasar 112
pass away	fallecer 60
patch	remendar 149
patrol	rondar 112
paw	manosear 147
pawn	empeñar 112
pay	pagar 145
pedal	pedalear 147
peel	pelar 112
penetrate	penetrar 112
perceive	percibir 160
perfect	perfeccionar 112
perform	ejecutar 112, interpretar 112
perish	perecer 60
permit	permitir 207
perpetuate	perpetuar 6
persecute	perseguir 178
persevere	perseverar 112
persist	persistir 207
personify	personificar 174
perspire	transpirar 112
persuade	persuadir 207
pervert	pervertir 180
petrify	petrificar 174
phone	telefonear 147
photocopy	fotocopiar 17
photograph	fotografiar 95
pick	escoger 42
pick up	recoger 42
pile up	hacinar 112
pinch	pellizcar 174

placate	aplacar 174
place	colocar 174
plan	planear 147
plant	plantar 112
play	jugar 122, tocar 190
please	agradar 112, complacer 135, contentar 112
plot	conspirar 112, tramar 112
plough	arar 112
plug in	enchufar 112
pocket	embolsar 112
point	señalar 112
point out	señalar 112
poison	envenenar 112
polish	lustrar 112, pulir 186
pollute	contaminar 112
ponder	meditar 112
popularize	popularizar 62
pose	posar 112
position	colocar 174
possess	poseer 125
postpone	aplazar 62, posponer 153
pour	verter 93
practise	practicar 174, ejercer 201
praise	alabar 112, elogiar 17
pray	orar 112, rezar 62
preach	predicar 174
precede	preceder 45
predict	predecir 67
predispose	predisponer 153
predominate	predominar 112
prefer	preferir 154
prepare	preparar 112
prescribe	prescribir 99
present	presentar 112
preserve	conservar 112
press	presionar 112, pulsar 112
pressurize	presionar 112
presume	presumir 207
presuppose	presuponer 153

pretend	fingir 76, simular 112
prevail	prevalecer 60
prevent	impedir 148, prevenir 203
prick	picar 174, pinchar 112
print	estampar 112, imprimir 207
proceed	proceder 45
process	procesar 112, tramitar 112
proclaim	proclamar 112
procreate	procrear 147
produce	producir 195
profess	profesar 112
program(me)	programar 112
progress	progresar 112
prohibit	prohibir 156
project	proyectar 112
proliferate	proliferar 112
prolong	prolongar 38
promise	prometer 45
promote	fomentar 112, ascender 25
pronounce	pronunciar 17
propel	propulsar 112
prophesy	profetizar 62
propose	proponer 153
prosecute	procesar 112
prosper	prosperar 112
protect	proteger 157
protest	protestar 112
prove	probar 155
provide	proporcionar 112
provide with	dotar 112
provoke	provocar 174
prune	podar 112
pry	curiosear 147
publish	publicar 174
pull	tirar 112
pull down	derribar 112
pull up	arrancar 23
puncture	pinchar 112
punish	castigar 38

purge	**purgar** 38
purify	**purificar** 174
purr	**ronronear** 147
push	**empujar** 86
put	**poner** 153, **meter** 45
put back	**atrasar** 112, **reponer** 153
put out	**apagar** 38
put up	**hospedar** 112
put up with	**soportar** 112

Q

quarrel	**pelear** 147
quench	**saciar** 17
question	**interrogar** 38
quote	**citar** 112

R

radiate	**rebosar** 112
raffle	**rifar** 112
rage	**rabiar** 17
rain	**llover** 128
raise	**levantar** 112
rape	**violar** 112
ratify	**ratificar** 174
ration	**racionar** 112
rationalize	**racionalizar** 62
reach	**alcanzar** 12
react	**reaccionar** 112
read	**leer** 125
realize	**percatarse** 32
reap	**segar** 138
reason	**razonar** 112
rebel	**insubordinarse** 32
recall	**evocar** 174
receive	**recibir** 160
recite	**recitar** 112
recognize	**reconocer** 51
recommend	**recomendar** 149
reconcile	**reconciliar** 17

reconstruct	**reconstruir** 74
record	**grabar** 112, **registrar** 112
recover	**recuperar** 112
recreate	**recrear** 147
recruit	**reclutar** 112
rectify	**rectificar** 174
recycle	**reciclar** 112
redden	**enrojecer** 60
redeem	**redimir** 207
redo	**rehacer** 113
reduce	**reducir** 162
refer to	**aludir** 207
referee	**arbitrar** 112
refine	**refinar** 112
reflect	**reflejar** 31, **reflexionar** 112
reform	**reformar** 112
refresh	**refrescar** 174
refrigerate	**refrigerar** 112
refund	**reembolsar** 112
refuse	**negar** 138, **rehusar** 164
refute	**rebatir** 207
regain	**recobrar** 112
regenerate	**regenerar** 112
register	**inscribir** 99, **registrar** 112
regret	**arrepentirse** 180, **lamentar** 112
regroup	**reagrupar** 112
regulate	**regular** 112
rehabilitate	**rehabilitar** 112
rehearse	**ensayar** 112
reheat	**recalentar** 112
reign	**reinar** 112
reinforce	**reforzar** 62
reinstate	**reintegrar** 112
reject	**rechazar** 62
rejuvenate	**rejuvenecer** 60
relapse	**recaer** 37
relate	**relacionar** 112
relax	**relajar** 31
release	**soltar** 59

relegate	relegar 38
relieve	aliviar 112, relevar 112
remain	permanecer 14, quedar 112
remark	comentar 112
remedy	remediar 17
remember	acordarse 8, recordar 161
remove	quitar 112
remunerate	remunerar 112
renew	renovar 166
renounce	renunciar 17
renovate	reformar 112
rent	alquilar 112, arrendar 149
repair	reparar 112
repatriate	repatriar 17
repeal	revocar 174
repeat	repetir 168
repel	repeler 45
replace	reemplazar 62, sustituir 74
reply	responder 45
report	informar 112
represent	representar 112
repress	reprimir 207
reprimand	amonestar 112
reproach	reprochar 112
reproduce	reproducir 195
repudiate	repudiar 17
request	solicitar 112
require	requerir 180
rescue	rescatar 112
research	investigar 38
resemble	semejar 31
reserve	reservar 112
reside	residir 207
resign	dimitir 207
resist	resistir 207
resolve	solventar 112
respect	respetar 112
respond	responder 45
rest	descansar 112

restore	**restablecer** 60, **restaurar** 112
restrain	**refrenar** 112
restrict	**restringir** 76
result	**resultar** 112
resume	**reanudar** 112
resuscitate	**resucitar** 112
retain	**retener** 189
retire	**jubilarse** 32
retract	**retractarse** 32
return	**regresar** 112, **devolver** 210
revalue	**revalorizar** 62
reveal	**revelar** 112
reverberate	**reverberar** 112
revere	**reverenciar** 17
review	**reseñar** 112
revise	**repasar** 112
revive	**reanimar** 112, **revivir** 207
revolutionize	**revolucionar** 112
reward	**recompensar** 112
rhyme	**rimar** 112
ride	**cabalgar** 38, **montar** 112
ridicule	**ridiculizar** 62
ring	**sonar** 185
rinse	**aclarar** 112, **enjuagar** 38
rip	**rasgar** 38
ripen	**madurar** 112
rise	**subir** 186
risk	**arriesgar** 38
rival	**rivalizar** 62
roam	**vagar** 38
roar	**rugir** 76
roast	**asar** 112, **tostar** 59
rob	**robar** 112
rock	**mecer** 201
roll	**rodar** 59
roll up	**enrollar** 114
rot	**pudrir** 158
row	**remar** 112
rub	**frotar** 112, **rozar** 62

rub out	**borrar** 112
ruin	**arruinar** 112, **estropear** 147
rule	**regentar** 112
rule out	**descartar** 112
run	**correr** 58, **administrar** 112
run away	**huir** 117
run over	**atropellar** 114
rush	**correr** 58
rust	**oxidar** 112

S

sabotage	**sabotear** 147
sack	**despedir** 148, **saquear** 147
sacrifice	**sacrificar** 174
sadden	**apenar** 112, **entristecer** 60
safeguard	**salvaguardar** 112
sail	**navegar** 38
salt	**salar** 112
sanctify	**santificar** 174
satisfy	**satisfacer** 176, **saciar** 17
saturate	**saturar** 112
sauté	**saltear** 147
save	**ahorrar** 112, **guardar** 112, **salvar** 112
savour	**saborear** 147
saw	**serrar** 149
say	**decir** 67
scan	**otear** 147
scare	**asustar** 112
scare away	**ahuyentar** 112
scatter	**desparramar** 112
scent	**husmear** 147
scold	**reñir** 167, **regañar** 112
scorch	**abrasar** 112
score	**anotar** 112, **marcar** 174
scorn	**menospreciar** 17
scrape	**raspar** 112
scratch	**arañar** 112, **rascar** 174
scream	**chillar** 114
screech	**chirriar** 95

screw	enroscar 174
screw on	atornillar 114
scrub	fregar 106, restregar 138
seal	precintar 112, sellar 114
search	registrar 112
search for	buscar 35
season	sazonar 112
seduce	seducir 195
see	ver 204
seek	buscar 35
seem	parecer 146
segregate	segregar 38
seize	asir 26, apresar 112
select	seleccionar 112
sell	vender 202
sell off	liquidar 112
send	enviar 95
sense	notar 112
sentence	sentenciar 17
separate	separar 112
serve	servir 182
set	colocar 174, fijar 31
set up	montar 112
settle	resolver 210
sew	coser 45
shake	agitar 112, sacudir 186
shape	configurar 112
share	compartir 207
share out	repartir 207
sharpen	afilar 112
shave	afeitar 112
shell	bombardear 147
shelter	refugiarse 32
shine	lucir 129, brillar 114
shiver	temblar 149
shock	escandalizar 62
shoe	herrar 149
shoot	disparar 112, fusilar 112
shorten	acortar 112

shout	**gritar** 112
show	**mostrar** 59
shower	**ducharse** 32
shrink	**encoger** 42
shuffle	**barajar** 31
shun	**rehuir** 163
shut	**cerrar** 40
shut away	**recluir** 74
shut in	**encerrar** 40
sicken	**hastiar** 95
sieve	**cribar** 112
sigh	**suspirar** 112
sign	**firmar** 112
signal	**señalar** 112
silence	**silenciar** 17
simplify	**simplificar** 174
simulate	**simular** 112
sin	**pecar** 174
sing	**cantar** 112
singe	**chamuscar** 174
sink	**hundir** 186
sip	**sorber** 33
sit	**sentarse** 179
situate	**situar** 183
size up	**tantear** 147
skate	**patinar** 112
sketch	**bosquejar** 31
skimp on	**escatimar** 112
skip	**saltar** 112
slander	**calumniar** 17
slap	**abofetear** 147
sleep	**dormir** 81
slide	**deslizar** 62
slim	**adelgazar** 62
slip	**resbalar** 112
slow down	**retrasar** 112
smart	**escocer** 41
smash	**estrellar** 114
smear	**untar** 112

smell	oler 144
smile	sonreír 165
smoke	fumar 112, ahumar 112
smooth	alisar 112
smother	sofocar 174
snap	tronchar 112
snatch	arrebatar 112
sneeze	estornudar 112
sniff	olfatear 147
snoop	fisgar 38
snore	roncar 174
snow	nevar 139
soak	empapar 112, remojar 31
soap	enjabonar 112
sob	sollozar 62
soften	ablandar 112
solder	soldar 112
solve	resolver 210, solucionar 112
sort	ordenar 112
sound	sonar 185
sound out	sondear 147
soundproof	insonorizar 62
sow	sembrar 149
space out	espaciar 17
spark	chispear 147
sparkle	centellear 147
speak	hablar 112
specify	especificar 174
speculate	especular 112
speed up	apresurar 112
spell	deletrear 147
spend	gastar 112
spill	derramar 112
spin	hilar 112
spit	escupir 207
splash	salpicar 174
split	partir 207
spoil	estropear 147, mimar 112
sponsor	patrocinar 112

spray	rociar 95
spread	difundir 186, extender 93
spread out	desplegar 138, extender 93
sprinkle	espolvorear 147, rociar 95, salpicar 174
sprout	brotar 112
spy	espiar 95
squander	malgastar 112
square	cuadrar 112
squeeze	apretar 20, estrujar 31
stab	apuñalar 112
stagger	tambalearse 32
stain	manchar 112
stamp	sellar 114
stand	colocar 174, soportar 112
stand in for	suplir 186
stand out	destacar 174, sobresalir 175
standardize	estandarizar 62
starch	almidonar 112
start	empezar 85, comenzar 44
startle	sobresaltar 112
state	afirmar 112
stay	permanecer 14
steal	robar 112
steam	humear 147
steam up	empañar 112
sterilize	esterilizar 62
stew	estofar 112
stick	pegar 38
stick out	sobresalir 175
stimulate	estimular 112
sting	picar 174
stink	apestar 112
stipulate	estipular 112
stir	remover 134, revolver 210
stop	parar 112
store	almacenar 112
straighten	enderezar 62
strain	colar 59
strangle	estrangular 112

strengthen	fortalecer 60
stress	recalcar 174
stretch	estirar 112
stretch out	extender 93, tender 93
strike	golpear 147
strike down	fulminar 112
structure	estructurar 112
struggle	luchar 112
study	estudiar 17
stuff	rellenar 112
stumble	tropezar 198
stun	aturdir 207
stutter	tartamudear 147
subdivide	subdividir 207
subdue	someter 45
subject	someter 45
subjugate	subyugar 38
submerge	sumergir 76
subordinate	supeditar 112
subsidize	subvencionar 112
subsist	subsistir 207
substitute	sustituir 74
subtract	restar 112, sustraer 196
succeed	suceder 45, triunfar 112
succumb	sucumbir 186
suck	chupar 112, mamar 112
sue	demandar 112
suffer	sufrir 207
suffocate	asfixiar 112, sofocar 174
suggest	sugerir 187
sum up	resumir 186
supervise	supervisar 112
supply	abastecer 60, proporcionar 112
support	apoyar 112, sostener 189
suppose	suponer 153
surprise	sorprender 45
surrender	capitular 112
surround	rodear 147
survive	sobrevivir 207

suspect	sospechar 112
suspend	suspender 202
swallow	tragar 38
swear	jurar 112
sweat	sudar 112
sweep	barrer 45
sweeten	endulzar 62
swell	engrosar 112
swim	nadar 136
swindle	estafar 112, timar 112
swing	bambolearse 32, columpiar 17
switch off	apagar 38
switch on	encender 87
sympathize	simpatizar 62
synchronize	sincronizar 62
synthesize	sintetizar 62

T

tabulate	tabular 112
take	tomar 191, llevar 112
take away	quitar 112, restar 112
take down	descolgar 43
take off	despegar 38, quitar 112
take out	sacar 174
talk	hablar 112
tame	domar 112
tan	broncearse 32
tangle	enmarañar 112
taste	probar 155
tattoo	tatuar 6
tax	gravar 112
teach	enseñar 112
tear	rasgar 38
tear up	rasgar 38
telephone	telefonear 147
televise	televisar 112
tell	contar 54
tempt	tentar 149
tend	tender 93

terrify	aterrar 112
test	examinar 112, probar 155
testify	testificar 174
thank	agradecer 11
theorize	teorizar 62
thicken	espesar 112
think	pensar 149
thread	enhebrar 112
threaten	amenazar 62
thresh	trillar 114
thrill	emocionar 112
throb	palpitar 112
throw	echar 112, tirar 112
throw away	tirar 112
throw out	echar 112
thunder	tronar 197
tidy up	ordenar 112
tie	atar 112
tighten	apretar 20, tensar 112
tilt	inclinar 112
tire	cansar 112, fatigar 38
toast	tostar 59
tolerate	tolerar 112
torment	atormentar 112
torpedo	torpedear 147
torture	torturar 112
totter	tambalearse 32
touch	tocar 190, conmover 134
tow	remolcar 174
trace	calcar 174
trade	comerciar 17
traffic	traficar 174
train	entrenar 112, formar 112
trample on	pisotear 147
transfer	transferir 116, trasladar 112
transform	transformar 112
transgress	trasgredir 207
translate	traducir 195
transmit	transmitir 207

transplant	**trasplantar** 112
transport	**transportar** 112
transpose	**transponer** 153
trap	**aprisionar** 112
travel	**viajar** 206
tread on	**pisar** 112
treat	**tratar** 112
tremble	**temblar** 149
trip	**tropezar** 198
triumph	**triunfar** 112
trivialize	**trivializar** 62
trot	**trotar** 112
trust	**fiarse** 95
try	**intentar** 119, **probar** 155
try out	**ensayar** 112
tune	**afinar** 112
turn	**girar** 112
turn off	**apagar** 112, **cerrar** 40
turn on	**abrir** 4, **encender** 87
turn out	**resultar** 112
turn over	**voltear** 147
turn round	**virar** 112
twin	**hermanar** 112
twinkle	**centellear** 147
twist	**torcer** 192, **retorcer** 192

U

uncork	**descorchar** 112
underestimate	**subestimar** 112
undergo	**experimentar** 112, **sufrir** 207
underline	**subrayar** 112
understand	**entender** 93, **comprender** 45
undertake	**acometer** 45, **emprender** 45
undo	**desabrochar** 112, **deshacer** 113
undress	**desnudar** 112
unearth	**desenterrar** 149
unfold	**desdoblar** 112
unify	**unificar** 174
unite	**aunar** 6, **unir** 207

unleash	desencadenar 112
unload	descargar 38
unplug	desenchufar 112
unravel	desentrañar 112
unscrew	desatornillar 114
untangle	desenredar 112
untie	desatar 112
unwrap	desenvolver 210
update	actualizar 62
upholster	tapizar 62
uproot	desarraigar 38
upset	disgustar 110, desajustar 112
urge	instar 112
urge on	acuciar 17
urinate	orinar 112
use	usar 112
use up	agotar 112
usurp	usurpar 112
utilize	utilizar 62
utter	proferir 180

V

vacate	desocupar 112
vaccinate	vacunar 112
value	tasar 112, valorar 112
vaporize	vaporizar 62
varnish	barnizar 62
vary	variar 95
venerate	venerar 112
ventilate	ventilar 112
veto	vetar 112
vibrate	vibrar 112
view	ver 204
violate	violar 112
visit	visitar 112
vomit	vomitar 112
vote	votar 112
vouch for	atestiguar 30

W

wag	menear 147
wait	esperar 101
wake up	despertarse 73
walk	andar 15, pasear 147, caminar 112
wall	amurallar 112
wall in	tapiar 17
wander	vagar 38
want	querer 159, desear 147
warm (up)	calentar 149
warn	advertir 180, avisar 112
wash	lavar 124
waste	derrochar 112, gastar 112
watch	mirar 112
watch over	velar 112
water	regar 138
wave	ondular 112
weaken	debilitar 112
wear	llevar 112, usar 112
wear out	desgastar 112
weave	tejer 45
weep	llorar 112
weigh	pesar 112
weigh up	sopesar 112
welcome	acoger 42
weld	soldar 112
wet	mojar 31
whine	gemir 108, gimotear 147
whip	azotar 112
whisper	cuchichear 147, susurrar 112
whistle	silbar 112
whiten	blanquear 147
win	ganar 112, vencer 201
wink	guiñar 112
wish	desear 147
withdraw	retirar 112
wither	marchitar 112
witness	presenciar 17

wobble	**vacilar** 112
work	**trabajar** 194, **funcionar** 112
worry	**preocupar** 112
worsen	**empeorar** 112
worship	**adorar** 112
wrap	**envolver** 210
wrap up	**liar** 95
wring	**estrujar** 31
wrinkle	**arrugar** 38
write	**escribir** 99
write off	**sanear** 147

X
X-ray	**radiografiar** 95

Y
yawn	**bostezar** 62
yield	**rendir** 148

Z
zigzag	**zigzaguear** 147